Economists and War

War and economic power have been interwoven in the thought of scholars since the beginnings of economic science, and views on the role of war in the economy have shifted dramatically as the world order has changed. The centenary of World War I has offered the opportunity for increased reflection on this topic, particularly as the war itself stimulated new directions for both research and the development of theory.

Economists and War brings together expert contributors who are united in their commitment to exploring this classic subject from innovative and heterodox points of view. The chapters presented in the book delve into a wide range of perspectives from Japan in the Second World War and Italy in the First; the debate on State intervention among German-speaking authors to the debate on the economic bases of perpetual peace; and from Keynes, who wrote on the 'irrationality of war', to Sismondi, who saw war as an opportunity for economic development, and not only for nation-states.

This volume is essential reading for scholars of the history of economic thought, international political economy and intellectual history. It is also of great interest to those studying military and naval history.

Fabrizio Bientinesi is Associate Professor of Economic Thought in the Department of Economics and Management at the University of Pisa, Italy.

Rosario Patalano is Associated Professor of the History of Economic Thought in the Department of Law at the University of Naples Federico II, Italy, and Guest Professor at the University Lumière Lyon 2, France.

Routledge Studies in the History of Economics

Economists and War

A heterodox perspective

Edited by Fabrizio Bientinesi and Rosario Patalano

LONDON AND NEW YORK

First published 2017 by Routledge

2 Park Square, Milton Park, Abingdon, Oxfordshire OX14 4RN
52 Vanderbilt Avenue, New York, NY 10017

Routledge is an imprint of the Taylor & Francis Group, an informa business

First issued in paperback 2019

British Library Cataloguing in Publication Data
A catalogue record for this book is available from the British Library

Library of Congress Cataloging in Publication Data
A catalog record for this book has been requested

ISBN: 978-1-138-64397-0 (hbk)
ISBN: 978-0-367-87677-7 (pbk)

Typeset in Times New Roman
by Deanta Global Publishing Services, Chennai, India

Contents

Illustrations

Figures

Tables

Contributors

Fabrizio Bientinesi is Associate Professor of History of Economic Thought in the Department of Economics and Management, University of Pisa (Italy).

Fanny Coulomb is Maître de Conferences in the Faculty of Political Sciences, University Pierre-Mendès-France of Grenoble (France).

Alberto Giordano is Lecturer in Political Theory in the Department of Political Science, University of Genoa (Italy).

Terenzio Maccabelli is Associate Professor of History of Economic Thought in the Department of Economics and Management, University of Brescia (Italy).

Fabio Masini is Associate Professor of History of Economic Thought in the Department of Political Sciences, University of Roma III (Italy).

Luca Michelini is Associate Professor of History of Economic Thought in the Department of Political Sciences, University of Pisa (Italy).

Tadashi Ohtsuki is Lecturer at the Tokyo University of Foreign Studies (Japan).

Letizia Pagliai is Lecturer in the Department of Social Sciences, University of Pisa (Italy).

Rosario Patalano is Associate Professor in the History of Economic Thought in the Department of Law, University Federico II, Naples (Italy).

Stefano Spalletti is Associate Professor in the History of Economic Thought in the Department of Political Sciences, University of Macerata (Italy).

Ted Winslow is Associate Professor in the Department of Social Science, York University, Toronto (Canada).

Introduction

Fabrizio Bientinesi and Rosario Patalano

Igitur navium militum armorum paratu strepere provinciae,
sed nihil aeque fatigabat quam pecuniarum conquisitio:
'eos esse belli civilis nervos'

(Tacitus, Historiae, 2.84)[1]

Ante igitur quam inchoëtur bellum, de copiis expensisque sollers debet esse trac-
tatus, ut pabula frumentum ceteraeque annonariae species, quas a prouincialibus
consuetudo deposcit, maturius exigantur et in oportunis ad rem gerendam ac muni-
tissimis locis amplior semper modus, quam sufficit, adgregetur. Quod si tributa
deficiunt, prorogato auro comparanda sunt omnia.

(Publius Flavius Vegetius Renatus, Epitoma rei militaris, III, 3)[2]

Economic issues have always had a fundamental – if not decisive – role in every
episode of war. It is, therefore, hardly surprising to find considerations on war
and on the economy closely linked even in ancient times. The military needs of
the nation-states of modern Europe were then to become central to what has been
defined as 'mercantilism'. In this context, war was seen as a simply inevitable
condition in the life of nations, and autarky – or at least reduction of foreign trade
to the barest essentials – as the most advantageous condition. This paradigm was
gradually abandoned in favour of very different approaches. Wealth no longer
coincided with the position of precious metals, and *doux commerce* became a
factor for progress and harmony amongst the nations (Hirschman 1977). This
approach would appear to have been very recently borne out by the facts found
(Jackson, Nei 2015).

However, war as an issue still loomed large in the work of Adam Smith (Smith
1776), traditionally taken to mark the scientific autonomy achieved in economic
thought. It has been written that there is an evident contrast 'between the rich and
suggestive reflections of Adam Smith from a broad-scientific perspective, and the
more constrained approach of Malthus, Ricardo and Mill, writing as they were
with limiting forces of a set of well-specified economic models. The appearance
of Schumpeter's "Ricardian vice" may have had its costs in this applied field too'
(Goodwin 1991: 35). Clearly, when in justification of the *Navigation Act* Smith

wrote that 'defence, however, is of much more importance than opulence', he was not subordinating the economic to the political sphere. If anything, he was proposing an analysis of economic choices that was *wertgebunden*. The 'Ricardian vice' became even more of a vice with the rise of the marginalist school in the second half of the nineteenth century. If the leading theme of *economics* – no longer *political economy* – was to be the maximisation of individual and social utility, then war as destruction of wealth and production of pure suffering could not be eliminated from the horizon of economic analysis (Goodwin 2008: 698). In the last decade of the nineteenth century the antimilitarist front based its aversion to war on the optimistic idea that the close and intricate economic interrelations that developed between industrialised societies made the implementation of projects for military hegemony totally irrational (and the identification of militarism with protectionism derived from this assumption). These ideas found their theoretical reference point in the weighty six volume work by the Polish economist Jan Bloch *Budushchaya Voina* (1898).[3] Apparently, even Tsar Nicolas II himself was profoundly influenced by the Polish economist's work. Bloch took part in the First Hague Conference (1899) on the laws of war without, however, achieving any success at the political level. In the early days of the twentieth century these ideas were revived by the British journalist Norman Angell in *The Great Illusion* (1910), a pamphlet that was to become a sort of manifesto of the world pacifist movement in the times of the *Belle Époque*. Both authors had succeeded in coming up with realistic, economistic answers to the problem of war, moving on beyond the traditional ethical view of the issue.[4] This pacifist and antimilitarist approach rested on the conviction that *doux commerce*, increased world trade, and the relative interdependence amongst the national economies would in practice have made war, or at any rate any long and devastating conflict, utterly futile. Just a few years later, World War I broke out.

The intensity and duration of the conflict required of all the countries at war an enormous effort in mobilisation of human and material resources. To this end, the entire productive apparatus had been rapidly converted and subordinated to the needs of the war. A supply policy was then devised to step up production and transfer the instruments of war to the front. Effectively, the war effort could not be sustained without the appropriate centralised management of foreign trade. To get the massive machinery of war functioning it was of course necessary to prepare all the right financial means. And to obtain satisfactory results it appeared increasingly necessary to plan and centralise the production and consumption choices, both civil and military, as much as possible, for otherwise collapse at the front and/or popular uprisings at home would inevitably follow. All this called for the preparation of planning mechanisms totally alien to the liberalism that dominated economic thought. We may therefore well understand why reflection on these issues was forced, belated and often marred by unrealistic assumptions.

The economists regained a central role in the management of the war effort during World War II, and went on to reach their zenith in the 1970s. In the last few years, recognition of the crucial role of economic analysis in addressing military problems has been attested by the rise of 'defence economics' as an independent branch of the science. In this new approach, which sees the economist transformed into neutral technician (much like a dentist or an engineer called upon to solve a technical problem), a substantial degree of agreement appears to have been reached within economic science[5]. The contributions to this volume present authors or aspects of economic thought that demonstrate that agreement is not, in fact, easily reached. The authors and subjects have been chosen favouring an essentially peripheral perspective – either because they are at the very limits of the mainstream if not explicitly opposed to it, or because they belong to peripheral geopolitical contexts marginal to the great military and economic powers.

The essay by Tadashi Ohtsuki then takes us to Japan, in the period between the two world wars, with analysis of the work of Kaname Akamatsu (1896–1974). Educated abroad, between the United States and Germany, following a path trodden by many Japanese economists at the time, Akamatsu formulated what is known as the 'Wild Geese Flying Pattern Theory'. This theory of development in stages represented with the image of the 'leading goose', the leading country in economic terms – Japan, in this case – the example to be imitated by the 'follower geese', the countries of Southeast Asia. Although Akamatsu showed a distinct *penchant* for peaceful development, at least until 1941, one cannot help seeing how perfectly the theory fits into supporting Japanese expansionism and the 'Greater East Asia Co-Prosperity Sphere'.

The contributions by Fabrizio Bientinesi and Stefano Spalletti address two authors, Stefan Possony (1913–1995) and Friedrich List (1789–1846), who share not only the same mother tongue, but also positions far removed from those of their times. In 1938, two months before the *Anschluss*, Possony published a book that challenged the then almost unanimously asserted position: the need for planning to support the total war economy. Possony, who was to become one of the moving spirits of the 'Star Wars' project under the Reagan administration, overturned this logic, starting from two basic points: the impossibility of meeting the needs of total war with no recourse to international trade, and the impossibility for a planned economy to adapt rapidly and efficiently to changeable strategic conditions. A century before, by contrast, the heretic List had challenged the growing consensus on the need for free trade. In his analysis, protectionism offered the only way for latecomers to pursue real economic development. Thus war, generating the effect of prohibitive duties, could prove a powerful motor for development. At the same time, Spalletti reminds us that List had stressed the inevitable inferiority of prevalently agricultural countries when it comes to waging war in comparison with the industrially advanced countries. The American Civil War was to provide dramatic proof of his thesis. According to Spalletti, then – in contrast with the interpretation offered by another author in this book, Fanny Coulomb – there is no confusion in List's analysis between economic power and military might, but there does seem to be a profound correlation.

While List took a heterodox position in his analysis of international trade, Jean Charles Léonard Simonde de Sismondi (1773–1842) departed from established doctrine on the issue of the possibility of crises associated with lack of demand. He failed to find the mention he may well have merited in Chapter XXIII of Keynes's *General Theory*, but, like Thomas Robert Malthus, he took a firm stand against the Say–Ricardo analytic line which was to dominate for over a century. The intellectual path that led Sismondi to his minority position found a direct match in his analysis of the relations between war and economics. In his early Smithian days, Sismondi vehemently attacked the abuses of war finance and resort to fiat currency. Later on, our Genevan author was to point out the uselessness, and indeed the harmfulness, of an 'export-oriented' economy, and the need to achieve self-sufficiency in peacetime to limit dependence on foreign suppliers should war break out.

The essays by Luca Michelini and Rosario Patalano both analyse of the much-debated relationship between economic thought and war in the context of a peripheral country like Italy. The contribution by Michelini reconstructs the diverging analyses by Achille Loria (1857–1943) and Maffeo Pantaleoni (1857–1924) of the experience of the First World War. Loria's analysis is very close to the socialist tradition (substantially betrayed with the dramatic split in the internationalist movement in August 1914), seeing war as a typical manifestation of the capitalist system, based on exploitation and deep-reaching social and economic conflicts at both the national and international level. War, dramatically aggravating social conflicts, should, according to Loria, hasten the final collapse of capitalism. Pantaleoni, by contrast, starting from the opposite, liberal viewpoint applies utilitarian analytic tools to war as to other aspects of social life, concluding that it should mark the end of every form of economic parasitism and confirm the validity of the market economy. Pantaleoni's theses attest to the fact that much of Italian economic thought remains anchored to rigid theoretical dogmatism, without fully understanding the problems deriving from the intensity and totality of modern warfare. Patalano's essay turns the focus on theoretical dogmatism in relation to the issue of war finance. Characteristic of the approach taken by the Italian economists up until the Libyan War of 1911 was the prevalence of the Smithian thesis that war finance should be based on taxation. But then, faced with the reality of the heavy demands entailed by the colonial war in Libya, thinking took a more pragmatic turn which is summed up in the fundamental contribution by Federico Flora (1867–1958), who asserted the legitimacy of alternative means of finance including loans and fiat currency circulation. The actual financing of the Great War confirmed the conclusions reached by Flora in his study, to the effect that the major financial burden of modern war was to be borne by borrowing both at home and abroad. Despite the empirical evidence, this opinion came in for criticism from the liberist economists, and in particular Pantaleoni and Luigi Einaudi (1874–1961), who went on to reassert their dogmatic position on recourse to loans while war was raging.

If Wilhelm Röpke (1899–1966) is an author not unknown to scholars, what is there to be said about John Maynard Keynes that has not already been said? And yet the essays by Alberto Giordano and Ted Winslow aim to offer some unconventional viewpoints on the two authors. Giordano examines how the Swiss–German author's reflections on war fit into the broader issue of the relationship between ethics and economics. He considered war more likely in the age of mass man and the 'far of competition'. For many other authors, from Sismondi to Luigi Einaudi,

Switzerland appeared to be the historical paradigm in which pacifism was associated with and found its origins in moral values that were essentially exogenous to the economic system. Such values could not be taken for granted but called for watchfulness to prevent degeneration of the economic (non-competitive forms of market) and social (megalopolises) structures, which in turn would make war more probable and more devastating. Winslow's contribution considers Keynes's evaluation of war in relation to his more general appraisal of the relationship between the human psyche and economics. He saw economic action and competition as the most effective way to channel the drive to dominate and the irrational elements at work in human beings. It was evidently these violent impulses that lay behind armed conflict, but they could readily be identified in behaviours that had marked Keynes's critical experience while the Versailles Treaty was being thrashed out, such as the *auri sacra fames* of the French or the refusal to let Germany use the little gold it had left to acquire foodstuffs and alleviate the consequences of the naval blockade.

Two essays of a *weltanschauunglich* nature complete this volume. In the first, Fabio Masini takes a close look at the other side of the coin, namely the approach of political economy to the means that can lead to the negation of war – in a word, peace. As the author puts it: 'Two main approaches emerge in the way peace is considered in political economy: *internationalism* and *constitutional supranational federalism*. The former is the one shared by all those who believe international peace is attainable *from below*, considering peace as the product of the implementation in each and every country of the principles of liberalism, democracy or socialism [...] The second approach is founded on the idea that peace is only sustainable when sovereignty is no longer a monopoly of nation States but is shared by a concentric system of multilayer governments, each providing collective goods, therefore requiring a binding and enforceable supranational juridical agreement'. Fanny Coulomb's essay takes the case of the First World War to address the more general issue of the relationship between the realities of war and theoretical development in economic science. Thus World War I can be seen as a great catalyser in the emergence of new theoretical approaches, above all on heterodox lines. The focus moves on from Hobson, whose theories on imperialism are compared with those of the Marxist authors, to Veblen, who dwells on the relationship between war and social composition, and then on, of course, to Keynes who, from his *Economic Consequences of the Peace* through debate with Ohlin on reparations, paved the way for his searching critique of mainstream economics.

Notes

1 'So then the provinces were filled with din as ships, soldiers, and arms were made ready for their needs; but nothing troubled them so much as the exaction of money. "Money," Mucianus kept saying, "is the sinews of civil war"', English translation by C.H. Moore, *Histories*, Harvard University Press, Harvard, 1925.
2 'The main and principal point in war is to secure plenty of provisions and to destroy the enemy by famine. An exact calculation must therefore be made before the commencement of the war as to the number of troops and the expenses incident thereto, so

that the provinces may in plenty of time furnish the forage, corn, and all other kinds of provisions demanded of them to be transported. They must be in more than sufficient quantity, and gathered into the strongest and most convenient cities before the opening of the campaign. If the provinces cannot raise their quotas in kind, they must commute for them in money to be employed in procuring all things requisite for the service' (Publius Flavius Vegetius Renatus, *Epitoma rei militaris*, III, 3. English Translation: *The Military Institutions of the Romans* translated from the Latin by Lieutenant John Clarke, W. Griffin, London, 1767). See also Preston, Wise (1970).

3 Originally published in Russian, and subsequently translated and summarised in English under various titles, cf. Bloch, Jan *Is War Now Impossible? Being an Abridgment of "The War of the Future"* (Bloch 1899a); *The future of war: in its technical, economic, and political relations* (Bloch 1899b).

4 Weinroth (1974).

5 'John Maynard Keynes remarked in 1930 that he looked forward to the day when economists would be "thought of as humble, competent people, on a level with dentists". It appears that in the 21st century economists concerned with the study of war have gained this status. It is now well accepted that war, like all human activity, requires the recognition of scarcity and the need to make choices based on forgone opportunities. This is the domain of economics. Defence economists stand ready to advise on these allocative decisions and to remind policymakers of the applicability of such concepts as externalities and public goods. The heroic years of defence economics are almost certainly gone forever; the economists are today, as they say, on tap but not on top. Nevertheless, their usefulness remains, even if at a more modest level than before. The study of war is now an accepted part of economics, assigned to its own subfield and dependent heavily on the tools and methods of public economics. In its current posture economics is less likely to find a cure for conflict than to make it more efficient and its prevention less costly. In a world full of shortages and sufferings this is no small accomplishment' (Goodwin 2008: 703).

References

Angell, N.R. (1910) *The Great Illusion: A Study of the Relation of Military Power in Nations to their Economic and Social Advantage*, G.P. Putnam's & Sons, New York.

Bloch, J. (1898) *Budushchaya Voina*, Tipografiya I. A. Efrona, Saint Petersburg.

— (1899a) *Is War Now Impossible? Being an Abridgment of the War of the Future*, Richard Grahant, London.

— (1899b) *The Future of War: In Its Technical, Economic, and Political Relations*, English translation by R. C. Long, Ginn, Harvard.

Hirschman, A.O. (1977) *The Passions and the Interests: Political Arguments for Capitalism Before Its Triumph*, Princeton University Press, Princeton (NJ).

Jackson, M.O., and Nei, S. (2015) 'Network of alliances, wars and international trade', *Proceedings of the National Academy of Sciences*, December, vol. 112, no. 50, 15277–15284.

Smith, A. (1776) *An Inquiry into the Nature and Causes of the Wealth of Nations*, Strahan & Cadell, London.

Goodwin, C.D. (1991) 'National security in classical political economy'. In Id. (ed.), *Economics and National Security. A History of Their Interaction*, History of Political Economy, Annual Supplement to Vol. 23, Durham, Duke University Press, 23–36.

— (2008) 'War and economics', *New Palgrave Dictionary of Economics*, Basingstoke, Palgrave Macmillan, 2008, vol. VIII, 696–703.

Preston, R.A., and Wise, S.F. (1970) *Men in Arms*, Praeger Publishers, London.

Weinroth, H. (1974) 'Norman Angell and the Great Illusion: An episode in pre-1914 pacifism', *The Historical Journal*, vol. 17, no. 3 (September 1974), 551–574.

1 An 'Austrian' Point of View on Total War

Stefan T. Possony

Fabrizio Bientinesi[1]

Introduction

'The generation of 1914 was entirely unaware of the necessity for extensive economic planning in time of war' (Einzig 1940: 13).[2] With these words, in 1940, Paul Einzig summarized what had become conventional wisdom about economic preparation for war.[3] Three years before, Stefan T. Possony had tried to confute this prevailing point of view with his book *Die Wehrwirtschaft des Totalen Krieges*,[4] which appeared, with perfect timing, in January 1938, two months before the *Anschluss* closed the debate, at least in Austria.

Who was Stefan Possony? According to Mirowski and Plehwe, 'the power behind Ronald Reagan's Star Wars project'.[5] This was the final outcome of a long career begun in the post-imperial Austria, half a century before. Born in Wien, in 1913, to a Jewish father, Ernst,[6] Possony was awarded a PhD on 23 December 1935, defending a thesis entitled 'Die Bedeutung der Wissenssoziologie für die Erkenntnistheorie der Geschichte'.[7] After the German invasion of Austria, he first fled to Czechoslovakia and then in August 1938 took part in the Walter Lippmann colloquium. The Wehrmacht forced him to move a second time, this time from Czechoslovakia to France. In 1940, after France had surrendered to Germany, and after many vicissitudes, he was able to reach Unites States,[8] where he became an important advisor on strategic issues.[9]

Thus, in 1938, Possony was a young scholar facing – without any particular complexes – a tragically central topic, namely *Wehrwirtschaft*. The concept of a branch of economics devoted to the specific conditions of war-economy originated in Germany, basically as a result of the awareness that the defeat in the first world war had deep economic roots[10] and gained ground mainly in German-speaking countries. The contributions of professional economists to the debate on *Wehrwirtschaft* were practically negligible. As Henry Spiegel wrote:

> There was nothing academic in this controversy, since it symbolized the struggle between various groups for mastery and control of the new discipline and its application in practice. Most of the participants in the discussion were army officers and economic writers of the more popular type, who were prominent in the Nazi party and eager to establish and expand a field

of economics, theoretical and applied, which would offer a great variety of opportunities. The academicians, on the other hand, were much more reticent. There was no academic economist of repute among the godfathers of the new discipline.

(Spiegel 1940: 715)

Many definitions of the *Wehrwirtschaft* and its aims were developed, but there were some common features that Henry Spiegel summarized thus:

To turn to the distinctive characteristics of the economics of the military state as they appear in recent German literature: (1) This economy is definitely an economy of scarcity, not of abundance. This applies to raw materials, human resources, and financial means. There is no unused capacity, industrial or otherwise. The utilization of men and materials is pushed to its limits. No problem of idle money and idle men arises since both are placed in the service of war preparation and war. (2) *There is centralized planning under maintenance of some elements of the price mechanism.* (3) *There are important modifications of the profit motive as the motor of economic activity.*

(Spiegel 1940: 717 italics mine)

German war-economy was actually managed in quite different way from the 'Idealtypus' of 'total rational planning'. Until the reshaping led by Albert Speer,[11] German war effort was seriously hindered by overlapping and jurisdictional struggles.[12] But in 1938 one choice appeared the only logical and reasonable one: total planning for a total war[13] – a theoretical and practical framework that was completely at odds with Possony's *Weltanschauung*.[14]

To-Morrow's War: an Austrian handbook on total war

In the preface to the book, Possony claimed the possibility – or rather, the need – for economists and statisticians to join the debate on military science (*Kriegwissenschaft*), thus following the examples of Henry Lloyd and Enrico Barone.[15] He defined the ambitious aim of his work in the preface to the Italian translation thus:

It will require an exact knowledge of the war-economy total requirements and investigation into the changes that would occur in the economic system, whose productive capacity is the basis of war-economy. Only after these investigations will it be possible to evaluate duly the proposed measures, whose usefulness to war-effort can be evaluated only from the point of view of their impact on the whole economic system. These are the aims of this book and, if its author is to believe to his critics, one might say that he succeeded in analysing scientifically and in depth the problem of war-economy with the methods and results of true economics.

(Possony 1939a: 18)[16]

And in the preface to the English translation:

> Every practical war-economy is based on a certain theory of warfare, hence it must be made clear what are the tasks which war actually sets the economy, whether it is able to fulfill them and if so, in what way. Of course, neither the tasks nor the performance of the economy can be expressed other than in approximate, round figures, yet these problems must be cleared up if only to avoid difficulties in the future which arise from ignorance either of military requirements or of economic facts. For if it is the duty of the economy to do all that would further the defence of the country, it is equally the duty of the army to keep its demands within the bounds of possibility and to adapt the principles along which the defence is to be organized to reality. Unfortunately at the present moment there is a deep gulf fixed between the army and the economists.
>
> (Possony 1938b: 11)[17]

To-Morrow's War is divided into two parts (see Figure 1.1): the first, dedicated to estimating the needs in terms of men and means for the war effort; in the second part, entitled 'Problem of Organizing the Economy of War', where the author expounds his theory on the most efficient policy to meet such needs. In the first part Possony estimates the needs for one year of war, on the hypothesis of a 1,000 km front, following two different scenarios: 'type I war, defensive on land, offensive in the air' and 'type II war, offensive on land, with strong general armament and air armament'.[18] Displaying a thorough knowledge of the technical developments of weaponry and their strategic consequences, Possony estimated the yearly needs of war time production for type I and type II war. Table 1.1 compares Possony's estimated needs (first two columns to the left) with data on output in Great Britain and Germany in 1940. Table 1.2 shows Possony's data on the ratio between estimated war needs for steel and iron/actual output, 1937.

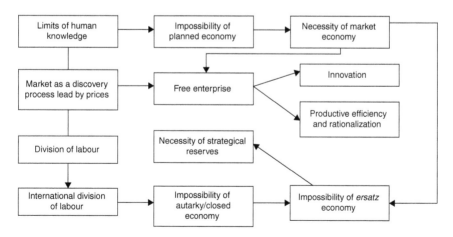

Figure 1.1 A conceptual map of Possony's *To-morrow's War*.

Table 1.1 Military hardware needed for 1 year, 1,000 km front

	Type I war	Type II war	German output 1940	British output 1940
Machine-guns	160–200	160–200	56,3	–
Guns	30	45	(over 75 mm) 6,3	1,9
Anti-aircraft guns	38	50	6,6	–
Armoured cars	25	120	6	0,5
Airplanes: bombers	70	70	(total production) 10,2	(total production) 15
Airplanes: fighters and reconnaissance	70	70		
Training	30	30		
Airplanes: auxiliary air fleet	56	210		

Source: Possony (1938b: 27); Müller (2000: 723–726).

Table 1.2 Percentage of coverage of iron required for the war effort with domestic production for different countries, peace time output

Country	Type I war	Type II war
USA	50	115
Germany	180	400
France	180	400
Great Britain	250	570
Russia	325	725
Japan	850	1850
Italy	1050	2300

Source: Possony (1938b: 108).

To these estimates, Possony added an even more astonishing one: he calculated the workforce needed for type I war at 52,000,000 and 82,000,000 for type II (Possony 1938b: 93). A real 'total war' – which was according to Possony, 'a combination of our two types of warfare' (Possony 1938b: 114) – was thus impossible, but it was not impossible to wage a war in a different way.[19] This implied nevertheless an obvious question: how could a country manage such a war effort?[20] According to Possony, the problem had to be broken down into three different challenges: (1) to cover the requirements of raw material in such a way that, if necessary, the state can manage without imports at war; (2) to make possible a rapid adaptation and enlargement of production from peace time to a war-time basis; (3) to keep open the way for obtaining as large parts as possible of the war-time requirements and manufactured articles from foreign countries' (Possony 1938b: 149).

On the first point, the *Wehrwirtschaft* theory had reached huge consensus on the so-called '*Ersatz* doctrine'. From the Italian orbace (national woollens) to German Buna (synthetic rubber), the Axis powers had made huge investments in surrogate production as a basis for total autarky plans.[21] Possony was totally opposed to this policy. His opposition was deeply rooted in the Austrian tradition of economic thought, whose exponents, from Mises and Hayek, to Machlup and Strigl were extensively cited in the book. Indeed, one might well read Possony's volume as an in-depth analysis and development of the concepts set out by Mises in the chapter 'War and Economy' in his book *Nation, State and Economy*.[22] Possony's analysis was developed from the hypothesis that the level of investments is linked to the total amount of savings. Thus, the production of surrogate materials – very often if not always with very low returns – required huge investments, which were clearly subtracted from sectors with higher returns. The national output decreased but this was not the only negative effect. The crowding-out effect was amplified by the rise in the level of national prices (Possony 1938b: 154–161) which, in turn, magnified the reduction of foreign trade. Thus, Possony stressed that 'the use of substitutes must cause a setback to international trade, that is the division of labour' (Possony 1938b: 171). This meant, *per se*, a decrease in production efficiency, as Mises had emphatically underlined[23] and as was confirmed by comparative costs theory.[24] An *Ersatz*-based war-economy could not survive without severe restrictions on imports and, as a result, exports, already hit by the rise in national prices, were hindered yet further. According to Possony 'if, for example, a car factory produces 1000 cars and exports 900, then if war breaks out, exports stop and this productive capacity which previously served other countries' needs, goes to benefit the country's own war-economy. Since on the whole people look upon exports with a favourable eye, they are greatly encouraged; often for the same goods as are protected. *Here the fact that import duties and the encouragement of exports are mutually opposed is overlooked. Every duty is a hindrance to the export trade*: hence if the productive capacity is to be increased by exports, one must be very chary of imposing importing duties' (Possony 1938b: 182 italics mine).

The passage in italics is central to Possony's analysis, but the logical connection according to which '*every duty is a hindrance to the export trade*' is not clearly explained in the book. It may depend on the fact that export goods made with high duty imports or with surrogates of lower quality could be less competitive on foreign markets. Or, as one may deduce from a different passage,[25] Possony was referring to an automatic restoration of equilibrium just like the 'specie flow mechanism'. This mechanism, like as clearly stated in Haberler's book *Der internationale Handel*, quoted by Possony in support of his analysis, was operative only in a gold standard environment, and this was not the case in the thirties (Haberler 1936: 26–29).[26] After all, a clear *penchant* for gold standard characterized Possony's thought on monetary problems. Re-establishment of the gold standard or an international currency standard with analogous features (therefore, not a fiat or managed currency) – as Hayek suggested (Hayek 1937)[27] – was considered a *condition sine qua non* to prevent 'too violent market fluctuations' (Possony 1938b: 250) and financial and credit laxity. Possony supported – for instance – the implementation of custom duties to hinder unbalanced gold outflow. Furthermore, he stressed that the war between Italy and Ethiopia had shown the economic relevance of the gold reserve to the financial war effort.[28] Consistently with this framework, Possony mocked the very idea of a shortage of foreign currency as 'one of the numerous popular errors in economics' (Possony 1938b: 205)[29] and vehemently opposed to dumping, a tool widely used before and after the First World War. In this case, the improvement of the trade balance was only apparent, since it was correlated to a worsening of the terms of trade:

> The various existing methods of increasing exports are, it is true, not suitable from the standpoint of war-economics. This is principally because, accompanied as they are by restrictions on imports, they become completely pointless; and also because the exports of the products of unremunerative lines of business are made possible by a charge on the community without any attempt being made to make the production of these products remunerative. Finally, the encouragement of exports, which is closely linked up with a bilateral trading and clearing agreements leads to a deterioration in the real ratios of exchange in the "gross barter terms of trade", which means that in course of time one has under these systems to export more goods in order to be able to obtain the same amount of imports. Before exports are stimulated one has to export 1A in order to be able to import 1B; n years later in order still to be able to import 1B, one has to export $(1 \text{ plus } m)$A.
>
> (Possony 1938 b: 203)[30]

Moreover, the implementation of custom duties or any other means to curb foreign trade fostered the formation of vested interests coalitions, which made reversing such means almost impossible.[31]

As an alternative policy, Possony suggested creating strategic reserves that would to reduce to a minimum level the distortion of market mechanisms, which remained the basis of a sound war-economy policy. But avoiding *Ersatz*-economy was only the first step. *Ersatz*-production was only one of the manifold faces of the real evil, the main target of Possony's book, the *Planwirtschaft*.[32] Possony's position was once again well rooted in Mises' – and more generally the Austrian School – analysis[33] and was based on two main assumptions. The first assumption went: no institution or organization – except from a purely theoretical point of view[34] – could efficiently manage the numberless variables of a developed industrial economic system. Within this framework, First World War experience became a sort of 'case study'. Possony explicitly wanted 'to unmask an historical falsehood which a great many people are willing to believe, namely, that no economic preparation was made for the Great War' (Possony 1938b: 174). There had been planning but it proved to be completely wrong.[35] Was the incapacity of the General Staffs to be blamed? No, Possony wrote.[36] The problem was to be found not in the brains of the top brass, but in the 'natural limits to the faculty of perception' (Possony 1938b: 246).[37] However, the economic experience of the First World War had had some positive aspects too. As the war went on far beyond expectations, the search for economic efficiency had, as it were, led to the right solution: the market mechanism. According to Possony:

> We may return now to the problem of how to make possible the improvisation of new lines of production and the expansion of old ones. It has to be remembered that this problem too was solved in the Great War, which is a splendid testimony to the adaptability of the capitalist–liberal economy. *This transformation was, as Mises points out, not the work of state intervention but the result of free enterprise*: the fact that the decisive part of the provisioning of the war-economy was *not* the work of the state is something to ponder over. The greatest difficulties, even in obtaining supplies of raw materials, arose from the maximum price regulations; these made production unremunerative, and the losses were not made good by the state. The supplies of war materials deteriorated in proportion as free business enterprise was curtailed. The Italian government suddenly saw "that private initiative was better suited to the urgencies of war". It was unfortunate that this principle was partly abandoned.
>
> (Possony 1938b: 187, italics mine)[38]

The second assumption on which Possony based his total refusal of the planning system as a possible answer to war-economy needs was its inability to introduce innovation, let alone to do so with the speed required by war-time. The rigidity of general plans to manage inputs and output distribution, linked with the impossibility of rational foresight, made innovations impossible to introduce,[39] thus hindering the war effort. Innovation could be introduced in the production cycle only through Schumpeterian entrepreneurs, which was compared to the 'apparatchik' of the planned economy: on one hand, an almost Promethean character, able and willing to undertake the burden of innovation; on the other, a man/woman whose only task is to obey.[40] For the same reason, Possony was equally wary about great corporation: the 'agency problem' had not been discovered yet, but it was already in action, just like Koch's bacillus before Koch.[41]

The third element which came in for Possony's criticism was the faulty incentive system of the planned economy. The market economy did not eliminate the possibility of misguided actions in the production cycle, but it reduced the reaction time to a minimum level, thanks to the profit-incentive on which was based: 'Under a system of free enterprise the danger of a misdirection of investment is by no means eliminated but it soon becomes apparent whether the investment was right or wrong. Even if with a planned economy a misdirection of investment should somehow come to light, the time taken to rectify matters would be much longer than under free enterprise, because the bureaucrat does not have to pay for his losses' (1938b: 201–211).[42]

The negative effects of the planned economy were not limited to wartime: they were fully operational in peace time. The *Planwirtschaft* removed the price system as scarcity indicator,[43] thus magnifying the mismatching between demand and supply.[44] In an open market economy, crises were not only natural but even beneficial, since they made possible to match ex-ante expectations with ex-post returns on investments:

> Crises are the consequence of booms, and occur because the market is uncertain about the prospects of investments; that is, because the principle of profit can only exert its effect *post hoc*. This effect, however, when it comes is very forceful and this is the essential characteristic of crises. They exercise a *purging function* in the sense of directing activity to the production of the combination of commodities which corresponds to consumers' demands.
>
> (Possony 1938b: 211 italics mine)

'A purging function': this view was relevant, according to Possony, to the ongoing crisis, on which Possony offered a structured digression. Again, on this subject, Possony adhered to Hayek's and Mises' analysis: wages had not decreased enough.[45] The data presented by Possony are summarized in Table 1.3.

If an excessively high wage level was the disease which prevented 'physiological' solution of the crisis, unemployment benefits as a cure were even worse than the disease: 'Unemployment benefit is unable to stop the evil; on the contrary it only makes it worse by enabling the wage level to be maintained and also by affecting the formation of capital' (Possony 1938b: 222). The latter passage is fully consistent with the theoretical reference framework: if the total investment has its limit in the amount of savings, any resource allocated to consumption reduces, *ipso facto*, the level of investment.[46]

For the very same reason Possony took a clear position against what was defined as 'the "famous purchasing power theory", which is misconceived and only contains a small grain of truth at the very best' (Possony 1938b: 223). On

Table 1.3 Wage and price levels in Germany, 1925–1934

	(A) Index of Prices of Industrial Materials	(B) Standard Wages	(A)/(B) × 100	(C) Index of Cost of Living	(A)/(C) × 100
1925	102.4	80.4	127.4	–	
1926	95.7	86.9	110.1	93.1	107.1
1927	96	92.1	104.2	97.3	105.6
1928	100	100	100	100	100
1929	98.7	105.5	93.6	101.5	96.2
1930	91.7	107.3	85.5	97.6	91
1931 (Dec.)	76.3	99.2	76.9	89.7	90.4
1932 (Apr.)	70.3	89.6	78.5	79.5	88.7
1933	–	–	–	77.8	–
1934	–	–	–	79.8	–

Source: Possony (1938b: 220–221).[49]

this point, as on many others not less crucial, Possony was somewhat elusive. Possibly because he shared Pantaleoni's opinion, 'that there were two schools of economics: that which could understand the science and that which could not' (Possony 1938b: 196).[47] Be that as it may, Possony's position on this topic can be fully understood regarding to the section Mises' *Human Action* titled 'Some Observations on the Underconsumption Bogey and the Purchasing Power Arguments', where Mises wrote that the increase in nominal wage – considered as fundamental to avoid overproduction crisis – did not need 'Government or labor union pressure' but was simply the outcome of an 'unavoidable and necessary phenomenon in the chain of successive events which the endeavors of the entre-preneurs to make profits by adjusting the supply of the consumers' goods to the new state of affairs are bound to bring about' (Mises 1949, 2007: 302).[48]

Thus, according to Possony's, (excessively) high wages, unemployment benefits and accommodating monetary policy could only reduce capital forma-tion and, therefore, the war effort, since *'the strength of the economic war will be identical with the amount of capital available'* (Possony 1938b: 191). The amount of capital was directly linked to the above mentioned question ('to make possible a rapid adaptation and enlargement of production from peace time to a war-time basis') to the third one ('to keep open the way for obtaining as large parts as possible of the war-time requirements and manufactured articles from foreign countries'). A 'proper' capital endowment was thus a *condition sine qua non* to keep international credit and a stable currency:

> One is easily inclined to underestimate the role of "confidence" in inter-national trade; actually it is impossible to overestimate its importance, for the granting of credit depends, above all, on there being confidence in the debtor's ability and willingness to pay and in the stability of the currency in which the debt will be paid. If this confidence is shaken, international trade is bound to decrease and with it the division of labour, prosperity, and the country's preparedness for war. In other words, the various foreign exchange restrictions, depreciations of currency, moratoria, and suspen-sions of payment are definitely disadvantageous from the standpoint of the war-economy, unless they are merely temporary measures to prevent a run or something similar.
>
> (Possony 1938b: 204)

Possony's criticism of planned economy as the optimal solution to war-economy problems was thus based on some well-defined theoretical bases. The first – although not directly mentioned[50] – was without any doubt one of the – at least – eight Say's laws.[51] In effect, if Say's law is considered as an analysis of 'an *unfolding market discovery process*, not an equilibrium condi-tion [...] with respect to both Austrian microeconomics and macroeconomics, Say's Law is a natural fit' (Horwitz 2003: 83, 96 italics mine). Say's law was then completed with the comparative costs theorem, which supported a free trade policy approach as a tool to achieve the most efficient international distribution of production. In Possony's analysis, production efficiency was quite different from that postulated on the basis of *homo œconomicus* as maximizing agent,[52] given his emphasis on the limits of the human mind, and hence on the impossibility of perfectly rational *a priori* human action.[53] The experience of the World War I had clearly shown how fallacious it was to pretend to plan economic war needs and production. *A fortiori*, the very idea of a planning without the aid of a price system as signal of scarcity was to be considered utterly foolish.[54] Production efficiency could be reached only through a 'trial and error' process, led by private enterprise according to prices variations. Thus, Possony's analysis fitted perfectly with two central concepts in the 'Austrian revival': '(g) markets (and competition) as processes of learning and discovery; (h) the individual decision as an act of choice in an essentially uncertain context (where the identification of the relevant alternatives is part of the decision itself). It is these latter ideas that have come to be developed in, and made central to the revived attention to the Austrian tradition' (Kirzner 1988: 150).[55]

Conclusions

Essentially, war-economy was, in Possony's opinion, a compromise between different and often 'conflicting requirements, just like a man of war' (Possony 1938b: 194): an antinomy which could be – at least partially – solved only by increasing output, fostering capital creation and dropping every investment which could prove 'relatively or absolutely unremunerative'. Thus, the measures to be implemented to reach war-economy goals, were:

> (a) introduction and maintenance of free trade; (b) establishment and preservation of competition; in other words, prevention of monopolies; (c) reduction of public charges to a minimum; this involves above all avoiding any taxation policy which amounts to a capital levy; (d) encouragement of economy, *i.e.* reduction of consumption by heavy taxes on consumers' goods; (e) renunciation of any policy which may discourage free enterprise, *i.e.* renunciation of any form of "planned economy"; (f) the capital for the purchase of stocks must be raised by loans or taxes, so as not to conflict with the other measures.
>
> (Possony 1938b: 200)[56]

In an essay published in 1940, Henry W. Spiegel described the schizophrenic position of a German economist – Adolf Lampe – whose aim was to include market economy mechanisms into the *Wehrwirtschaft*, thus creating a new *marktliche Wehrwirtschafttheorie*. According to Spiegel, Lampe's theory was a 'a curious blending of political opportunism and subservience with strong leanings in favour of a type of traditional economics of ultra-conservative hue' (Spiegel 1940: 719).[57] Possony definitely and clearly adopted only the latter as a logical result of a theoretical framework which was entirely within the Austrian School.

Notes

1 Dept. of Economics and Management, University of Pisa. I wish to thank: Graham Sells for language editing; Jenny Fichmann for research in the Possony archive at Stanford; Christine Reitemeier for translations from the German.

2 One year before, Einzig had written: 'It is essential that the Government, political parties and the public should realise the necessity for an organisation of production in the interests of national defence, if not before the outbreak of war at least immediately after it. It should be remembered that to all intents and purposes production in the totalitarian States is already organised more or less on a war basis, so that from this point of view Germany will have an initial advantage. The extent of that advantage will depend upon the extent to which the democratic countries realise the necessity of following Germany's example' (Einzig 1939: 29).

3 A paradigmatic example in Humphrey 1941. Fanny Coulomb writes on this topic: 'Governments learned from the First World War to be better prepared for a second war, by underlining the importance of economic self-sufficiency and of the use of governmental agencies of control of production goods, as well as of the industry's monopolized organization' (Coulomb 2004: 172).

4 Possony 1938a but preface is dated November 1937; English translation: Possony 1938b; French translation: Possony 1939b; Italian translation: Possony 1939a.

5 Mirowski and Plehwe (2009: 48).

6 According to the documents contained in the Austrian National Archive, regarding the inventorying of the property of the Jewish introduced by the Nazis after the *Anschluss*, Stefan's father, Ernst Possony, was a retired opera singer. The last document concerning him, bearing the date of 23 January 1939, reports that he was held in 'protective custody' in Dachau ('in Schutzhaft in Dachau befindet', a letter by the office in charge of Vermögensverkehrsstelle, Kanz, to Mercurbarnk di ÖSTA/ADR/BMF/Min. für Wirtschaft und Arbeit 1938–1945, Vermögensverkehrsstelle, V.A. II, Ll/Hko). No information is supplied about his mother.

7 Possony's thesis was reviewed by Robert Reiniger and Karl Bühler, Archiv der Universität, Wien. I owe this information to Thomas Maisel, whom I want to thank here.

8 German political philosopher Eric Voegelin wrote a letter of introduction to William Yandell Elliot, a political theorist at Harvard University, in November 1940, introducing Possony as 'the author of the treatise of the Defence Economy of the Total War [...] and one of the leading authorities on the economic problems of modern warfare' Voegelin (2009: 258–259).

9 Possony was one of the leading experts on Soviet expansion policy and the correlation between strategy and technological development and one of the founder members of the Foreign Policy Research Institute at the University of Pennsylvania. Among his most important works are: Possony 1953; Possony 1964; Possony 1966; Possony and Pournelle 1970; Possony 1974. He also dealt with the problem of human inequality and wrote, with Nathaniel Weyl, *The Geography of Intellect* – Possony and Weil 1963 – the conclusions to which were summarized thus in a review: 'The chief claim made is that the major differences in intellectual ability are genetically determined. Races adapted to cold and temperate climates have adequate mental endowments, those adapted to the tropics are inadequate. The way to advance civilization is by way of intellectual élites, which although aided by amelioration of living conditions and of opportunity are nevertheless largely genetically determined. To increase the proportion of such individuals it will not be sufficient to sterilize the mentally inferior; more positive eugenic measures must be adopted, including artificial insemination with the sperm of men of genius', L.C. Dunn (1964: 287–288). On Possony and his role in Foreign Policy Research Institute, see Wiarda (2010). A feature of a certain significance in the relations between Possony and the Regnery publishing house lies in the fact that Henry Regnery had 'studied in Germany for two years dur-

ing the mid-1930's, establishing friendships with anti-Nazi intellectuals and political figures' Schneider (2009: 46).

10 Stern 1960.

11 See Zilbert 1981.

12 See Müller 2000.

13 The term 'total war' became a household word after general Erich Ludendorff's book, *Der totale Krieg* (Ludendorff 1936). Rosenbaum pointed out that the term had already been used by the French general Bernard Serrigny in an article published in 1923 in the *Revue des deux mondes*, Rosenbaum (1942: 69). Léon Daudet had previously published a book entitled *La guerre totale* (Daudet 1918), cf. Bell, Crépin, Drevillon, Forcade, Gainot 2011. Possony offered a very general – vaguely tautological – definition of 'total war': '*War is "total" in the sense that it mobilizes a country's forces, but not in the sense that it really hits the whole of the enemy country*', Possony (1938b: 114, original italics). It is very interesting to compare this definition with the one given by Henry Spiegel: 'Total war can be defined as an armed conflict between sovereign states, sponsored and waged by a society in arms. Total war has no specific objective. Its aim is "the utter destruction of the vanquished nation and its final and complete disappearance from the stage of history". Total war is unrestricted in its means, and is fought on land, at sea and in the air with weapons supplied by modern technology, psychology and economics. The whole population is exposed to its terrors, and the line of demarcation which used to divide war and peace, belligerents and non-belligerents, is fading away' Spiegel (1942: 37).

14 See also Possony 1941a, Possony 1941b. Perhaps Possony would agree with an observation by Gedaleh, a character of Primo Levi's novel *If not now, when?*: 'What if, what if, what if … Only the Germans foresee everything, and that's why they lose wars'.

15 Possony (1938b: 13).

16 Italian edition titled the preface 'Prefazione all'edizione italiana e inglese' (Preface to Italian and English editions), but in the copy I consulted, from the library of Göttingen, the prefaces to the two translations are very different.

17 It is very interesting to note that, in the same years, an even more radical idea was stated by two Swiss scholars, Eugen Bircher and Ernst Clam, according to which 'although good generalship would help in a future war, brilliant economists were more essential' Bircher and Clam (1937: 296), quoted in Müller (2000: 435).

18 The scenario hypothesized by Possony was clearly shaped on a European continental war. Maritime war, in such a hypothesis, was practically negligible.

19 'The total war is thus merely an ideal which cannot be realized with the means available and apparently it has even become impossible to wage a war according to the rules of the military art. This does not by any means mean that war is impossible – it is not a sensible thing for a non-swimmer to bathe in a deep lake, but it is not impossible. *War is "total" in the sense that it mobilizes all a country's forces, but not in the sense that it really hits the whole of the enemy country*. The effect of modern warfare remains far behind the expenditure involved, and this gap between idea and reality means that in future wars *a rapid and decisive victory is impossible when the opponents dispose of equal economic and moral strength; in other words, that the advantage will continue to be with the defensive and blockade must be considered the chief weapon*', Possony (1938b: 114, original italics). However, Luc Favel pointed out that, following Possony's reasoning *strictu sensu*, a war in Europe appeared practically impossible Favel (1940: 8–10).

20 In a review that appeared in the *Journal of Political Economy*, Melchior Palyi asserted that Possony had confused two different maximization problems: on the one hand, the 'attempt to determine first the resources needed to attain the maximum military results against an enemy of indefinite strength' and on the other 'the maximum military results to be achieved with given resources' Palyi (1939: 450). As I hope to clarify, the two problems are, in Possony's analysis, the same.

21 Just as the Allies, too embarked upon large-scale research programs for surrogates, as in the case of rubber, when the Japanese invasion of South-East Asia hindered supplies of natural rubber. The difference between the Allies and Axis economic policies clearly lay in the juridical and political framework in which they were implemented: 'The concept of autarchy denotes something much more pernicious than economic self-sufficiency, and the drive towards self-sufficiency must be understood as an expression of the desire for mastery over a constantly expanding territory. There can be no real self-sufficiency until the expansion extends over the whole world', Spiegel (1942: 15–16). On the different approaches to the organisation of national economies during the WWII, cf. Harrison (1998).

22 Mises 1919, Mises 1983.

23 'The locational development of the division of labor leads toward a full world economy, that is, toward a situation in which each productive activity moves to those places that are most favorable for productivity, and in doing so, comparisons are made with all production possibilities of the Earth's surface', Mises (1983: 166).

24 'In what follows we shall assume a certain knowledge of economics as there is neither space to explain the working of the economic system nor need to repeat what others have already explained better and more fully. Therefore, in cases of doubt we shall suggest references to literature on the subject, for we shall not here explain what is the theory of comparative costs, and so forth', Possony (1938b: 197–198). On the comparative costs theory and its role as basis of the mainstream international trade theory see Maneschi 1998.

25 'The use of substitutes must cause a setback to international trade, that is to the division of labour. Apart from the reduction in output which results from this, it has the further disadvantage from the point of view of the war-economy *that exports are reduced*', Possony (1938b: 171 italics mine).

26 With the same clarity, Haberler stressed that the external trade balance hypothesis in the standard model was adopted for precise identification the dividing line between comparative advantage/disadvantage goods, Haberler (1936: 136–139).

27 For a general view of Austrian theories on this topic, cf. Salerno (1994: 249–257).

28 'It is noteworthy that all the same gold became of such importance again for the Italian war-economy, that the state organized a collection of it among the population to provide itself with fresh supplies. One can reasonably say this gold and the huge supplies of all war requirements it made possible, considerably facilitated and accelerated Italy's final success, and that without it there would have resulted a year-long colonial war which would have worn and sapped her strength. Thus gold, falsely given as dead, has shown itself as a very important condition for armament and economy of war', Possony (1938b: 250).

29 At a time when the dollar gap had such heavy consequences, Possony's words are a bitter reminder – at least for the Italian reader – of Don Ferrante's illusions (Don Ferrante, one of the characters in Alessandro Manzoni's masterpiece, *I promessi sposi*, is killed by plague and dies while denying the possibility of contagion and attributing the origin of the disease to a malign astrological configuration). In 1950 Possony, who wrote, in the *Encyclopædia Britannica*, entry 'Europe', the part concerning the history of Europe between the two World Wars, (cf. Stefan Thomas Possony Papers, b. 64, Hoover Institution Archives, Stanford, USA), pointed out that 'nothing had replaced the former automaticity of the gold standard', a situation that, together with the flows of 'international ready money' and the spread of "beggar-my-neighbour" policies, had transformed 'the crisis into catastrophe'.

30 Possony referred to bilateral and clearing agreements which were widespread in the thirties as a tool to compensate for international currency shortage, see League of Nations 1935; League of Nations 1945. Judging the clearings agreements, Possony did not take into account the 'influence effect', as Hirschmann called it, i.e. is the dependence which inevitably arose from any kind of trade and which could be deliberately

increased, especially in some conditions, cf. Hirschman [1945] (1980: 37). In this book Hirschman mentioned Possony, with Mises, Robbins, and Röpke, among the free traders who 'have usually fallen back upon the argument that foreign trade enriches a country and thus helps its defense', Hirschman [1945] (1980: 7). Years later, Possony must have changed his mind, since in a typewritten document, without date but surely subsequent 1947, he wrote: 'In order to control the economy of a foreign power, it is first necessary to control or regulate the economy at home. Thus, a country that fosters free-enterprise is at a distinct disadvantage when compared with a nation whose foreign trade is entirely controlled (or operated) by the state [...] Bilateral trade agreements for the purpose of economic isolation, the use or misuse of world cartels, or world agencies, the spoliation of markets by dumping are a few of economic weapons employed', cf. Stefan Thomas Possony Papers, b. 92, Hoover Institution Archives, Stanford, USA.

31 Possony wrote: 'As regards the maintenance in war-time of foreign trade, most of the factors opposed to this are of course likely to come into play. It cannot be sufficiently emphasized that is the main duty of politics to avoid a war in which trade is bound to cease; this is a task to which all others must be subordinated' Possony (1938b: 195–196).

32 The danger of the planned economy was so intensely felt by Possony that some years later he wrote: 'even so perspicacious a thinker as Peter Drucker could not avoid the pitfalls of the planning concept', Possony (1941a: 114).

33 Mises had offered a seminal contribution on this topic with his essay on the possibility of 'rational economic activity' in a socialistic system (Mises 1920), which was republished in the famous volume edited by Hayek (Mises 1935). On this subject, see Lavoie 1985; Murrell 1983; Horwitz 1998. It's hardly surprising that Mises wrote in his review of the book that 'the greatest credit of the Author is the destruction of a deeply rooted prejudice', Mises (1938: 96).

34 As Possony wrote: 'perhaps only the ghost imagined by Laplace' could conceive a real economic total plan. It's interesting to compare Possony's opinion with Kirzner's remarks on this topic: 'More important is the point that Mises and Hayek were implicitly attacking the relevance of the entire concept of Walrasian general equilibrium from which these equations [the equations supposed by Enrico Barone in his essay *The Ministry of production in the Collective State* Barone 1908, Barone 1935], flowed. For Mises and Hayek there was no disjunction between the "theoretical" and the "practical" following the Austrian tradition, a theory that necessarily violated practical reality was an unsound theory', Kirzner (1976: 68).

35 Possony supported this hypothesis extensively quoting Mises 1919.

36 On this subject, an interesting episode in World War II, which seems to confirm the problems and limits of economic war-planning, is described by Zilbert: 'in January 1940, at a meeting with various military experts at which the supplies of raw materials were discussed, Goering was given conflicting statements about the requirements for copper in the armament program. This was some four months after Germany's attack on Poland and England's entry into the war. The responsible military authorities reported that the copper requirement could be substantially reduced because of new technical substitutions, and on the other hand there was an unprecedented increase in the requirement for copper. In an attempt to resolve these discrepancies and conflicting opinions, Todt was made head of a commission to investigate the matter and to make recommendations for a solution to the copper program', Zilbert (1981: 87).

37 Possony stressed that 'if the prophetic gifts of the members of the General Staffs failed in their narrow, specialized field, that of strategy and tactics, who could have done better? They failed still more in other fields. Nobody foresaw the material war; nobody foresaw the part to be played by oil, or the magnitude of the war and the partial end of international trade. In July 1914 nobody would have regarded the situation as it was in October 1914 as anything but absurd. Owing to a lack of the power of prophecy the

economic preparations for the Great War were poor, but it *was* prepared for [...] The prospects of the present plans cannot be considered any better than those of the plans for the Great War', Possony (1938b: 176). Possony was living evidence of this truth. In fact, three years before Pearl Harbor he wrote that air bombing was ineffective against ships (Possony 1938b: 127) and, two years before the *Blitzkrieg*, that 'the possibilities of conquering an equally matched adversary by means of a "short, sharp" war are nil', Possony (1938b: 128). A vaguely ironical reference to this point appears in a review of the book published on International Affairs (Reynolds 1939).

38 The passage 'private initiative was better suited to the urgencies of war' recalled the title of the section 52 of Luigi Einaudi's *La condotta economica e gli effetti sociali della guerra italiana* (Einaudi 1933), a book published in the series financed by 'Carnegie Endowment for International Peace', containing a passage that Possony might have written verbatim: 'Due to accounting regulations or the unavoidable red tape, the government is inevitably slower than the private industrialists, and possibly also less efficacious, with the result that production in its hands would probably be reduced rather than increased, and be more costly', Einaudi (1933: 108). The same positions – obviously – are to be found in Mises: 'The greatest economic achievements that the German people accomplished during the war, the conversion of industry to war needs, was not the work of state intervention: it was the result of the free economy', Mises (1983: 171).

39 The 'proper' compromise between productive maximization and innovation was one of the major problems for the war-economy strategy. On this topic, Backman and Stein wrote: 'When, as in war, time is precious, use must be made of what is currently available, even though better alternatives could be chosen if time could be ignored. Such a question has arisen with respect to aircraft production, where improvements in design calculated to increase the speed, maneuverability, and fire power of fighter planes are being constantly developed. It has been suggested that where these improvements necessitate drastic, if temporary, curtailments in production, it might be wiser to sidetrack the improvements on the theory that is better to have large numbers of airplanes of non quite the latest design than a mere handful of the best which can be made', Backman and Stein (1942: 14).

40 'The means of determining the utility of a measure are no different in a planned economy than they are in a system of free enterprise. In both cases the decisions have to be taken by individuals; though in one case they are business men who stand to lose or gain and in the other case they are government officials who run no personal risk [...] The business man exercises a special function in the present economic system just as that of the past; he must act with initiative, "carry through new combinations" as Schumpeter calls it; that is to say, the function of the business man is the constant improvement of existing economic conditions, the increase of production and the improvement of the standard of living, etc. The business man plays the same part in economic progress as the inventor does in technological progress, while the official is of necessity no more than a policeman on point duty. This situation can never be changed, for the fulfillment of the business man's function by a bureaucrat is a contradiction in terms, and, in any case, the business man's real incentive, gain, has to be excluded from any government department', Possony (1938b: 207, 209). Possony again stressed the problems of 'natural opposition' to innovation and their relevance to war-economy in Possony 1941b.

41 'Even under normal business conditions, it has been proved that mammoth concerns cannot be supervised by one individual and that hence any rational direction is impossible; in fact, the larger the concern the more difficult it is to direct it', Possony (1938b: 207–208). It is worth noting that the sociologist Hans Speier, another of the host of German-speaking exiles, disagreed on this point, although he agreed with Possony on the end the entrepreneur as such ('The logic of total preparedness transforms the capitalist into a functionary of the government. Is he still a capitalist when everything is prescribed to him, the amount and the kind of his production, the time and scope of his

investments, prices as well wages, and even the number of workers to be employed?',
Speier (1939: 380)). In the 1950s Speier and Possony were to collaborate on the issue
of controlling the 'arms race', cf. Rostow (2003: 149–164).

42 Possony (1938b: 201–211). On the other hand, Jules Backman realistically highlighted
the role of the State as the necessary warrantor for private investments in the wartime: 'basic to a system of private production is the profit motive. Among the measures
designed to appeal to the profit motives are subsidies, guaranteed prices, and special
arrangements for rapid amortization of new plants. But the profit motive is often not
a sufficient inducement to insure the building of new plants. Businessmen fear that,
because of a sudden termination of hostilities, they will not be able to recover their
investment in such plants. The government may therefore pay the cost of building the
plant and then turn it over to private business to manage', (Backman 1942: 36).

43 'With decreasing scarcity one may, therefore, if one wishes, abandon the principle of
profit; war-economy means an increased scarcity of goods, since not only civil but also
military needs must be satisfied ...] The principle of profit does not exist in a planned
economy since, as Pierson and Mises have shown, no computation of returns can be
made, for this is possible with free market prices [...] even if one could successfully
maintain the entreprennial [sic] function in a planned economy there would be no crite-
rion as to what should or should not be produced', Possony (1938b: 209–210).

44 'In a planned economy, as experience proves, lasting disproportionality crises arise, in
the shape of over-production of certain goods and under-production of others. This is
inevitable in view of the absence of any basis for calculation, and the impossibility for
a government department to survey the whole world of economics with its changing
conditions', Possony (1938b: 211).

45 'The inevitable consequence of this wage situation is unemployment, because profit
is dependent on costs. If the prices obtainable do not cover the costs, as happens with
very high wages, then production ceases and unemployment, reduction in exports and
budgetary difficulties follow', Possony (1938b: 221–222).

46 'Even if the level of public expenditure is constant, there is still some question as to what
means should be employed in covering it. Taxes which affect the formation of capital or
even, as we have seen, make it impossible, may be rejected without argument. In so far
as there is a shortage of capital, it is necessary to throttle consumption, and a reduction
of consumption would have been the most suitable way too to cover the capital losses of
the war. Einaudi, referring to Italian conditions, observes: "The Italians, then, could have
conducted the war without piling up debts, without monetary inflation, without increasing
or decreasing prices more than is inevitable in any shift from one line of production to
another, and without any serious disturbance of the old order, they ...could have resolved
to live for ten years at an average standard of life only 86 per cent. superior to that enjoyed
by the Italian peasant at the outbreak of war". Here one must take into consideration the
fact that the Italian war costs were relatively small and that the "average standard of life"
of that time must be called very low. But with an extension of the given period of ten
years, Einaudi's argument is correct for every country', Possony (1938b: 219).

47 Possony limited himself to adding in a footnote a very short reference to Strigl's *Kapital
und Produktion* as 'a very good refutation of the theory of purchasing power regarding
of the demand for expansion of credit in favour of the consumption for the purpose of
compensating the recurrent phase of the economic cycle', Possony (1938b: 252–253).
About Strigl, see Hayek 1944, 1992; Steindl 1987.

48 Even if his analytical framework was completely at odd with Keynes' theory, Possony
mentioned the author of the *General Theory* twice – not negatively – with regard to
hoarding and to the justification of duties in some specific cases.

49 Possony supplied even more data, again without acknowledging his source, according
to which, assigning 100 to 1913, in 1932 the price level of industrial raw materials was
95, while that of manufactured goods was 125, the level of wages was 150–160, while
interest on capital came to 200–250 Possony (1938b: 221).

50 Not only in Possony's book: 'Given the strong similarities between Say's work and that of the Austrians, including their similar classical outlook, one would expect to find a good deal of discussion of Say's Law in the classic Austrian literature. In fact, there is almost none', Horwitz (2003: 86). Horwitz's hypothesis is that the attention on Say's law followed Keynes' criticism in the *General Theory*.

51 The reference is clearly to Baumol 1977.

52 Three years after the publication of the book, Possony compared *homo œconomicus* to Sorel's concept of 'myth' as the main motive for human action: 'One of the most dangerous thoughts which Sorel contributed to the modern world is the idea that political movements can be created only by myths. This doctrine of the necessary myth has permeated nearly the whole of our political thinking. It is not possible here to investigate the correctness of Sorel's theory. It must, however, be pointed out that the expression "myth" should not be indiscriminately applied to all ideas and motives which cause individuals or collectives to move. That part in man which can be roughly described as the *homo oeconomicus* is not moved by a myth but by interests, even if he does interpret his interests according to mythical conceptions', Possony (1941a: 107).

53 Thus eliminating the schizophrenia underlined, among the others, by Sombart, cf. Sombart 1929.

54 From this point of view, Possony's analysis fitted perfectly in the theoretical framework that Hayek developed some years later and which Garrison and Kirzner efficaciously summarize thus: 'In his treatment of the use of knowledge in society, Hayek made a sharp distinction between two kinds of knowledge: (1) scientific, or theoretical, knowledge and (2) the knowledge of the particular circumstances of time and place. The first-mentioned category is the proper concern of the economist; the second-mentioned category is the proper concern of the market participant. Failure to recognize this "division of knowledge" can lead to one of two serious errors. The assumption that *economists* can assimilate both kinds of knowledge leads to the conclusion that "rational planning" can outperform – or at least duplicate – the market itself; the assumption that *market participants* can assimilate both kinds of knowledge leads to the conclusion that "rational expectations" can nullify the systematic effects of monetary manipulation', Garrison and Kirzner (1998: 611).

55 These two concepts are added by Kirzner to those identified by Machlup as central to the Austrian tradition: 'Fritz Machlup has, on several occasions listed six ideas as central to the Austrian School prior to World War II. There is every reason to agree that it was these six ideas that expressed the Austrian approach as understood, say, in 1932. These ideas were: (a) methodological individualism (not to be confused with political or ideological individualism, but referring to the claim that economic phenomena are to be explained by going back to the actions of individuals); (b) methodological subjectivism (recognizing that the actions of individuals are to be understood only by reference to the knowledge, beliefs, perception and expectations of these individuals); (c) marginalism (emphasizing the significance of prospective *changes* in relevant magnitudes confronting the decision maker); (d) the influence of utility (and diminishing marginal utility) on demand and thus on market prices; (e) opportunity costs (recognizing that the costs that affect decisions are those that express the most important of the alternative opportunities being sacrificed in employing productive services for one purpose rather than for the sacrificed alternatives); (f) time structure of consumption and production (expressing time preferences and the productivity of "roundaboutness")', Kirzner (1988: 150).

56 Possony (1938b: 200).

57 Moreover, Lampe's attempt was a total failure: 'Lampe's expositions were fiercely criticized by the military, who simply brushed aside his theoretical efforts, disputed his empirical proofs founded on examples drawn from the First World War', Müller (2000: 435). Lauterbach stressed how 'A few authors, such as Stephen Th. Possony and, in a very different way, Professor Lampe, tried to show that private initiative was superior to any other policy in securing the greatest possible efficiency for defense', Lauterbach (1943: 81).

References

Backman, J. (1942) 'Maximizing wartime production' in Backman, J. and Stein, E. (eds.) (1942), pp. 28–60.

— and Stein, E. (1942) 'Transition from peace to war' in Backman, J. and Stein, E. (eds.) (1942), pp. 3–27.

— and Stein, E. (eds.) (1942) *War Economics*, New York, Farrar & Rineheart.

Barone, E. (1908) 'Il Ministro della produzione nello Stato collettivista', *Giornale degli economisti*, settembre, pp. 267–293.

— (1935) 'The Ministry of production in the Collective State' in Hayek, F. von (ed.) (1935) (Engl. transl. of Barone, E., 1908).

Baumol, W.J. (1977) 'Say's (at least) eight laws, or what Say and James Mill may really have meant', *Economica*, 44, pp. 145–162.

Bell, D., Crépin, A., Drevillon, H., Forcade, O. and Gainot, B. (2011) 'Autour de la guerre totale', *Annales historiques de la Révolution française*, 366, pp. 153–170.

Bircher, E. and Clam, E. (1937) *Krieg ohne Gnade. Von Tannenberg zur Schlacht der Zukunft*, Scientia, Zürich.

Coulomb, F. (2004) *Economics Theories of Peace and War*, Routledge, London & New York.

Daudet, L. (1918) *La guerre totale*, Nouvelle Librairie Nationale, Paris.

Dunn, L.C. (1964) review of Possony, S.T. and Weyl, N. (1963), *Political Science Quarterly*, June, pp. 287–290.

Einaudi, L. (1933) *La condotta economica e gli effetti sociali della guerra italiana*, Laterza, Bari.

Einzig, P. (1939) *Economic Problems of the Next War*, Macmillan & Co, London.

— (1940) *Economic Warfare*, Macmillan & Co, London.

Favel, L. (1940) *Problèmes économiques de la guerre totale*, Sirey, Paris.

Garrison, R.W. and Kirzner, I.M. (1998) entry 'Hayek, Friedrich August von', *The New Palgrave: A Dictionary of Economics*, vol. II, Macmillan, London, pp. 609–614.

Haberler, G. von (1933) *Der internationale Handel: Theorie der weltwirtschaftlichen Zusammenhange sowie Darstellung und Analyse der Aussenhandelspolitk*, Springer, Berlin.

— (1936) *The Theory of International Trade with its Applications to Commercial Policy*, William Hodge & Company, London (Engl. transl. of Haberler, G. von 1933).

Harrison, M. (ed.) (1998) *The Economics of World War II. Six great powers in international comparison*, Cambridge University Press, Cambridge.

Hayek, F. von (ed.) (1935) *Collectivist Economic Planning*, Routledge, London.

— (1937) *Monetary Nationalism and International Stability*, Longman, Green & Co London.

— [1944] (1992) "Richard von Strigl", in Klein P.G. (ed.) (1992) *The Collected Works of F.A. Hayek*, vol. IV, *The Fortune of Liberalism. Essays on Austrian Economics and the Ideal of Freedom*, Routledge, London & New York, pp. 168–171.

Hirschman, A.O. [1945] (1980) *National Power and the Structure of Foreign Trade*, University of California Press, Berkeley.

Horwitz, S. (1998) 'Monetary calculation and Mises's critique of planning', *History of Political Economy*, Fall, 30, pp. 427–450.

— (2003) 'Say's law of markets: An Austrian appreciation' in Keates, S. (ed.) (2003), pp. 82–98.

Humphrey, L.M. (1941) 'Planning for economic warfare', *Military Affairs*, n. 3, Autumn, pp. 141–151.

Keates, S. (ed.) (2003) *Two Hundred Years of Say's Law. Essays on Economic Theory's Most Controversial Principle*, Edward Elgar, Cheltenham.

Kirzner, I.M. (1976) 'Ludwig von Mises and economic calculation under socialism' in Moss, L.S. (ed.) (1976), pp. 145–151.

— (1988) entry 'Austrian School of Economics', *The New Palgrave: A Dictionary of Economics*, vol. I, Macmillan, London, pp. 145–151.

Lauterbach, A.T. (1943) *Economics in Uniform*, Princeton University Press, Princeton (NJ).

Lavoie, D. (1985) *Rivalry and Central Planning*, Cambridge University Press, Cambridge.

League of Nations (1935) *Enquiry into Clearing Agreements*, Geneva.

— (1945) *Commercial Policy in the Post-War World*, Geneva.

Ludendorff, E. (1936) *Der totale Krieg*, Ludendorff Verlag, München.

Maneschi, Andrea (1998) *Comparative Advantage in International Trade: A Historical Perspective*, Elgar, Cheltenham.

Mirowski, P. and Plehwe, D. (2009) *The Road from Mont Pelerin. The Making of the Neoliberal Thought Collective*, Harvard University Press, Cambridge (MA).

Mises, L. von (1919) *Nation, Staat, und Wirschaft*, Manzsche Verlags-und Universitäts-Buchhandlung, Wien-Leipzig.

— (1920) 'Die Wirtschaftsrechnung im sozialistischen Gemeinwesen', *Archiv für Sozialwissenschaften*, vol. 47, pp. 86–121.

— (1935) 'Economic calculation in the socialist commonwealth' in Hayek, F. von (ed.) (1935), pp. 87–130 (Eng. transl. of Mises 1920).

— (1938) review of Possony, S.T. (1938a) *Paneuropa*, März, h. 3, pp. 95–96.

— [1949] (2007) *Human Action. A treatise on economics*, Liberty Fund, Indianapolis (IN).

— (1983) *Nation, State and Economy*, New York University, New York (Eng. transl. of Mises 1919).

Moss, L.S. (ed.) (1976) *The Economics of Ludwig von Mises. Toward a critical reappraisal*, Sheed and Ward Inc., Kansas City (MO).

Müller, R.-D. (2000) 'The mobilization of the German Economy for Hitler's war aims' in Müller, R.-D. and B.R. Kroener and H. Umbreit (eds.) (2000), pp. 405–786.

— Kroener, B.R. and Umbreit, H. (eds.) (2000) *Germany and the Second World War*, volume VI/I, *Organization and Mobilization of the German Sphere of Power Wartime Administration, Economy and Manpower Resources 1939–1941*, Clarendon Press, Oxford.

Murrell, P. (1983) 'Did the theory of market socialism answer the challenge of Ludwig von Mises? A reinterpretation of the socialist controversy', *History of Political Economy*, Spring, 15, pp. 92–105.

Palyi, M. (1939) review of Possony, S.T. (1938a) (1938b) *Journal of Political Economy*, June, pp. 450–453.

Possony, S.T. (1938a) *Die Wehrwirtschaft des Totalen Krieges*, Gerold & Co., Wien.

— (1938b) *To-Morrow's War: Its planning, management and cost*, William Hodge & Co., London (Engl. transl. of Possony 1938a).

— (1939a) *L'economia della guerra totale*, Einaudi, Torino (Italian transl. of Possony 1938a).

— (1939b) *L'économie de la guerre totale: ses possibilités, ses limites*, Librairie de Medicis, Paris (French transl. of Possony 1938a).

— (1941a) 'The limits of post-war planning', *The Review of Politics*, January, pp. 103–119.

— (1941b) 'Rational planning for war', *Military Affairs*, Winter, pp. 222–23s.

— (1953) *A Century of Conflict: Communist Techniques of World Revolution*, Henry Regnery Chicago.

— (1964) *Lenin: The Compulsive Revolutionary*, Henry Regnery, Chicago (IL).

— (1966) *Aggression and Self-defense: The Legality of U.S. Action in South Vietnam*, University of Pennsylvania, Foreign Policy Research Institute (PA).

— (1974) *Waking up the Giant; The Strategy for American Victory and World Freedom*, Arlington House, New Rochelle (NY).

— and Pournelle, J.E. (1970) *The Strategy of Technology: Winning the Decisive War*, University of Cambridge, Cambridge (MA).

— and Weyl, N. (1963) *The Geography of Intellect*, Henry Regnery, Chicago (IL).

Reynolds, B.T. (1939) review of Possony, S.T. (1938b) *International Affairs*, January–February, pp. 113.

Rosenbaum, E.M. (1942) 'War economics: A bibliographical approach', *Economica*, n.s., vol. 9, n. 33, February, pp. 64–94.

Rostow, W.W. (2003) *Concept and Controversy. Sixty Years of Taking Ideas to Market*, University of Texas Press, Austin (TX).

Salerno, J.T. (1994) 'International monetary theory' in Boettke, P.J. (ed.) *The Elgar Companion to Austrian Economics*, Edward Elgar, Aldershot, pp. 249–257.

Schneider, G.L. (2009) *The Conservative Century: From Reaction to Revolution*, Rowman & Littlefield, Lanham (MD).

Sombart, W. (1929) entry 'Capitalism', *Encyclopedia of Social Sciences*, New York, pp. 195–208.

Speier, H. (1939) 'Class structure and "total war"', *American Sociological Review*, vol. 4, no. 3, June, pp. 370–380.

Spiegel, H.W. (1940) 'Wehrwirthschaft: Economics of military state', *The American Economic Review*, 4, December, pp. 713–723.

— (1942) *The Economics of Total War*, D. Appleton-Century Company, New York & London.

Steindl, J. (1987) entry 'Strig, Richard von', *The New Palgrave: A Dictionary of Economics*, Macmillan, London, vol. IV, p. 520.

Stern, W.M. (1960) 'Wehrwirtschaft: A German contribution to economics', *The Economic History Review*, 2, pp. 270–281.

Voegelin, E. (2009) *Selected Correspondence 1924–1949*, vol. xxix, University of Missouri Press, Columbia (MO, USA).

Wiarda, H.J (2010) *The Foreign Policy Research Institute and Presidential Politics*, Lexington Books, Lanham (MD).

Zilbert Edward, R. (1981) *Albert Speer and the Nazi Ministry Of Arms. Economics Institutions and Industrial Production in the Germany War Economy*, Associated University Press, London.

2 The Evolution of the Economic Thought Confronted with World War I and the Reparations' Issue

Fanny Coulomb

The development of the neo-classical theory by the end of the nineteenth century had excluded issues of economic policy and international economic relations from the field of the mainstream economic analysis. The new 'economic science' is apolitical and aims to explain the markets' functioning within the framework of pure and perfect competition. In terms of doctrine, the Liberals advocate for a minimal state and free trade. But the First World War, that broke out in a context of unprecedented economic and financial interdependencies at the world level, raises questions about the liberal optimism regarding the pacification of international relations through economic links. Moreover, the Russian revolution of 1917 enhances the popularity of the Marxist theory, which directly competes with liberalism: it is the return to the 'political economy'. Some heterodox theories arise out of this very period: as soon as the early twentieth century, Hobson had criticized the imperialist policies of capitalist countries, within a perspective of reform. World War I accelerated the development of another major theoretical critic of capitalism, the one of Veblen, the founding father of institutionalism. The time is right for political debates, in which economists take part. Amongst Marxist economists, disagreements are numerous, in particular concerning the evolution of capitalism.

After the war, the issue of the reparations imposed on Germany by the Treaty of Versailles turned out to be important for the evolution of economic thought. Only in 2010 did Germany finish paying the last debts related to the post-World War I reparations, whose initial amount, determined in 1921 to 132 billion Goldmarks, has never been fully settled. These debts resulted from foreign loans to Germany, along with the Dawes (1924) and Young (1929) plans, aiming at reducing the reparations' burden on the German economy. In 1931, the payments were nevertheless interrupted, while only 20 billion had been paid; they resumed in 1953. Become an adviser to the British Treasury in 1915 and directly implied with the issue of war funding, Keynes argues in vain against the option of total war for Britain. He is almost about to resign from the Treasury when the British government launches the call for conscription. After the German defeat, his book *The Economic Consequences of the Peace (ECP)* (Keynes 1919), published in 1919, is a major criticism of the conditions of the Versailles Treaty, allowing him to play a central role in the debate on the economic future of

Germany. In the 1920's, the study of international economic relations developed a great deal, thanks to the debates on the issues of reparations and inter-allied debts, notably in France, Great Britain and in the United States.

The question of Germany's capacity to pay poisoned interwar international relations and fed the resentment against the 'diktat' of the Treaty of Versailles. Later, the partial waiving of reparations sent out a signal favouring the German rearmament. The peace through free markets remains far, capitalism being plagued by financial disorders resulting from the war. Keynes will seek in his reflection on the inter-war economic and financial problems some principles underlining the *General Theory*, notably his mistrust towards world financial interdependencies ruled by speculation.

This paper first presents the debates amongst Liberal as well as Marxist economists, fuelled by the First World War, on the role of conflicts and wars in the capitalist system. A second part will show how the discussion on the post-war European order acted as a catalyst for the evolution of the economic thought, with the rise of Institutionalism and the foundation stones of Keynesianism, favoured by the very lively debate between economists on the issue of the German reparations.

The discussion on the reasons for war in a capitalist system

The explanation of the causes of the First World War is not easy for the liberal economists. In fact, the conflict occurs during an expansion phase of a Kondratiev cycle started in the last decade of the nineteenth century, with a first globalization began in the early 1870s and characterized by increasing international financial integration, facilitated by the stability of the gold standard system (but nevertheless leading to repeated financial crises), the rise in international trade interdependence and therefore the opening up of many economies, especially through investments in territories rich in raw materials. For the Liberals, why the pacifying effect of international economic relations has not worked is a challenge that few manage to overcome.

The liberal theory is not the only one to question its doctrinal foundations. Marxism is indeed so challenged that strengthened by the world conflict, which arouses diverging interpretations. The theorists of imperialism in fact often disagree on the issue of the inevitability of inter-imperialist wars and on their destructive impact on the capitalist system.

The failure of the Liberals' assumption of the achievement of peace through economic interdependence

The pacifism of liberal economists during the nineteenth century: the influence of Bastiat

The question of war and peace had been widely discussed by the Liberal economists during the second half of the nineteenth century, particularly in France. A disciple of Jean-Baptiste Say, Frédéric Bastiat, who is quoted by Karl Marx as '*the most superficial and therefore the most adequate representative of the apologetic vulgar economy*' (Marx (1873) quoted in Fine, Saad-Fihlo, Boffo 2012: 247), who has been claimed as a reference by the enthusiasts of ultraliberalism in the twentieth century, raised the issue in his writings, without however completing his chapter on the war in his *Harmonies Economiques*, the text titled 'Comment la guerre finit' remaining unfinished (Chapter XIX) (Bastiat 1893: 576). But Bastiat represents those Liberals who consider that war can only come from the pressure of private interests to the detriment of the general interest, an idea already present in Adam Smith's *Wealth of Nations* (Smith 1776). The idea behind the Bastiat's thought is that wars will end when public opinion in European countries will acknowledge the superiority of liberalism and free trade, incompatible with international conflicts and their side-effects: economic disorganization, greater state control and disruption to international trade. He does not fear the invasion of France and even suggests the unilateral disarmament of the country in 1849 to set off a wave of pacifism at the European level (Bastiat 1849). In a letter titled *Propriété et Spoliation* (Bastiat 1848), defending the principle of ownership, Bastiat explains that it is the principle of dispossession, an inherent tendency of mankind, which is the origin of inequality among men: the economic freedom combined with the principles of justice can only lead to peace and global prosperity. Every means of dispossession must be banned from human societies: not only war and slavery by also excessive taxation, public borrowing and war on capital.

In his wake, many proposals have emerged within the liberal current, for institutions capable of arbitrating international disputes, to avoid open conflicts that would increase the state control on public life.[1] By the end of the twentieth century, many congresses for peace have been held, where economists' influence was great.[2] In 1901, the first Nobel Peace Prize was awarded to Frederic Passy,[3] a French politician and ardent pacifist aiming to mobilize public opinion to promote a culture of peace, together with the promotion of liberalism.

Keynes' pacifism and support of Angell's views

Keynes' critique of the Versailles Treaty in the *ECP* is precisely part of this liberal pacifist tradition. He did not hide his enthusiasm for the League of Nations, founded in 1920, which raised much Pacifists' hope in the interwar period, but which however quickly showed its limitations. Keynes had moreover welcomed, a decade earlier, the book of his compatriot Norman Angell, titled *The Great Illusion* (Angell 1910), which denounced the European arms race and criticized the principle of war reparations. The basic premise underpinning Angell's work is the idea of peace through economic globalization, given the fact that:

- The economic benefits of colonialism are illusory.
- The potential economic cost of wars between industrial superpowers has become too great for policies of aggression to be considered, as economic isolation would very swiftly lead to economic exhaustion.

- The wars of predation are over, military conflicts' costs being too high because of destructions and induced economic disturbances, which cannot be fully covered by a potential war indemnity. Moreover, war indemnities can only be paid by the defeated country through an exports surplus that would compete directly with national products in the recipient country, with adverse economic consequences.

This questioning of war reparations' effectiveness has influenced Keynes, when he wrote the ECP. Enthusiastically welcoming Angell's work, Keynes supported his (successful) candidacy for the Nobel Peace Prize, in the early 1930s.[4] But the liberal pacifist optimism expressed in Angell's work of 1910 was tempered in a second edition, published in 1933. For his part, Keynes had already ceased writing on the reparations issue since many years.

A heterodox call for peace: Hobson's denunciation of the Western world's imperialism

As explained above, the liberal thought on war at this time was focused on challenging its cost and economic nonsense, as well as on the idea that war can only result from a diversion of the State machinery to private interests: it is not the capitalist system that is at issue, as the free operation of markets should on the contrary generate a common welfare, making wars always more absurd.

But an alternative interpretation of the imperialist policies of capitalist countries had been suggested at the beginning of the twentieth century, by a British essayist supporting war resisters in the 1910s and, at that time, supporting the 'new liberals' alongside Keynes[5]: this is John Hobson, whose book published in 1902, *Imperialism: A study* (Hobson 1902), made him famous, all the more so as large parts of his analysis have been used by Lenin in his own analysis of imperialism.

In his book, Hobson condemned the fact that liberalism needed jingoism, which allows maintaining the docility of workers who are subjugated by an increasingly mindless labour. He also explained that colonial expeditions are not only made to respond to the megalomania of national leaders and to make the people dream; they also have a distinct economic objective: let the surplus of the capitalist production slim down in the international markets. This idea, which is already present in Marx's 1848 text *On the question of free trade*, will be largely taken up by Lenin. Hobson thinks that the solution is to raise public's purchasing power so as to create internal opportunities for the capitalist production; one of the main reasons of wars would therefore be eliminated.

Hobson has published several papers in the review *The Nation*, that was acquired by Keynes in 1922. But their political paths separated in the late 1910s, when Hobson joined the future Labour Party. However, in the *General Theory of Employment* (1936), Keynes pays respect to Hobson's ideas, emphasizing his 'ardour and courage against the ranks of orthodoxy' (Keynes 1973: 355).[6]

The discussion within the Marxist current on the issue of the inter-imperialist war

The Marxist analysis of war and militarism in the early twentieth century lacks of unity: there are considerable divergences between theoreticians, regarding notably the inevitability of a conflict's outbreak and its impact on the proletarian movement.

From Marx's economic war to Lenin's inevitable collapse of imperialist powers

Karl Marx himself did not write specifically on these issues, maybe because he reserved his analysis of militarism for the last volume (never written) of *The Capital*, dedicated to the issue of the state. However, in his speech *On the question of free trade* (Marx 1848), he states a central idea for the Marxist rhetoric during the twentieth century: the world trade will become increasingly contentious as capitalist systems mature, because export markets represent an efficient counter-tendency to the rate of profit to fall, while imports of cheap foreign products exert downward pressures on workers' wages. All capitalist countries at the same stage of development having the same commercial and colonial appetites, economic conflicts may occur and the class war transform into a war among nations. Mocking the optimistic and pacifist views of the Liberals, Marx writes:

> To call cosmopolitan exploitation universal brotherhood is an idea that could only be engendered in the brain of the bourgeoisie. All the destructive phenomena which unlimited competition gives rise to within one country are reproduced in more gigantic proportions on the world market.
>
> (Marx 1848)

However, free trade is considered more progressive than protectionism, which is viewed with distrust, as well as nationalism, chauvinism and independence movements, by Marx and Engels. The Leninist theory of imperialism only partially comes from the Marxist idea of increased international disputes because of the transfer of internal economic contradictions on the world market. Besides, Lenin doesn't refer to the tendency of the rate of profit to fall in his theory of 1916, *Imperialism, the highest stage of capitalism* (Lenin 1916: 667–766).

It is the unequal development of national economies and of monopolies that lead to international relations' instability, at the stage of imperialism. With the rise in capital exports and in the economic concentration, the States are no more the central actors but the monopolies which control the world trade and make progressively disappear the free competition. The fight for raw materials exacerbates antagonisms on colonies' sharing; the new industrial powers, wishing to reverse the international economic hierarchy, are responsible for the outbreak of inter-imperialist conflicts, until the ultimate world war that will end capitalism.

The non-orthodox scenarios of some Marxist economists

Within the Marxist current, Lenin's theory was challenged by several competing and more or less incompatible analyses. If he does not criticize Hilferding – from whom he has borrowed the concept of financial capital – who had stated that, in the long term, an agreement between the more powerful capitalist interests, is very likely, Lenin targets Kautsky.

Hilferding is the theoretician of the 'financial capital', appeared at the end of the nineteenth century[7]: this capitalist model is characterized by a deterioration in competition, an increased concentration of industry and bank sectors and the growing power of just a few shareholders. The role of the state is enhanced because the state apparatus serves the interests of certain monopolies or cartels, with the setting up of protectionist measures that are circumvented by foreign direct investments. Moreover, the militarism is inherent to the financial capitalism, notably because the colonial expeditions allow to secure national economic interests abroad, the supply of raw materials but also to open foreign markets for domestic industrial goods. Only a strong pacifist opposition of the proletariat and of the medium class will permit to avoid a war between imperialist powers. However, in the longer term, the rise in firms' size and the internationalization of their activities, will lead to an agreement between the most powerful capitalist interests, beyond national borders, with the setting up of agreements between national cartels. The international agreements ensuring the inter-cartels peace must nevertheless be regularly reviewed, with the change in the balance of international power. This idea about an agreement between the most powerful interests, at the world level, was revisited by Kautsky, with the concept of 'ultra-imperialism'.

Like Hilferding, Kautsky sees the state's power politics as being in the service of bourgeois interests, as it helps prevent the under-consumption crises and the proletarianization of the middle class. If Kautsky had an important role, from 1890 to 1914, within the Third International, he was no more considered an orthodox Marxist from 1915, when he published a paper in *Neue Zeit* that was fiercely contested by Lenin (Kautsky 1915: 144).[8] Kautsky indeed defended the hypothesis of another stage of capitalism, subsequent to imperialism: ultra-imperialism. At that stage, not yet been reached (and maybe will never be), it is likely that the struggle between national capital is replaced with a joint exploitation by a worldwide integrated financial capital, therefore limiting incentives for an arms race between capitalist economies. This theory irritated Lenin, who called Kautsky an 'ex-Marxist'.

Another Marxist economist attracted the attention of 'official' theorists: N. Kondratiev, whose long wave theory, exposed as soon as 1925, portrays capitalism as a system always ready to be reborn from its ashes (Kondratiev 1993 [1925]). In this theory, wars and political or social conflicts are more likely to occur in upward phases of long cycles, notably because economic growth exercises a pressure on the supply of raw materials. The downturn in raw materials' prices is therefore an early sign of the beginning of a new long-term economic crisis. If it is known that Kondratiev was deported to Gulag and executed by the Stalinist regime, because of his pessimist views concerning the inevitability of capitalism's disappearance, his reputation was enhanced by the works of Joseph Schumpeter based on his long-term cycles' theory. Schumpeter is focused on the issue of major innovations liable to initiate a new phase of long-term economic growth: he rejects the idea that wars are important determinants for the gestation of those innovations, opening up a still current debate (Coulomb, Bensahel, Fontanel 2011).

Lastly, the First World War and the previous arms race, by requiring an increasing interventionism, have addressed the problem of the role of the state in the evolution of capitalism. Hence, in his 1915 book *Imperialism and world economy* (Bukharin 1915), Nikolai Bukharin develops the idea according to which capitalism has reached a new stage of its development, the one of 'State capitalism', with a strong control of the state apparatus on economic activities, inducing the continuation of interventionism by the time peace returns. In the context of the worldwide fall in the rate of profit, illustrated by the internationalization of firms' activities, the state plays an essential role in the promotion of national interests on world markets; but the diverging interests of the various nations may create the conditions for international economic disputes, the economic war being liable to end in an open military conflict, inter-imperialist agreements being unlikely. Bukharin's views on international conflicts do not correspond to the pure economic determinism of Lenin's thesis of 1916 that states are able to change the world markets' structure through their foreign policy (Howard, King 1989: 245–250). The historical materialism therefore indirectly comes into question.

The debate on the post-World War I European order, a catalyst for the evolution of the economic thought

In the ECP, Keynes was in favour of reducing the reparations burden for the German economy, in view of the double objective of a quick recovery of the European economy and of the durability of democracy. His position was criticized in two ways: by Veblen, who accused him of defending the status quo of an unfair and ineffective capitalist system and whose thought on inter-war international relations was pivotal in developing his institutionalist theory; by Ohlin and other economists, who challenge Keynes' analysis of reparations, opening the way to a highly focused debate on international transfers.

Veblen's attack on the institutions of capitalism through the question of war

Veblen's critique of Keynes' ECP

Keynes will strongly mark the debate among economists on the relevance of the Treaty of Versailles' clauses on the reparations imposed on Germany, with the publication of his 1919 book, *The Economic Consequences of the Peace*. He incisively denounces the French position aiming at economically weakening the defeated country to prevent its rearmament and he advocates for a reduction in the reparations burden, giving ammunitions for the supporters of the idea that Germany has no capacity to pay. Keynes is concerned with the political consequences of the Treaty, fearing a power takeover by reactionary forces both in Germany and in Russia, leading to their rapprochement:

> From the military point of view an ultimate union of forces between Russia and Germany is greatly feared in some quarters. This would be much more likely to take place in the event of reactionary movements being successful in each of the two countries, whereas an effective unity of purpose between Lenin and the present essentially middle-class Government of Germany is unthinkable.
>
> (Keynes 2005 [1919]: 289)[9]

This position supportive of a political status quo in Germany has been criticised by a heterodox economist, founding father of the institutionalist political economy, Thorstein Veblen. In his review of the ECP published in 1920, Veblen condemns the fact that the Allies' policy is more aimed at combating Soviet Russia than at reforming German institutions, as the victors are eager above all to safeguard the capitalist interests. He writes:

> So also his oversight of this paramount need of making the world safe for a democracy of absentee owners has led Mr Keynes to take an unduly pessimistic view of the provisions covering the German indemnity.
>
> (Veblen 1920: 471)

Veblen resumes a concept developed twenty years earlier in a key work, *The theory of the leisure class: An economic study of institutions* (Veblen 1899). It was an analysis of the capitalism's functioning, highlighting the predatory behaviour of the ruling class (absentee owners), which is losing contact with the concrete labour, left to engineers: speculation and economies' financialization are the inevitable outcomes.

The critique of capitalism through the analysis of the role of patriotism and warlike spirit

The outbreak of WWI brings to maturity Veblen's theory, already inclined to address war and militarism's issues, as it enquires into the internal factors of societal evolutions. In a key work published in 1915, *Imperial Germany and the Industrial Revolution* (Veblen [1915] 1964), Veblen introduces the distinction between predatory dynastic states (like Germany) and modern states (Great Britain, USA).

The predatory instincts of man have had a major impact on societies gone beyond the primitive stage, provoking the wars and conflicts that have marked the history of humanity and the changes in the institutions, the weakest ones being eliminated. Far from being mutually exclusive, war and trade have always interacted with each other, in spite of a perennial competition between commercial interests (prevailing in modern industrially developed societies) and dynastic interests (prevailing in dynastic societies of less industrially developed countries). In dynastic societies, mental habits inherited from the feudal period (sense of duty, subordination, preparation for war…) still prevail, leading to more warlike policies than in modern societies: these latter being long accustomed to peace have benefited from an evolution in the mental habits, and are consequently more likely to develop peaceful activities, like trade or finance. The differences in the political systems (autocratic or democratic) result from these institutional differences and there is a risk of an international conflict initiated by dynastic states.

However, Veblen's theory is evolutionary but not determinist. The 'normal' evolution of societies should in the long term transform all of them into modern States, as the changes in mental habits with the shifts in economic structures lead to institutional and social transformations. But as the evolution of societies ensues from a permanent adjustment between instincts and institutions, it is impossible to predict their future direction. In the dynastic states, forces of change (modernization) are exerted thanks to industrialization and technology boom, while in modern societies, the predatory instincts may spring back to life at any moment and lead to aggressive foreign policies.

This latter point is studied in detail in a book written two years later, *An inquiry into the nature of peace and the terms of its perpetuation* (Veblen [1917] 1964), in which Veblen develops the three following ideas:

- In dynastic societies, the preparation to war should cause organisational changes in dynastic societies, because of the growing sophistication of armaments needing advanced technologies and skilled manpower: these are factors for them to become modern societies (Chapter 1), that are more peaceful than dynastic ones.
- In modern societies, the evolution of the economic system tends to erase all economic solidarity (the ordinary man becomes always more mindless); Only remains patriotism to federate the system. Modern societies are thus forced to maintain a kind of warlike spirit in the population, capable of bringing up one day feudal instincts prone to war (Chapter 2).
- The last chapter (7) develops a strong critique of the evolution of capitalism, which fosters a concentration of wealth in the hands of a few. International initiatives for peace, and notably international institutions, are therefore regarded with caution by Veblen, even if he doesn't venture to predict the future of the economic system.

Veblen's attack on patriotism and institutions has arisen hostile reactions, of which the one of Roosevelt.[10] Veblen's thought is however said to have had an influence on the content of the New Deal, through its critical approach of the institutions, even if there is no direct link.[11]

The influence of Veblen was more direct on the Technocratic movement, created by Howard Scott in the 1920s[12] and very popular in the United States in the 1930s ; this movement advocates for solutions largely inspired by Veblen's 1921 book, *The Engineers and the Price System* (Veblen 1921), in which he recommends the abandonment of the price system and the seizure of power by engineers and experts, who are the only ones capable of managing the production with a long-term vision, without being permanently focused on profit maximization.

A further point to note is that Hobson was a huge fan of Veblen, to whom he devoted a book published in 1936. Both were heterodox authors rejecting the liberal theory and aiming at proposing alternative social models, out of the Marxist current.

The debate on reparations and the premises of the Keynesian theory

The reparations imposed on Germany were a key issue in interwar international relations. The non-payment of indemnities by the Weimar Republic, undermined by hyperinflation, caused the occupation of the Ruhr by France (until 1925, following the German refusal to pay the sums due for 1923), while the Dawes Plan (1924) confirmed a restructuring of the indemnities, in contradiction to France's demands, to allow the stabilization of the German currency and prevent the return of hyperinflation caused by money printing: lower amount of annuities, vagueness about their duration and, above all, an international loan of 800 million (consisting mainly of bonds with a maturity of 25 years), to ensure the payment of the first annuity. Unable to generate lasting trade surpluses, Germany soon carried a heavy debt-service burden.[13] For the critics of the debt relief solution, this initiative has made it possible for Germany to pursue a rearmament program far costlier than the amount of indemnities set in 1921. The diagnosis about the German economic collapse in the 1920s was therefore wrong: it is a French economist, Etienne Mantoux, who has expounded this idea in *La paix calomniée ou les conséquences économiques de Monsieur Keynes* (Mantoux 1946), written in 1943 and published in 1946). The complete renunciation of reparations decided in 1932 was held to have given to the German public opinion the signal of a permissiveness concerning the rearmament issue: Clémenceau has thus denounced in 1930 the revenge and militaristic spirit of the German elites in the aftermath of the defeat, and the immediate secrete rearmament (Clémenceau 1930).

The Keynes–Ohlin debate

It is this issue of Germany's capacity to pay the reparations that has concentrated the economists' concerns at that time. This debate was called the 'transfer problem', because the challenge for Germany was to get enough foreign currencies and gold to be able to transfer due amounts to recipient countries. Its most famous episode is probably the publication of an article written by Keynes in the *Economic Journal* in March 1929, titled 'The German Transfer Problem' (Keynes 1929) and Ohlin's answer in the same review, in June (Ohlin 1929). The French economist Jacques Rueff has also contributed to the debate in this review (Rueff 1929), directly criticizing Keynes' view and supporting France's position.

The arguments presented during the course of the debate have been subsequently discussed at very great length, so much so that this debate has become quasi-mythical. It is known that Keynes did not use arguments compatible with the *General Theory* published in 1936: his argument is based on a classical view, with the anticipation of negative terms-of-trade effects for Germany as a result of the transfers.[14]

Besides, the issue of the international loans to Germany expected from the Dawes Plan has also launched a controversy. According to the American economist H.G. Moulton, the induced debt may become dangerous for the German economy and these loans are high risk. But the American bank lobby dismissed his arguments, while the largest financial institutions transferred the risk on those loans to small financial institutions and ignorant investors.[15]

Ohlin blamed Keynes for not having taken into account the existence of these loans to Germany from 1924, and to have kept on analysing the reparations issue in the same way as in 1919. Ohlin argues that the capital flows to Germany, mainly American, have rendered erroneous the assertion of Germany's inability to pay, as the United States have invested in Germany twice as much as the amount paid by Germany for reparations.

Concerning the structural consequences of these payments, Keynes and Ohlin had two different interpretations. Keynes' argumentation is similar to that of ECP in 1919: in Germany, the devaluation and/or the deflation induced by the additional taxes financing reparations will not be enough to generate the trade surplus necessary to transfer the owed amounts, as marks must be converted to foreign currencies: indeed, the problem with Germany is that it is a key importing country, with a not export-oriented economy. If the industry of exports grows to the detriment of the domestic production, the flow of German products on the world market can lead to falling prices and to a worsening of the terms of trade for Germany. The burden of reparations on the German economy is therefore much more important than it seems at first sight. Keynes rejected the idea that the American loans have settled the transfer problem, contrary to what Ohlin thought.

For Ohlin, the lack of any significant change in Germany's structure of production in the 1920s (high production of capital goods for the home market without a development of the export goods' sector) is explained by the size of American loans to Germany: the issue of its capacity to pay has become irrelevant.

Ohlin challenged Keynes' view on reparations by using an analysis the development of incomes in the different involved countries: the rise in taxes in Germany for the reparation payments induce a decrease in incomes and demand in the country and therefore a fall in imports; conversely, the recipient countries benefit from a rise in factors incomes and therefore favours German exports. There is no transfer problem nor change in the terms of trade.

According to Metzler (Metzler 1973: 109), Ohlin's 'orthodox' explanation is innovative because international income transfers were mentioned for the first time. From a theoretical perspective, it represents an intermediary between the classical theory and the Keynesian one: Keynesian because it deals with trends in purchasing power and Classical as it assumes full employment and the validity of the Say's law.

In the opinion of Robert Mundell (Mundell 2002), Ohlin was the clear winner of the debate with Keynes.

One year earlier, in 1928, the French economist Jacques Rueff (Rueff 1928) had contested the existence of a transfer problem, by reference to the automatic adjustment of balance of payments' mechanism, related to the quantity theory of money. The purchase of foreign currencies by Germany on financial markets (financed through a rise in taxes or by loans) would cause an increase in German currency and therefore its decline in value against other currencies. The weaker Reichsmark has a stimulating effect on German exports, which would enable the transfers. Rueff put forward again this point in the Economic Journal in September 1929, in addition to the Keynes–Ohlin debate.

The transfer problem and the emerging Keynesian thought

Keynes' analysis of the transfer problem was not 'Keynesian' yet. However, three key ideas are reflected in it:

- The fear of an 'economic war': Keynes thought that Germany's necessity to create a trade surplus would induce a price war damaging for the whole European industry.
- The fear of a decrease in the standard of living in Germany: for him, honouring the debts is less important than public welfare, which is a rampart against fascism or communism.
- The distrust of capital international flows: loans to Germany has been a key element in the overexpansion of the world financial sphere, leading to the great crash of 1929.

Regarding this third point, the transfer debate was major in the genesis of the Keynesian theory. According to Robert Skidelsky (Skidelsky 2012), Keynes' analysis of the transfer problem contributes to the debate on the nature of the imperialism of capitalist economies: the superiority of Keynes' approach compared with the Hobson/Lenin thesis of imperialism is to have shown that the export of savings is not offset by an induced rise in foreign investment. Yet, according to Hobson's theory, only foreign investment can lead to rising exports preventing crises that result from over-production.

Skidelsky explains:

> Keynes pointed out that the expansion of exports which a net transfer of money abroad required could be blocked at both ends: the capital exporting country might be unwilling or unable to increase its competitiveness sufficiently to allow the 'real' transfer of goods and services to take place; and the capital importing country might not be willing to suffer the loss of its own

competitiveness. His argument was conducted in terms of a fixed exchange rate system, but it can be adapted to a system of managed floating.

(Skidelsky 2012)

According to Skidelsky, Keynes' mistrust in capital exports results from his analysis of unemployment in Great Britain in the 1920s, which stems directly from his thinking on the transfer problem linked to reparation payments imposed on Germany. The transfer debate has therefore proved essential in the emergence of an original Keynesian thought.

Conclusion

The interwar period was a favourable time for economists' discussions, which were important in the history of economic thought. The liberal orthodoxy is weakened by the outbreak of WWI, which refuted its optimistic view concerning the peace-making effects of economic globalization. The Marxist theory, which has incorporated Hobson's analysis of imperialism, is significantly challenged by an abundance of contradicting interpretations regarding the evolution and survival of the capitalist system. The emerging Institutionalist theory is enriched by Veblen's critical analyses of international relations, based on a categorization of countries' institutions. Arising from the Treaty of Versailles, the debate on reparations reveals the prominent place of economists in the political debate of the period, concerning the Allies' policy towards Germany; and also, the complexity of interwar financial and trade linkages and the great volume of international capital flows.

On both points, Keynes' view prefigures the idea of public welfare as a major objective of public policy and the mistrust towards international finance, paving the way for his subsequent critic of financial markets, expressed in the *General Theory*.

Lastly, one final remark is that this debate has revealed the vagueness of the data on national economies and international economic flows, at that time. It will only be dispelled with the progressive upgrading of national accounting systems, based on Keynes' works, well after the Second World War.

Notes

1 As, for example, Gustave de Molinari, a Belgian disciple of Bastiat and vice secretary of the Association pour la liberté des échanges (Association for free trade). See Coulomb (2004).
2 See Coulomb, Hartley, Intriligator (2008).
3 Jointly with Henry Dunant, who created the Red Cross movement.
4 See Alcouffe, Coulomb (2014).
5 See Dostaler, Vignolles (2009).
6 Keynes (1936) Chapter 23.
7 Hilferding (1910).
8 This article is quoted is in Lenin (1916).
9 Keynes J.M. (1919), *Economic consequences of the peace*, Cosimo Classics, 2005, p. 289.

10 About the debates to which Veblen's books have given rise, see: Borus (2009).
11 See Tilman (2004: 61–63).
12 Veblen was a member of the first movement founded by Howard Scott in 1919, The Technical Alliance.
13 See Fiore (2002: 37).
14 See Brakman, Van Marrewijk (2007: 122).
15 See Fraga (1986: 25).

References

Alcouffe A. and Coulomb, C. (2014) *De la paix par le libre-échange à l'interventionnisme pour la paix: l'évolution de la pensée de J.M. Keynes de la première à la seconde guerre mondiale*, draft paper for the XVe International Conference of the Association Charles Gide, Lyon, June.

Angell, N. (1910) *The great illusion*, G.P. Putnam's son, New York and London.

Bastiat, F. (1848) *Propriété et spoliation*, July, www.Bastiat.org.

— (1849) *Paix et liberté ou le budget républicain*, www.Bastiat.org.

— (1893) 'XIX: Guerre', in *Harmonies Economiques*, tome sixième, 10ème édition, Librairie Guillaumin et Cie, Paris.

Borus, D. (2009) *Twentieth-century multiplicity: American thought and culture, 1900–1920*, Rowman & Littlefield, pp. 236–237.

Brakman, S. and Van Marrewijk, C. (2007) *Transfers, non-traded goods and unemployment, an analysis of the Keynes–Ohlin debate*, History of Political Economy, 39(1).

Bukharin, N. (1915) *Imperialism and the world economy*, London, Martin Lawrence Ltd.

Clémenceau, G. (1930) *Grandeurs et misères d'une victoire*, Paris, Librairie Plon.

Coulomb, F. (2004) *Economic theories of peace and war*, Routledge.

—, Hartley, K. and Intriligator, M. (2008) 'Pacifism in economic analysis: A historical perspective', *Defence and peace economics*, 19(5).

—, Bensahel, L. and Fontanel, J. (2011) 'Economists' Controversies about the causality between war and economic cycles', in Chatterji, M. ed., *Business, Ethics and Peace,* Emerald.

Dostaler, G. and Vignolles, B. (2009) 'Keynes et ses combats', *Idées economiques et sociales*, vol. 3, no. 157.

Fiore, M. (2002) *Les banques suisses, le franc et l'Allemagne*, Genève, Paris, Droz.

Fraga, A. (1986) *German reparations and Brazilian debt: A comparison*, Princeton University, Princeton, NJ.

Hilferding, R. (1910) *Finance capital, A Study of the Latest Phase of Capitalist Development*. Ed. Tom Bottomore, Routledge & Kegan Paul, London, 1981, www.marxists.org.

Hobson, J. (1902) *Imperialism: A study*, James Pott and Company, New York.

Howard, M.C. and King, J.E. (1989) *A history of Marxian economics*, vol. 1, Princeton, NJ, pp. 245–250.

Kautsky, K. (1915) *Die Neue Zeit*, 30 avril 1915, p. 144. This article is quoted is in Lenin (1916), Imperialism, the highest stage of capitalism, VII, www.marxists.org.

Keynes, J.M. (2005 [1919]) *The economic consequences of the peace*, Cosimo, New York.

— (1929) 'The German transfer problem', *Economic Journal*, 39, March, 1–7.

— (1973) *The general theory of employment, interest and money*, In Moggridge (Ed.) *The Collected Writings of John Maynard Keynes, Volume VII*, London, The MacMillan Press, p. 355.

Kondratiev, N. (1993 [1925]) *Les grands cycles de la conjoncture*, Paris, Economica.

Lenin, V.I. (1916) *Imperialism, the highest stage of capitalism*, in Lenin's *Selected Works*, Progress Publishers, 1963, Moscow, vol. 1, pp. 667–766, www.marxists.org.

Mantoux, E. (1946) *La paix calomniée ou les conséquences économiques de M. Keynes*, Gallimard, Paris.

Marx, K. (1848) *On the question of free trade*, Speech to the Democratic Association of Brussels at its public meeting of January 9, www.marx.eserver.org.

— (1873) *Capital I, afterword to the second German edition*, quoted in Fine, B., Saad-Fihlo, A. and Boffo, M. (2012) *The Elgar companion to Marxist economics, Edward Elgar*, Cheltenham, Northampton, p. 247.

Metzler, L.A. (1973) *Collected Papers*, Harvard University Press.

Mundell, R. (2002) 'Keynes and Ohlin and the transfer problem', in Findlay, R. et al. (eds), *Bertil Ohlin: A centennial celebration 1899–1999*, MIT Press, pp. 227–262.

Ohlin, B. (1929) 'The reparation problem: A discussion', *Economic Journal*, 39, June, 172–178.

Rueff, M.J. (1928) 'Une erreur économique: l'organisation des transferts', dans *Théorie monétaire*, pp. 181–200, p. 183.

— (1929) 'Mr. Keynes' views on the transfer problem', *Economic Journal*, 39, September, 388–399.

Skidelsky, R. (2012) *Keynes, Hobson, Marx*, October 10, www.skidelskyr.com.

Smith, A. (1776) *An inquiry into the nature and causes of the wealth of nations*, London, Methuen & Co Ltd.

Tilman, R. (2004) *Thorstein Veblen, John Dewey, C. Wright Mills and the Generic Ends of Life*, Rowman & Littlefield Publishers, pp. 61–63.

Veblen, T. (1899) *The theory of the leisure class: An economic study of institutions*, Macmillan.

— [1915] (1964) *Imperial Germany and the industrial revolution*, Augustus M. Kelley, New York.

— [1917] (1964) *An inquiry into the nature of peace and the terms of its perpetuation*, Augustus M. Kelley, New York.

— (1920) 'Review of John Maynard Keynes, the economic consequences of the peace', *Political Science Quarterly*, 35, pp. 467–472.

— (1921) *The engineers and the price system*, B.W. Huebsch, New York.

3 Third Way, Liberalism and the Crisis of Civilization

Wilhelm Röpke Facing the Second World War

Alberto Giordano

Premise

The outbreak of World War II left Wilhelm Röpke astonished but not surprised. For so many years the German economist, who was forced by the Nazi to flee to Turkey and eventually to Switzerland, where he taught at the *Institut d'Hautes Etudes Internationales* sited in Geneva, had been fearing that the political, economic and moral disintegration of the international community, and Europe in particular, was to produce a war of unprecedented scale.[1] He saw the reestablishment of customs; the increasingly invasive interventionism into market economy; the aggressive upsurge of fascist autarkies and populist totalitarianism, though black or red; the progressive loss of competition within and outside the national borders as the most alarming symptoms of a crisis doomed to burst violently and overwhelm Western civilization.

However, while struck by the drama he suffered, Röpke strove to find a cure for so great a disease. No coincidence that between 1942 and 1945 he wrote and published four fundamental books, where he tried to outline a proposal of a liberal third way in order to overcome the fruitless option between totalitarian collectivism and historical capitalism – phenomenon, the latter, that embodied the degeneration of free market economy. Quite unexpectedly, even though Röpke has been experiencing a massive revival,[2] the impact of his reflections on the intellectual and economic nature of war has been somehow underrated even by the best literature. Hence the purpose of this chapter, which aims to re-evaluate his analysis of the moral and economic roots of the second World War and to show how much it inspired the development of his peculiar liberalism.

Röpke's economy and sociology of war

The intellectual and political evils of war

In the first page of one of his masterpieces, *International Order* (first ed. 1945, rev. ed. 1959 bearing the title *International Order and Economic Integration*), Röpke revealed how much his enduring distrust for militarism and nationalism had matured inside the dark trenches of WWI, where he kept alive the myth of the golden age, aka the nineteenth century, commonly regarded as *le siècle libéral*:

> The author of this book belongs to the generation which in its youth saw the sunset glow of that long and glorious sunny day of the western world, which lasted from the Congress of Vienna until August 1914, and of which those who have only lived in the present arctic night of history can have no adequate conception. His experience has therefore been similar to that of so many of his contemporaries in all those countries which were drawn into the whirlpool of the first world war. Like other Germans, Englishmen, Frenchmen and Belgians he knew as a young man the horrors of the gigantic battles on the plains of France. This experience became a determinant factor for the rest of his life as it did for his contemporaries. At the most impressionable age for such influences, he received a shock which suddenly caused him to see many things which his upbringing had up to then kept hidden from him. Never again were the pictures of those days to forsake him, nor the ideas which from that time on made him a fervent hater of war, of brutal and stupid national pride, of the greed for domination and of every collective outrage against ethics. He made a solemn promise, that if he should escape from that inferno, the main purpose of his life from then on could only consist in his devoting himself to the task of helping to prevent a recurrence of this disaster, and in reaching out beyond the narrow confines of his own nation to join forces with all other fellow-workers in the same cause. Thousands and thousands of his contemporaries and fellow-sufferers within and beyond the frontiers of his country had come to the same conclusion.
>
> (Röpke 1959a [1945]: 3)

As properly stated in Gregg (2010: 4), 'like many other young men of his generation, Röpke's experience of military service in World War I cannot be underestimated when attempting to comprehend the post-war direction of his thought'. Such a tremendous shock did not make him forgetful of the benefits enjoyed by citizens and consumers alike thanks to the globalized market economy emerged through the nineteenth century; but he suddenly became aware of the need to examine the moral and political dilemmas that marked so deeply the evolution of economic life in the last decades. Therefore, he started to study in detail the social and cultural values of post-war Europe and suddenly many factors popped under his own eyes.

Ambitious as it was, this mission implied an engagement that moved well beyond the boundaries of pure economics; in fact, 'to Röpke's eyes, the crisis was not merely economic' (Solchany 2014: 100). In an early analysis of the causes of the Great Depression, dated 1933, he had already stressed the interdependence of ethics, politics and economics focusing on 'the many forces at work to undermine the intellectual and moral foundations of our social system and thereby eventually to cause the collapse of the economic system indissolubly connected with the social system as a whole'.[3] All this resulted in the intellectual crisis of liberalism, conceived as 'a cultural energy center that has been operative in all periods of the flowering of Western civilization and drew its sustenance from the thought of the best men of all times' (Röpke 1969: 80, 84) rather than a narrow middle-class ideology.

Furthermore, he noticed that the seeds of nationalism and militarism were widely spread among the masses almost everywhere. This perversion was due, in greater part, to the fact that many intellectuals and politicians began 'to deny at times the supremely catastrophic character of war';[4] in the meantime, he had to admit that 'wars would be impossible if international interrelations were subject to an effective judicial system which would curb the arbitrary use of force between the nations in exactly the same way as does a national judicial system between individuals', regardless of any 'sociological and psychological argument' (Röpke 1959a [1945]: 26).

In other words, the evil influence of Machiavellianism – a ghost doomed to taunt, though periodically, lots of European souls – had produced so great an upheaval that nor the ruling classes neither the populace were ready to resist its seduction:

> Europe would not have become a charnel house and a heap of smoking ruins if these doctrines had not during the last century gained an ever stronger hold over people's minds and an increasingly unrestrained influence over foreign politics. [...] As apparent to all today as is the destruction which this doctrine of a double-barreled morality has brought about, so indubitable is it that no international order of any kind will be possible in the future unless the confusion of moral ideas is abolished which this doctrine has created.
>
> (Röpke 1959a [1945]: 33–34)

But there was something more, in the political realm, that really frightened Röpke, that is 'the paramount force of the modern state and also the influence of single pressure groups within the nation'; from this he came to infer that 'the power of the State must be limited and influential power groups must be suppressed'. Both things, by the way, concurred to make clear the origins of war – which had brought together 'a hitherto unknown degree of restriction upon elementary freedoms' (Röpke 1959a [1945]: 6) – and the factors that steered to the irreversible crisis of liberalism in the interregnum between the two world wars. It is worthwhile to quote again at length from the introduction to *International Order*, where the milestones of his approach to the above mentioned points are very well synthesized and displayed:

> From the very beginning the difficulty was – to express it in sharp paradox – that we agreed with the Socialists in rejecting Capitalism and with the followers of Capitalism in rejecting Socialism. We began with the first rejection in the trenches, where we learnt to hate every form of repression, abasement and exploitation of mankind; we learnt the second form of rejection later, when experience and reflection taught us the true nature of Socialism. It seemed

to us that Capitalism and Socialism were each right in a certain way and wrong in another way. Everything depended upon discovering in what way to achieve the best combination of what was right on both sides. The natural result was that we continually sought for the solution which later, as its out-lines became more clearly defined, came to be known as "the third way" or "economic humanism".

(Röpke 1959a [1945]: 9)

For Röpke, in sum, a number of moral and political issues triggered a long series of metamorphoses into the inner structure of market economy. The 'third way', indeed, stood as the only rational cure to the economic insanity which led to the outbreak of war at the end of the Thirties, whose intrinsic nature and roots he duly described – something to which we must now turn.

The economic roots of WWII

The withdrawal from free markets had begun very early and, according to Röpke, proceeded in at least three ways:

1   a sheer increase in State interventionism (together with the outcome, by no way negligible, of the growing fascination towards collectivism);
2   the conflicts between nations for the acquisition and the display of raw commodities, a factor tied up to the demographic explosion experienced by most Western countries and the rise of nationalism as a public philosophy;
3   the consequent disintegration of the globalized economy, a system based on entrepreneurial freedom, division of labour and international competition.

Röpke was persuaded that the increase of State interference was due on the one hand to the influence that certain moneyed interests had been exercising for a long time on national governments; on the other (as we shall see in depth in the next paragraph), to the blindness of many classical liberals, who had faithfully believed in the so-called theory of 'the automatic regulation of a free market', forgetting that, quite the reverse, 'a market economy needs a firm moral, political and institutional framework' (Röpke 1950 [1942]: 51–52).

Paradoxically enough, this failure in the recognition 'of the necessary socio-logical limits and conditions circumscribing a free market' (Röpke 1950 [1942]: 51) urged many social groups and classes to request an active role of the State and gave rise to a political theory that shaped the minds and the actions alike of many policymakers, intellectuals, businessmen as well as simple citizens: the 'administrative control (i.e. political direction) of the economic process'. This trend towards the establishment of a hypertrophic State led to the dismissal of at least one crucial pillar of any real market economy:

> This development towards the interventionist, welfare and fiscal state shows already essential features of socialism. It lies exactly on the line which the

latter follows to its logical end: the subjection of the economy to political forces. What is already true for the step-by-step "political direction" with its increasing accentuation of the economic importance of national boundaries is all the more to be expected from the complete political direction of the economy, to which the superseding of the free market economy by dirigisme actually amounts. In fact, it is only now that the process of the "nationalization of man" is being completed. It is no longer a mere tendency, which within certain limits can be avoided, but a logical necessity.

(Röpke 1959a [1945]: 94, 97)

Nationalism, interventionism and collectivism, for Röpke, were properly distinctive features shared by totalitarian regimes of any colour[5] (but traces of which were detectible alike in progressive democracies such as the US under the *New Deal*). And the spread of collectivism, or at least of interventionism, made it much more likely for some States to pursue a policy of power on the international stage, particularly as to the supply of commodities. Röpke believed that 'the much abused liberal epoch of the 19th century' had found a good solution to the problem: 'to lessen the economic importance of unequal domination of the world's resources to the greatest possible extent, by separating where possible the spheres of politics and economics and creating what we call world-economy' (Röpke 1959a [1945]: 122).

This global market of commodities had made it possible 'for international economic transactions to be so carried out, as if there were a world-state' so that, in the end, 'no one spoke of a "raw materials problem" of the "have-not peoples", no one of the necessity of "the equal access of all peoples to the world's raw materials", and if anyone would have done so, he would not have been at all understood'. But then a small number of '"hungry" states' like Germany, Italy and Japan – 'i.e. those countries, whose "dynamic force" finally led to the Second World War' – came to demand 'in the name of "proletarian peoples" or, according to the German variation, with the claim to "Lebensraum" (room to live), a fresh distribution of political domination in the world in favour of the have-nots', that is an 'international social justice' regarding the distribution of commodities (Röpke 1959a [1945]: 117–118, 122).

Such a request was equally due, according to Röpke, to the well-known demographic boom that put so much pressure on the power élites, more than ever the ones which were about to build and rule totalitarian regimes. The 'enormous increase in population of the last 100 years', through a 'historically unique process' (Röpke 1959a [1945]: 132), determined an escalation in the causes of conflict among nations (the supply of commodities included), that reached its peak in the years immediately preceding and following the outbreak of WWI:

This was the first time broader strata of the society were beginning to feel a very real uneasiness concerning the world economic and industrial development. Not a few began to realize that the unparalleled increase in the population had brought the world into a situation full of dangers and problems, which would one day show themselves in all their enormity, as soon as the conditions, under which the additional millions had come to life, started to waver. Even then the realization was ripening, that modern mass-civilization, which has bestowed upon us the growth of the population, leads to serious manifestations of social instability and burdens it with moral and political tensions of all kinds, which also have a dangerous reaction on foreign policy. In this way, however, it was possible to argue even at that time, there arises a really tragic confusion: the earth has only been able to bear and nourish an increased population, because its entire productive power could be adapted to the purpose of supplying the masses by a complicated scheme of inter-national division of labour, but the conditions necessary for the enormous mass-supplying apparatus are peace, order, freedom and security, in short a series of laboriously acquired principles of human communal life, which must be guarded as laboriously as they have been acquired. Mass-civilization however, implies powerful tendencies, which loosen rather than strengthen those principles, for which concentrated masses tend in general to have very slight respect.

(Röpke 1959a [1945]: 135–136)

Nationalism, then, looked like the easiest, though misleading, answer to challeng-ing and over-complicated questions. All these phenomena, identified as primary factors of subversion, had impacted significantly the state of the global economy. Röpke was always deeply convinced that, at least until 1914, 'the world-economy was basically a system of interdependence and intercommunication', a multilat-eral system and, 'thanks to a really international monetary system (Gold standard) practically a global payments community'. As a final point, 'the world-economy was a system of basic freedom not only in the international movement of goods, but also in the international movement of capital and human beings' (Röpke 1959a [1945]: 156–158).

At least, this was the state of affairs until the systematic destruction of the world economy endorsed by those governments who had implemented the above described policies (i.e. protectionism, nationalism, interventionism): some of them acted 'from evil intention', others 'from negligence, weakness or lack of insight and still others from self-defence or after extreme resistance and in pes-simistic resignation' (Röpke 1959a [1945]: 160). Hence the gradual birth of an irrational fear of both domestic and (mostly) international competition; however, while until the outbreak of World War I 'it was as a rule more a case of fear of competition in definite branches of production than of general fear of competi-tion which imagined a possible inferiority of the national economy as a whole vis-à-vis foreign countries', within the next two decades 'from being an excep-tion, this general fear of competition has become the rule' (Röpke 1959a [1945]: 177–178).

Add to all this the 'very fear of an adverse balance of payments' that had 'contributed towards spreading the plague of currency control throughout the world' (Röpke 1959a [1945]: 195) and the collapse of global economy, together with every hope of a progressive spread of political liberty, was quite easily explained. The war, then, was the only logical end to 'a general crisis of civilization beginning in August 1914', but whose roots were well planted into 'the preceding hundred years' and needed to be examined in detail:

> We shall then realize with astonishment that this unique period between 1814 and 1914 was predominantly a century of peace and at the same time the century of liberal capitalism, and this century, whose spirit of progress, order, stability and increasing prosperity is unequalled in history, is succeeded by a period of disruption which in turn surpasses most of its historical predecessors. Truly a sudden descent from the proud pinnacle on which the nineteenth century – despite the predictions of a few far-sighted prophets – had felt so secure!
>
> (Röpke 1950 [1942]: 3)

The disease could be cured only overcoming the social and political philosophy that had superseded the corruption of market economy and the subsequent outbreak of war. Such was the mission of the Third Way, a revisionist theory ready to dismiss 'the sterile alternative between laissez-faire and collectivism' (Röpke 1950 [1942]: 23) and to initiate a novel economic humanism.

The Third Way: the ethics, politics and economics of reconstruction

As a matter of fact, many factors concurred in Röpke's elaborating his program. The clash of civilization and the sorrows of war, as we have seen, made him revise every field of economic thought and policy. But he believed, in the meantime, that even despite all the economic causes he had identified, a fundamental element was needed to be added in order to explain the ultimate reason of wars: the decline of liberal culture, inextricably linked to the decadence undergone by those institutions that were meant to embody the same liberal values.

Liberalism, for Röpke, was the heir of the classical tradition represented by Aristotle, the Stoics, Cicero and Boethius, not to mention the Christian anthropology of Aquinas and Marsilio of Padua. As a political and economic philosophy, liberalism reached its apex in the eighteenth century, so that 'humanity, freedom, order, rational control of the instincts, balance, peace, progress and the other attributes of the nineteenth century appear…to be largely the fulfilment of the intellectual and moral theories of the eighteenth century' (Röpke 1950 [1942]: 54). In the nineteenth century, in fact, those who, as 'Benjamin Constant, Tocqueville, John Stuart Mill, Alexander Hamilton, Madison, Calhoun, Lecky and many others' (Röpke 1950 [1942]: 85), had passed on the torch of liberalism, despite disagreeing on several subjects, invoked a common, shared intellectual heritage.

However, the seeds of corruption had already been planted. In eighteenth century, great liberals – like, at least with his idea of the 'invisible hand', the father himself of political economy, Adam Smith – began to view markets as self-regulating, so that policymakers had only 'to remove obstacles from its path'

(Röpke 1950 [1942]: 51).[6] Such a distorted belief was welcomed and cherished throughout the nineteenth century by a vast majority of economists and social scientists, who held as an undeniable dogma 'the automatic regulation of a competitive market' and rejected any other attempt to emphasize the significance of extra-economic premises:

> The glory of liberalism would indeed be unblemished if it had not also fallen victim to rationalism and thereby increasingly lost sight of the necessary sociological limits and conditions circumscribing a free market. It was seriously believed that a market economy based on competition represented a world of its own, an *ordre naturel* which had only to be freed from all interference in order to stand on its own feet. [...] Thus the market economy was endowed with sociological autonomy and the non-economic prerequisites and conditions that must be fulfilled if it is to function properly, were ignored.
>
> (Röpke 1950 [1942]: 51–52)

Classical liberals, in sum, were mistaken in forgetting 'that the ultimate moral support of the market economy lies outside the market', since 'market and competition are far from generating their moral prerequisites autonomously' (Röpke 1963 [1958]: 126). Quite the reverse, 'competition reduces the moral stamina and therefore requires moral reserves outside the market economy'; or, more precisely, 'a market economy needs a firm moral, political and institutional framework' (Röpke 1950 [1942]: 52). Röpke, consequently, argued that, because of the rationalist spirit of the time, 'what was in reality a highly fragile, artificial product of civilization was held to be a natural growth'; this was the original sin of what he came to call 'historical liberalism':

> Historical liberalism (particularly the nineteenth century brand) never understood that competition is a dispensation, by no means harmless from a moral and sociological point of view; it has to be kept within bounds and watched if it is not to poison the body politic. [...] It was for the same reason that economic liberalism, true to its rationalist origin, exhibited a supreme disregard for the organic and anthropological conditions which must limit the development of capitalist industrialism unless a wholly unnatural form of existence is to be forced upon men. This spirit of historical liberalism, so alien to everything vital, is responsible for our monstrous industrial areas and giant cities, and even for that perversion in economic development which condemns millions to a life of frustration and has, above all, turned the proletariat into a problem which goes far beyond material considerations.
>
> (Röpke 1950 [1942]: 52)

The evidence seemed so striking that Röpke did not doubt even for a moment the correctness of his analysis. He was comforted, in so doing, by two of the main sources he referred to, José Ortega y Gasset and Walter Lippmann (both non-economists, by the way). The former blamed historical capitalism for the birth of the perfect 'mass-man...whose life lacks any purpose and simply goes drifting along', a man intrinsically adverse to the philosophy of political liberalism – labelled as 'the supreme form of generosity' since it implied for the State to award an equal right of citizenship to every individual regardless of her/ his choices in front of those held by the majority – and even 'anxious to get rid of it' (Ortega y Gasset 1957 [1930]: 49, 76).[7] The latter, originally supportive of F. D. Roosevelt's *New Deal*, of which he later came to be a staunch critic,[8] condemned in his masterpiece – *The Good Society* (1937) – 'the cardinal fallacies of nineteenth-century liberalism' and most of all the philosophy of laissez-faire, 'a theory formulated for the purpose of destroying laws, institutions, and customs that had to be destroyed if the new mode of production was to prevail', but in the end 'incapable of guiding the public policy of states once the old order had been overthrown' (Lippmann 1944 [1937]: 184–185).[9]

The evolution of the economic system, left unbound, had produced serious perversions – like monopolies and giant industrialism – and disruptive social illnesses (unemployment and deflation, among others). That's why, according to Lippmann, a deep reform had to be called for by liberals themselves:

> Obviously, it is the duty of a liberal society to see that its markets are efficient and honest. But under the laissez-faire delusion it was supposed that good markets would somehow organize themselves or, at any rate, that the markets are as good as they might be. That is not true. The improvement of the markets must be a subject of continual study in a liberal society. It is a vast field of necessary reform. [...] Along with measures to make the markets genuine it is necessary to take steps to reduce the evil of necessitous bargaining. Thus a liberal state cannot be neutral as between those who have too little bargaining power and those who have too much power. [...] Not only is there no reason why a liberal state should not insure and indemnify against its own progressive development, but there is every reason why it should.
>
> (Lippmann 1944 [1937]: 221, 222, 224)

No wonder that, in the new preface to the third English edition, Lippmann maintained that he had written the book 'daring to believe that the causes of the coming war and the principles of the reconstruction to follow it were known' (Lippmann 1944 [1937]: VIII). Röpke shared Lippmann's overview, absorbed his recipe and went further. In *The Social Crisis of Our Time*, he explicitly pictures the third way as an ensemble of the core principles that would guide the reconstruction of Western civilization by avoiding all those mistakes that marked the last hundred years and eventually led to both World Wars.[10]

As a first step, Röpke tried to secure the general boundaries of his proposal:

> We are thinking of an economic policy which is in one sense conservative and radical in another, equally definite sense: conservative in insisting

on the preservation of continuity in cultural and economic development, making the defense of the basic values and principles of a free personality its highest, immutable aim – radical in its diagnosis of the disintegration of our 'liberal' social and economic system, radical in its criticism of the errors of liberal philosophy and practice, radical in its lack of respect for moribund institutions, privileges, ideologies and dogmas, and finally, radical in its unorthodox choice of the means which today seem appropriate for the attainment of the permanent goal of every culture based on the freedom of the individual. The advocates of this program are as aware of the fundamental errors of nineteenth century liberalism as they are opposed to collectivism, however dressed up, and the political-cultural totalitarianism that inevitably goes with it – not only as an impracticable solution but also as one harmful to society.

(Röpke 1950 [1942]: 21–22)

The economic policy he imagined had to be grounded on a crucial dichotomy, the one between 'two groups of state intervention…for which we have suggested the terms 'compatible' and 'incompatible' interventions: i.e. those that are in harmony with an economic structure based on the market and those which are not', the formers being 'interventions which do not interfere with the price mechanism and the automatism of the market derived from it', the latter's 'interventions which paralyze the price mechanism and therefore force us to replace it by a planned (collectivist) order' (Röpke 1950 [1942]: 160). But even under such a sword of Damocles, the agenda envisaged by Röpke appears to be made up of wide reforms:

Economic liberty and competition are self-evident postulates where the arch-evils of collectivism and monopolism are involved, but they are only part of a many-sided and comprehensive general program. This program lays down the firm frame which will give the necessary support to the freedom of the market. Decentralization, promotion of smaller production and settlement units and of the sociologically healthy forms of life and work (after the model of the peasant and the artisan), legislation preventing the formation of monopolies and financial concentration (company law, patent law, bankruptcy law, anti-trust laws etc.), strictest supervision of the market to safeguard fair play, development of new, non-proletarian forms of industry, reduction of all dimensions and conditions to the human mean (*à la taille de l'homme*, as the Swiss poet Ramuz has put it so well); elimination of over complicated methods of organization, specialization and division of labor, promotion of a wide distribution of property wherever possible and by all possible means, sensible limitation of state intervention according to the rules of, and in keeping with, the market economy (compatible state interventions instead of incompatible interference à la planned economy), while care is exercised to reserve a sphere for the actual planned economy.

(Röpke 1950 [1942]: 178–179)

Relying on this account, some scholars have argued that Röpke, Lippmann and the majority of the 'neo-liberals' (as they called themselves) 'sought to accommodate certain elements of the welfare state agenda within their liberalism as a means of legitimating the market' (Jackson 2010: 133); others, for example, Somma (2014: 53–55), have emphasized the conservative flavour of his extensive but moderate series of reforms. Both are partly correct, but both seem to miss one crucial point, together with even those who, like Mierzejewski (2006: 277), properly admit that 'he was convinced that the market was not applicable to all spheres of life and that even where it was appropriate, it should be limited': for Röpke the limits to market economy were to be found in human nature itself.

He used to stress, in fact, the importance of an ethical framework surrounding markets and political society as a whole, for a free society cannot survive if its members live and act, in any field of the public realm, while not sharing a bunch of non-negotiable values: in his own words, 'self-discipline, a sense of justice, honesty, fairness, chivalry, moderation, public spirit, respect for human dignity, firm ethical norms – all of these are things which people must possess before they go to market and compete with each other' (Röpke 1963 [1958]: 125). Wherever 'men who measure their strengths in the competition of the open market' are not 'united by a common ethic', competition itself 'degenerates into an internecine struggle' (Röpke 1959b: 234) and this struggle threatens the survival of any given community.

Worried as he was by the disintegration of civil society, he looked relieved to find out – thanks to the Swiss model of cantonal federalism[11] – that 'community, fraternity, charity' were compatible with market freedom, but only if it be granted the existence of those 'small, easily comprehended circles that are the original patterns of human society' and which can support every individual in her/his everyday life by supplying the natural and human landscape anyone dreams of:

> If man is to be restored to the possibility of simple, natural happiness, it can only be done by putting him once more in a humanly tolerable existence, where, placed in the true community that begins with the family and living in harmony with nature, he can support himself with labor made purposeful by the institution of private property. The almost desperate character of this effort does not testify against its necessity if we wish to save our civilization.
>
> (Röpke 1959b: 234–235)

This reconstruction of the ideal milieu for human life should, on one side, unquestionably avoid 'the rape of irreplaceable natural reserves [whose] consequences are already making themselves felt in many instances and in an alarming manner'; on the other, restore the inner constitution of society, for 'a healthy society, firmly resting on its own foundation, possesses a genuine "structure" with many intermediate stages; it exhibits a necessarily "hierarchical" composition (i.e. determined by the social importance of certain functions, services and leadership qualities), where each individual has the good fortune of knowing his position' (Röpke 1950 [1942]: 10, 144).

We might agree with Foucault in noticing the conservative, and even authoritarian, flavour of this sentence;[12] but we should also remember that Röpke had mostly in mind the virtues of the middle class, that social aggregate made up of 'the best types of peasants, artisans, small traders, small and medium-sized businessmen in commerce and industry, members of the free professions and trusty officials and servants of the community', men and women who live 'a life that gives them inward and, as much as possible, outward independence' (Röpke 1950 [1942]: 178). This independence must provide them, besides material prosperity, with the largest intellectual freedom and made them ready to rule civil society in the time of need. For the same society 'is in supreme danger if the "Clerks" remain dumb, if they are not allowed to express themselves freely, or from fear or confusion commit the treachery of silence' (Röpke 1948 [1944]: 72). All along the twentieth century many clerks remained dumb, and two World Wars were the most evident sign of their sin.[13] The third way program had to assure that no such thing happened again.

Final remarks

In this chapter, I have tried to shed some light on the connections between two usually estranged poles of Röpke's economic thought: the analysis of the moral and economic roots of the second World War and his 'Third Way' program, by which he intended to reform both liberal theory and contemporary economic institutions.

In fact, I have suggested that the *trait d'union* might be found in his denunciation of the damages produced by what he called 'historical liberalism', i.e. the dogma of the automatic regulation of markets, and 'historical capitalism', i.e. the monopolistic, gigantic and unnatural shape capitalism had acquired all along the nineteenth century, together with the even more nefarious growth of collectivism as a misleading answer to the errors of classical liberalism.

He believed that, as Molina Cano (2001: 30) correctly put it, 'European wars required a novel point of view' if one wished to change the status quo; and his recipe was thought of as a medicine to rescue the real values of liberal philosophy against the perversion that caused 'so many economic distortions, social sufferings and political upheavals' and that moreover 'gained much discredit and begot the decline of real liberal ideas' (Audier 2012: 458). In so doing, he was ready to admit a certain degree of State interventionism though only if 'compatible', that is in harmony with market economy and individual liberties. He conceived the market as 'an artistic construction and an edifice of civilization' (Röpke 1948 [1944]: 133), something that put him somehow at odds with the very idea of a 'spontaneous order' backed by most adherents to the Austrian school.

What is more, he came to realize that his plan would be successful solely as far as economists, policymakers and the public opinion understand that 'the vital things are those beyond supply and demand and the world of property', for the only economic structure bound to survive would be the one that recognizes and respects those assets which 'give meaning, dignity, and inner richness to life, those purposes and values which belong to the realm of ethics in the widest sense' (Röpke 1963 [1958]: 5). We may blame him for his conservatism, or for the fallacies of his historical enquiries; but we cannot deny that, perhaps unintentionally, while meditating upon the evils of war he grasped the ultimate question that plagues any season of economic decadence – our age, unfortunately, included.

Notes

1 Cf. Gregg (2010), 1–2.
2 For wide-ranging enquiries on Röpke's economic and political liberalism see Peukert (1992); Molina Cano (2001); Zmirak (2001); Gregg (2010); Audier (2012); Solchany (2015). Following the steps of Foucault (2010 [1979]), Bonefeld (2012) and (2013) and Somma (2014) have assimilated Röpke to mainstream ordoliberals, convicting them all for the naissance of authoritarian power-driven biopolitics. Among others, Goldschmidt and Rauchenschwandtner (2007) did their best to rebut this intellectual trend, while Mierzejewski (2006) has tried to shed light on the nature of the connections that linked Röpke to Ludwig Erhard and social market economy.
3 This feature was noticed and appreciated by Hayek (1992: 195), for whom 'Röpke realized at an early stage, perhaps earlier than most of his contemporaries, that an economist who is nothing but an economist cannot be a good economist'. Quite the reverse, the Dutch Keynesian economist Jan Pen defined Röpke 'a great economist but one who has also done harm to the science of economics' because he had maintained that 'economics as a science of human activity is denatured by the quantitative method'. For Pen, 'this form of pseudo-spirituality is nonsense', since 'regularity is an indisputable fact, whatever Röpke, Von Mises and others may claim on this account' (Pen 1970: 231, 232). It should be noted that Hayek, Pen and many other scholars tend to stress the acquaintance of Röpke with the Austrian school of economics, something, nonetheless, that remains quite doubtful. On this point, see the opposite arguments of Wohlgemut (2006) and Audier (2012: 399–508).
4 Röpke developed at length this argument in *The German Question* (Röpke 1946 [1945]).
5 The criticism of massive State interference was quite common among German liberals, even those who worked and lived under the Nazi regime. The post-war 'social market economy' may be seen as a response to this kind of economic policy, though remaining alternative to the old *laissez-faire*. See Peacock and Willgerodt (1989) and Nichols (1994). Somma (2014: 36–45, 50–68) argues, instead, that many issues linked together ordo-liberals and national socialists in their vision of the economic process. He is deeply mistaken, however, in implying an apparent resemblance in Röpke's third way and national socialist economic (and un-democratic) policies.
6 As correctly stated in Bonefeld (2013), this view of Smith is rather misleading, more than ever in the light of the new deal of Smith's studies – from Winch (1978) to Rothschild (2001). However, I do consider unacceptable his attempt to paint Smith as the forerunner of that (hypothetical) kind of 'authoritarian' liberalism which the ordoliberals would eventually endorse.
7 On the social and political philosophy of Ortega see Graham (2001).
8 See Audier (2012: 72–82).
9 Lippmann's public philosophy is vividly portrayed in Wellborn (1969). See also Jackson (2012).
10 Solchany (2014: 98) seems to stress too much the point when he notes that 'all the publications of Röpke from the late twenties to his death, and to a lesser extent the writings of many other neoliberal intellectuals, may be interpreted as a thought on the crisis of modern world and the ways to remedy it'.

11 The impact of Swiss politics on his thought has been duly noted and studied by Zmirak (2001: 25–66).
12 Not surprisingly, this vision has been endorsed as well by a certain conservative opinion; see Carlson (2009).
13 As he himself confessed, on this topic Röpke was heavily influenced by the works of Julien Benda and Johann Huizinga. See Benda (1927) and Huizinga (1936 [1935]).

References

Audier, S. (2012) *Néo-libéralisme(s). Une Archéologie Intellectuelle*, Grasset, Paris.
Benda, J. (1927) *La Trahison des Clercs*, Grasset, Paris.
Bonefeld, W. (2012) 'Freedom and the Strong State: On German Ordoliberalism', *New Political Economy*, 17(5), 633–656.
— (2013) 'Adam Smith and Ordoliberalism: On the Political Form of Market Liberty', *Review of International Studies*, 39(2), 233–250.
Carlson, A. (2009) 'Wilhelm Röpke's Conundrums Over the Natural Family', *Intercollegiate Review*, 44(1), 21–30.
Foucault, M. (2010 [1979]) *The Birth of Biopolitics: Lectures at the Collège de France, 1978–1979*, Picador, New York.
Goldschmidt, N. and Rauchenschwandtner, H. (2007) *The Philosophy of Social Market Economy: Michel Foucault's Analysis of Ordoliberalism*, Walter Eucken Institut, Freiburg.
Graham, J.T. (2001) *The Social Thought of Ortega Y Gasset: A Systematic Synthesis in Postmodernism and Interdisciplinarity*, University of Missouri Press, Columbia, MO.
Gregg, S. (2010) *Wilhelm Ropke's Political Economy*, Edward Elgar Publishing, Cheltenham.
Hayek, F.A. von (1992) *The Fortunes of Liberalism. Essays on Austrian Economics and the Ideal of Freedom*, edited by Peter G. Klein, University of Chicago Press, Chicago, IL.
Huizinga, J. (1936 [1935]) *In the Shadow of Tomorrow*, Heinneman, London.
Jackson, B. (2010) 'At the Origins of Neo-Liberalism: The Free Economy and the Strong State, 1930–1947', *The Historical Journal*, 53(1), 129–151.
Jackson, B. (2012) 'Freedom, the Common Good, and the Rule of Law: Lippmann and Hayek on Economic Planning', *Journal of the History of Ideas*, 73(1), 47–68.
Lippmann, W. (1944 [1937]) *The Good Society*, Billing and Sons Ltd, Guildford.
Mierzejewski, A.C. (2006) 'Water in the Desert? The Influence of Wilhelm Röpke on Ludwig Erhard and the Social Market Economy', *Review of Austrian Economics*, 19(4), 275–287.
Molina Cano, J. (2001) *La Tercera Vía en Wilhelm Röpke*, Instituto Empresa y Humanismo, Navarra.
Nichols, A.J. (1994) *Freedom with Responsibility: The Social Market Economy in Germany 1918–1963*, Oxford University Press, Oxford and New York.
Ortega y Gasset, J. (1957 [1930]) *The Revolt of the Masses*, Norton, New York.
Peacock, A. and Willgerodt, H. (eds.) (1989) *German Neo-Liberals and the Social Market Economy*, Macmillan, London.
Pen, J. (1970) *Modern Economics*, Penguin Books, Harmondsworth.
Peukert, H. (1992) *Das Sozialökonomische Werk Wilhelm Röpkes*, 2 vols, Peter Lang, Frankfurt.
Röpke, W. (1946 [1945]) *The German Question*, translated by E.W. Dickes, George Allen & Unwin Ltd, London.

— (1948 [1944]) *Civitas Humana: A Humane Order of Society*, translated by C.S. Fox, William Hodge & Company, London.

— (1950 [1942]) *The Social Crisis of Our Time*, translated by A. and P. Schiffer Jacobsohn, The University of Chicago Press, Chicago, IL.

— (1959a [1945]) *International Order and Economic Integration*, translated by G.E. Trinks, J. Taylor and C. Kaufer, D. Reidel Publishing Company, Dordrecht.

— (1959b) 'The Necessity of Economic Freedom', *Modern Age*, 3(3), 227–236.

— (1963 [1958]) *A Humane Economy. The Social Framework of the Free Market*, translated by E. Henderson, Henry Regnery Co, Chicago, IL.

— (1969) *Against the Tide*, edited by G. Dietze, translated by E. Henderson, Henry Regnery Co, Chicago, IL.

Rothschild, E. (2001) *Economic Sentiments: Adam Smith, Condorcet and the Enlightenment*, Harvard University Press, Cambridge, MA.

Solchany, J. (2014) 'Wilhelm Röpke as a Key Actor of Transnational Neoliberalism after 1945', in Schulz-Forberg, H. and Olsen, N. (eds.) (2014) *Re-Inventing Western Civilization: Transnational Reconstructions of Liberalism in Europe in the Twentieth Century*, Cambridge Scholars Publishing, Newcastle upon Tyne, 95–115.

— (2015) *Wilhelm Röpke, l'autre Hayek: Aux Origines du Néolibéralisme*, Publications de la Sorbonne, Paris.

Somma, A. (2014) *La Germania e l'Economia Sociale di Mercato. 1. Da Weimar ad Helmut Schmidt*, Centro di Ricerca e Documentazione 'Luigi Einaudi', Turin.

Wellborn, C. (1969) *Twentieth Century Pilgrimage. Walter Lippmann and the Public Philosophy*, Louisiana State University Press, Baton Rouge.

Winch, D. (1978) *Adam Smith's Politics: An Essay on Historiographic Revision*, Cambridge University Press, New York and Cambridge.

Wohlgemut, M. (2006) 'L'influence de l'économie autrichienne sur le libéralisme allemand', in Nemo P. and Petitot J. (eds.) *Histoire du libéralisme en Europe*, PUF, Paris, 985–1030.

Zmirak, J. (2001) *Wilhelm Röpke: Swiss Localist, Global Economist*, ISI Books, Wilmington, DE.

4   From Pacifism to Political Realism

The Economics and Sociology of War in Vilfredo Pareto[1]

Terenzio Maccabelli

> War [...] constitutes a truly great experiment, as in a physics laboratory.
>
> (Pareto 1973 II: 895)

Foreword

In his major economic works – the *Cours d'économie politique* and the *Manuale di Economia Politica* – Vilfredo Pareto mentions the subject of war only *en passant*, without dwelling upon it systematically. Just as in the case of Maffeo Pantaleoni, Pareto identified the field of economics with the space of the contractual relations between agents who make no resort to force to settle their exchange. A decidedly different viewpoint appears in the sociological works, and above all the late ones, as from the *Trattato di Sociologia generale*. In his sociological writings, in fact, war is discussed extensively, as documented both in the field of Paretian historiography[2] and in some recent comparative studies on the sociologists and the war.[3] Thus, reading Pareto from the perspective of war would appear to limit the scope to a sociological approach and to a span of time from the outbreak of the First World War to 1923, the year of his death.

Here, too, we will discuss Pareto's sociological conceptions about war, but from a viewpoint which we intend to open out to embrace his entire intellectual biography. We will attempt to show that those writings constitute a sort of point of arrival, which Pareto comes to after traversing a decidedly laboured intellectual path. In this traversal, Pareto's views on war changed significantly: from a phenomenon to be eradicated by virtue of universalistic *liberal reason*, in Pareto's late writings war became 'a laboratory' for dissection and investigation with the lofty, detached *habitus* of the social scientist. In between we have an ambiguous attitude descending to some extent to compromise, with which Pareto formulates a vision which, in that magmatic cultural climate of the early twentieth century, shows a certain sympathy with the revival of the idea of war as a regenerating force. However, by the time war was raging throughout Europe, Pareto had withdrawn from the political arena, stating that he wanted to be no part of the tremendous clash shaking Italian and European society. His sole intent was to apply *scientific reason* to examine the impulses and sentiments that drive society to war.

Thus our aim in this chapter is to reconstruct the intellectual path that led Pareto to look at the war as a scientific phenomenon. The conceptual framework constructed by Pareto in the years immediately preceding the First World War – and subsequently reasserted continually in the following years by virtue of its explanatory potential – is well known, and has already come under scrutiny in the literature on Pareto, and above all in the essentially sociological literature. In this chapter, therefore, we will recall it only in broad outline. We will, however, focus particular attention on a specific aspect of this framework, which may not have been adequately investigated in relation to the war. Here we are referring to the dialectic between *rentiers* and *speculators* within the elite class, among which Pareto detects certain unintentional processes that in some conditions drive towards war.

This particular aspect of Pareto's conceptual framework is also interesting for another reason, in that it is proposed as an explanatory model in which arguments of both a sociological and an economic nature converge. It is thus among the most telling in delineating the horizon of a general science of society which was, in fact, Pareto's goal. Within it, scholastic distinctions between *war sociology* and *war economics* fall away. Equally important, however, is the issue of Pareto's political position, which we can hardly disregard if we wish to reconstruct his thought. Schematic as it may prove, we will nevertheless propose an approach in which economics, politics and sociology overlap, and where both Pareto's *political realism* and his disenchanted view of war as a scientific laboratory find their place along the tortuous path traced out in his intellectual and political biography.

The chapter is organised in four parts. In the first two sections we will briefly outline Pareto's intellectual biography, summarising as far as possible the developments in his attitude towards war. We will consider his initial pacifism, consistent with his universalistic liberalism, and the subsequent shift in his political position, which sees him standing as a charismatic figure alongside the men who forged Italian nationalism. In the third section we will discuss the attitude of increasing detachment with which Pareto viewed social phenomena, eventually approached as facts to dissect with scientific method, no longer the object of political opposition or support. In the fourth, concluding part we will discuss the conceptual framework constructed by Pareto to address the subject of war, with particular focus on the role played by the rentiers/speculators dialectic within this framework.

'Free trade, Peace, Goodwill among nations'

In 1893 Pareto published a lengthy essay on the post-unification situation in Italy in the *Political Science Quarterly*. By 1893 Pareto had established a reputation as a theoretical economist and was about to take over the chair from Léon Walras in Lausanne. He was, however, also an attentive and sympathetic observer of Italian politics, which he followed closely with frequent articles in journals and newspapers. His 1893 paper is very important for at least two reasons: first, because it delineates the basic outlines of his scientific project, which he would perfect only in the following decade, and second, because it provides valid orientation in the political field, which also helps to determine the position taken by Pareto himself and through his publicist activity.

In this essay Pareto provides detailed description of the various political forces and currents in post-unification Italy, while also offering profiles of the major political leaders. Particularly striking is the emphasis on the figure of Francesco Crispi, the then Prime Minister, whose programme was taking a somewhat aggressive turn in foreign policy, with a strong leaning in the direction of militarism and colonialism.

> The Premier, Signor Crispi, [...] wished to follow a policy which was characterized as "imperial." According to Crispi, Italy was to became a great military and naval power, and was to play a role of great importance in the European political world. To carry out this policy the nation must make the necessary sacrifices; it must not be niggardly in bearing taxes and incurring debts.
>
> (Pareto 1893: 687)

Pareto was profoundly opposed to this policy. His aversion derived, in the first place, from the problem of the financial sustainability of this ambitious foreign policy, but there was also a more basic objection to aggressive colonialism, militarism and the power politics of the European countries. Thus Pareto's attention turned to those political forces that were taking a critical attitude towards Crispi in Italy, the so-called 'extremes' (radicals, republicans and the budding socialist party). The common ground that drew the liberal and liberist Pareto into dialogue with these political forces was, in fact, pacifism.

Political liberalism, economic liberism and pacifism in international relations effectively represented the principal coordinates of Pareto's thought in the closing decades of the nineteenth century.[4] 'For us economists' – Pareto wrote in 1889, when he had yet to set out on the road of theoretical and mathematical economics – the best policy for trade is *laissez-faire*, a commercial policy that works in 'favour of peace. [...] In other words, we see that the population of the state living in commercial isolation from the others has a greater propensity for war, and the more trading relations it develops, the less inclination it will have for warlike adventures' ([1889] 1974a: 295–296).

These were the principles that prompted Pareto to get into contact with Ernesto Teodoro Moneta, one of the most active advocates of nineteenth century *pacifism* who was awarded the Nobel Peace Prize in 1907.[5] His kinship with Moneta ripened when Pareto channelled his activity as political commentator through *Il Secolo*, the Milanese newspaper edited by Moneta himself, and a reference point for the radicals led by Felice Cavallotti.[6] Pareto's publicist activity in the radical daily took on the tones of a vehement anti-government campaign, attacking Francesco Crispi's pursuit of *grandeur*, and in particular Italy's militarism and colonial aspirations.

Moreover, this fierce hostility towards Crispi's policy and sympathy for the radicals characterised the entire liberist group that had formed around the *Giornale degli economisti*, and which Pareto had also joined.[7] To a far greater degree than the other Italian liberists, however, he conceived of liberalism and liberism as institutional configurations inseparable from a vocation for peace. In his view, the strict alliance between liberalism and pacifism is mirrored in the alliance between protectionism and militarism.[8]

Pareto's antimilitarism rested upon motivations of both an economic and a political nature. From the economic point of view, he asserted that only a system of peaceful relations amongst nations, which is eased by *laissez-faire*, guarantees benefits for all the populations. There exists, then, a virtuous circle in which free trade, over and above the principle of economic efficiency, becomes in turn a powerful means to bring about peaceful relations between nations. Moreover, from the fiscal point of view, militarism weighs upon the state budget, diverting resources from more urgent and fruitful use. On various occasions Pareto stressed the distributive distortion of military spending, whose negative effects on public finance are both direct (higher taxes and/or budget deficit) and indirect (impossibility of using these resources for more urgent objectives, e.g. fighting poverty).[9] And, at the political level, Pareto opposed the foreign policy centred on the Triple Alliance, which gave rise to a spiral of increasing military expenditure that was bringing no advantage to Italy.[10] It was, however, the incompatibility between liberalism and militarism that Pareto stressed at the political level, insofar as it is the civil liberties that are sacrificed when a country attributes priority to military power.[11]

In support of these ideas, Pareto looked to British liberalism. Richard Cobden and William Ewart Gladstone took on the guise of tutelary deities for the Italian economist. From the Cobden Club motto – '*Free trade, Peace, Goodwill among nations*' – Pareto drew the keywords of an 'intransigent' liberalism which postulates these objectives as 'inseparable', since 'they can be achieved' only jointly (Pareto [1892a] 1974a: 535). And, thanks to his personal relations with Gladstone, he would be able to add as epigraph to a booklet bearing the significant title *Le spese militari e i mali dell'Italia* (Military Expenditure and the Ills of Italy) an extract from a letter by the British liberal which effectively evokes the political horizon of the Italian economist himself. 'Protectionism and militarism are united in un unholy but yet a valid marriage: and the one and the other are in my firm conviction alike the foes of Freedom'.[12]

Throughout the last decade of the nineteenth century, Pareto remained set in his intransigent pacifism. As editor of the 'Cronaca' (Chronicle) of the *Giornale degli Economisti*, containing the political commentaries of Italy's major economics journal, Pareto continued with his commitment to demystifying the Africa campaign backed by Crispi. This colonial campaign had produced no benefit for Italy ([1896b] 1974b: 123), and had been sustained by the Italian bourgeoisie's 'vain pursuit of military glory' ([1896a] 1974b: 79). The disastrous effects of the African venture led to the discovery of the vicious circle in which 'colonial expenditure and military expenditure sustained one another reciprocally' ([1897] 1974b: 200), leading the entire nation into a blind alley.

A point worth stressing here is the perfect consistency between the positions that Pareto was adopting in the theoretical field and the position he took in the political field. Indeed, his commitment to the pacifist cause (and the idea of complementarity between peace and free trade) contributed to reinforcing his friendship with Teodoro Moneta on the one hand, and consolidating the political alliance between radicals, liberists and socialists on the other. This consistency began to waver in the delicate transition as the nineteenth century came to an end. Both the crisis in European liberalism and the specific dynamics of the political battle in Italy contributed to Pareto's reappraisal of his scientific approach, with significant repercussions on his political orientation. The alliance between socialists and liberists had crumbled, while pacifism ceased to function as a catalyst of democratic political opposition to the authoritarianism of the 1890s. Behind this turning point lay a change in Italy's political scenario, as conditions came about for a role for 'the socialist movement in the political life of the country' when Giovanni Giolitti came to power (Michelini 1997: 103). It was, however, precisely when a 'modern political dialectic' took shape in Italy that Pareto, like Pantaleoni, took a very decided distance from it. His views 'changed radically. From being a crusader for democracy and free trade he became indifferent to active politics and an increasingly bitter enemy of parliamentarism and democracy' (Finer 1968). Pareto shifted to 'increasingly conservative positions', abandoning his polemical attitude towards Crispi, to find a place for himself in the variegated archipelago of the various opponents of Giolitti (Michelini 1997: 111).

In the decisive, troubled transition to the new century, the initial analogy between economic liberism and political liberalism gave way to the magmatic repositioning in the theoretical and political field, opening up to certain cultural trends, such as nationalism, which would contribute to the democratic involution of Italy and of Pareto himself. In the political field, the repositioning was also reflected in the attitude towards war, which saw profound transformation.

The crisis of liberalism and the rise of nationalism: the regenerative war

Pareto approached nationalism gradually, step by step. The turn of the century found Pareto taking a detached view of nationalism, but with occasional signs of profound aversion. Nevertheless, he immediately identified in European – and in particular French – nationalism the one force able to stem the socialist tide. As he saw it, democracy became a drive for socialism, and it is on the basis of this fundamental identification between socialism and democracy that we are to understand the antidemocratic stances Pareto subsequently adopted.

Fundamental in this respect was the line of argumentation Pareto pursued in these years with regard to the bourgeoisie, and in practice it pointed him in the direction of Italian nationalism. At the heart of all his reflections lay a concept that became a sort of obsession for European culture – the degeneration or decadence of the élites. Normally applied in the field of biology, the concept of degeneration was used to describe a risk seen to be hanging over the European élites. Eugenic ideas had crystallised in the conviction of a possible genetic decay of the élites if no barriers were raised to the mixing of the social classes or, from a nationalistic point of view, if no strict limits were placed on the inflow of populations from abroad deemed biologically inferior.

Pareto transposed the idea of degeneration from the biological to the cultural and political fields. More than genes, it was ideas that could pollute and debase the élites, and it was the democratic and humanitarian principles the bourgeoisie was nourishing within its breast that was contributing to its inevitable decline (Busino 1989: 628). This theme recurs like a *topos* in Pareto's contributions as publicist in the early years of the twentieth century. We find it both in his theoretical works, whether economic or sociological, and in his political contributions, as well as being harped upon in his vast correspondence.[13]

The ardent set of Florentine intellectuals who cultivated the seeds of Italian nationalism proved particularly sensitive to Pareto's concerns. In the pages of *Leonardo* and above all in *Il Regno*,[14] first by Giuseppe Prezzolini and subsequently by Pareto himself, the idea of bourgeois degeneration would be thrashed out in all its implications, exposing all the contradictions of an approach intended to be a scientific–descriptive but in practice proving political–programmatic. A redoubtable contribution towards settling this contradiction would be made in the philosophical framework of reference for early twentieth century Italian nationalism, i.e. pragmatism.[15]

It was in fact Prezzolini who reformulated Pareto's discussion of degeneration in the framework of pragmatism. The central issue was the capitulation of the Italian bourgeoisie, which Pareto deemed imminent in the light of his theory of the circulation of the élites. Rather than passively submit to its capitulation, – Prezzolini writes – the bourgeoisie was to resist and fight, 'openly and desperately waging war with all its strength and all its means, attaining an aristocratic vision and preferring noble death in battle to slowly rotting in senility'.[16] It was precisely the dialectic between scientific objectivity and pragmatic volunteerism that marked Pareto's relations with nationalism – relations he embarked upon in his correspondence with Prezzolini himself.

> I see that the journal you sent me is *nationalist*. I have now withdrawn completely from active political life and dedicate myself *solely* to science; I view social phenomena precisely as I would contemplate chemical phenomena.
>
> (V. Pareto to G. Prezzolini, 17 December 1903. In Pareto 1973, I: 507)

Despite his declared position outside political debate, Pareto did not refrain from suggesting the editorial line that the journal *Il Regno* should pursue given its nationalist orientation. The premise was that if it was to be successful nationalism had to exploit the force of sentiments and beliefs. Thus the nationalists are well advised to bring issues like war into play to revive national sentiments, taking as an example the British war in South Africa. However, this was not to dominate the nationalist agenda, for Italy was not yet ready to bear the economic burden of a war of expansion. It was, therefore, better to leave the theme of war in the background, 'speaking of it sparingly, as is the practice with sacred matters', concentrating efforts on lexical and linguistic purification with a purge of words like democracy, justice, solidarity, etc. 'We have a tough job ahead of us, ridiculing humanitarianism, Tolstoyism and other follies dissolving today's bourgeois society': we must 'do away with those follies, as they deserve', so as to expose 'the humanitarian idols' in their disgusting nakedness' (V. Pareto to G. Prezzolini, 17 December 1903, Pareto 1973, I: 508).

The letter to Prezzolini, despite firmly asserting the purely scientific nature of the theory of the circulation of the élites, reveals some surprising glimmers of hope for Italian nationalism. Although the Italian bourgeoisie was on the brink of a precipice, it had not yet plunged to the depths.[17] The *will to believe* inspiring both pragmatism and nationalism might yet succeed in regenerating the Italian bourgeoisie. Prezzolini could not have hoped for a better response from Pareto, promptly proposing publication in *Il Regno* (Busino 1989: 630). Pareto's answer was published at the beginning of 1904, with the emblematic title *La borghesia può risorgere?* ('Can the bourgeoisie rearise?'), marking the beginning of assiduous collaboration with *Il Regno*, which was to continue until 1906, when the journal ceased publication.[18]

Despite his involvement in a militant journal like *Il Regno*, Pareto continued to affirm his role as detached and objective scientist, standing outside the political melee. Detached as he may have been, however, Pareto's contribution was to prove decisive in cementing what has been defined 'the backbone of nationalist ideology'.[19]

In the pages of the *Regno* Pareto reiterated his censure of caring, democratic humanitarianism, responsible for the decline of the bourgeoisie. Obligatory education, which the bourgeoisie had called for, had generated new élites of proletarian extraction now ready to take over power.[20] The workers' movement had organised itself in leagues and unions while the bourgeoisie had done nothing of the sort, showing, rather, a compliant attitude that precluded any chance of fighting on the same ground.[21] More in general, resort to force and the virile qualities had become the exclusive prerogative of the working classes, while the bourgeoisie had foregone any such action.[22]

These seem to be the dominant themes in the dialogue between Pareto and the nationalists.[23] But lurking in the background was the theme of war, already hailed as a force to regenerate the bourgeoisie. In his letter to Prezzolini, Pareto had warned the nationalists not to bandy about the subject of war too boldly, so as not to drain it of significance. But he had also stressed the absolute need to continue quietly evoking it, so as to implant the ineluctability of war in the collective imagination. In keeping with these objectives, Pareto himself kept the subject alive in his contributions. War must not be taboo. The bourgeoisie had to recognise the regenerative function of war, the one true bulwark. 'If there is a great European War, socialism will be driven back for at least half a century, and the bourgeoisie safe for that span of time' (Pareto [1904b] 1974b: 414–415).

In the space of just a few months, however, Pareto's tone changed significantly. War ceased to be a hypothesis – *if there is a war* – to become a certainty. In fact, the following year Pareto wrote 'that one must be blind not to see' that the prospect of a European war was no longer so remote 'as it had erstwhile seemed' ([1905a] 1974b: 459). And a few months later he reiterated in peremptory terms the ineluctability of the coming world war, the only uncertainty being, apparently, *when* it would break out:

> The present period is much like that which preceded the Franco-Prussian war of 1870. People fondly talk of universal peace while a tremendous conflict may be in the offing. [...] Of more use to our country than the hollow sacred images of the humanitarian and socialist Olympus are patriotism, virile resolve, good arms, virtue and the sense to use them when necessary.
>
> (Pareto [1905b] 1974b: 465)

In short, Pareto contributed to forging the language and rhetorical modules which the nationalist movement would exploit – language in which war would become increasingly recurrent together with the need to revive the virility of the Italian bourgeoisie. Pareto's reflections on war found fertile ground amongst the journalists and readers of the *Regno*. Indeed, magnification of war became one of the most effective ways to stir the national conscience. However, the time was not yet ripe for Italy, left to look on with envy and admiration as the armies deployed by the imperialist nations did their work. 'War has broken out at last' – the *Regno* journalists proclaimed hailing the outbreak of the Russo-Japanese War – and 'this great war really seems to be waged for us.'[24]

Nevertheless, the option of war was to remain far from the Italian horizon for some years yet. Eventually it came about in 1911, with the war over Libya. War was no longer an evocative word but concrete reality. The language of the nationalists, hitherto reserved to the cultural élites, found its way into everyday life and a place on the agenda in political debate, thanks also to the creation of the Italian Nationalist Association. The idea of national regeneration now appeared to be indissolubly bound up with warlike themes and the pursuit of power.[25]

Pareto continued to describe himself as an unbiased onlooker, taking no interest in political struggles. This attitude, as we have seen, dated back to the closing years of the nineteenth century, and was reasserted by Pareto with ever greater insistence over the following decade. And so he played no substantial role in the creation of the Italian Nationalist Association. Even when world war broke out, he took no part in the dramatic clash over intervention. Rather, he clung to the role of the detached social scientist satisfied with having given scientific form to a complex conceptual system in which war emerged as rigorously logical 'prediction'. It was only an editorial delay in publication of his *Trattato di Sociologia generale* that obliged him to refer to it no longer using the term 'prediction' but, rather, 'deduction'.[26] No awareness was shown, however, of the performative role of language – language permeated by the inevitability and naturalness of war, to which Pareto had given a fundamental contribution.

War as scientific laboratory

In the summer of 1914, when the First World War broke out, Pareto had effectively completed his *Trattato di Sociologia Generale*, the first draft of which dated back to 1912. The outbreak of war was seen as the practical proof of his theories formulated over the last decade that constitute the core of the *Trattato*. A number of letters evidence Pareto's intention to revise parts of it in the light of the events brought on with the war, but he decided to make no change.[27]

In the *Trattato*, publication of which dragged on until 1916, various parts are in fact dedicated to the issue of war and the social forces that bring about breakdown of the social equilibria and the ravages of war. There is, however, no specific reference to the events of the First World War, although they found discussion in essays published alongside the *Trattato*. What Pareto said about in these essays was empirical translation of the conceptual categories formulated at the theoretical level in the *Trattato*. We will endeavour to bring out the strict interdependence between the *Trattato* and the essays on war in the closing sections of this chapter.

An initial attempt to contextualise the world war and trace back its deep-rooted causes is to be seen in a letter to Pierre Boven of 27 August 1914, written a month after the outbreak of the war:

> This war will be one of the great events of world history. Different forces are at play. The mains seem the nationalist forces. The Slavs and Latins defend their existence on the one hand, Germans on the other. England took sides according to the special point of view of its colonial empire. Then there is the fight of the Socialist radicalism against conservative governments.
>
> (V. Pareto to P. Boven, 27 august 1914, in Pareto 1973, II: 879–880)

The correspondence sums up the guidelines of the essay published in the *Giornale d'Italia* the following month, under the title 'Conflitto di razze, di religioni e di nazioni' (War of races, religions and nations) (Pareto [1914] 1974b). The geopolitical destabilisation which lay behind the First World War resulted from three, interdependent crisis factors: (1) the clash between the pan-nationalist ideologies of the Germans and the Slavs; (2) the clash between the aristocratic militarism of the central Empires and the democratic regimes in countries like France and England (in his letter to Boven Pareto referred to socialist radicalism, but it is worth recalling that in Pareto's lexis democracy and socialism often recur as synonyms; (3) the divergent interests of the various states. The same formulation reappeared the following year in an essay entitled 'La guerra ed i suoi principali fattori sociologici' (The war and its principal sociological factors) (Pareto [1915] 1980), published in *Scientia*. These essays constitute the reference point for the subsequent reflections on the origins and consequences of the world war, which Pareto would continue to formulate to the very end of his life.

Of particular significance for argument is the second factor in Pareto's framework, namely the competition between systems of aristocratic – military government (Germany and Austria) and democratic – social government (France and England). In Pareto's political theory this distinction relates not so much to the traditional forms of government as to the 'styles of government', or in other words the process 'by which consent is obtained by the governing élite and the extent to which force is used' (Tarascio 1991: 122). Although there is a general tendency to reduce resort to force as a means of power, the Western countries are far from showing homogeneity. Appreciable differences remain in the demographic composition of the élites – differences that bring Pareto back to the theory of residues formulated in the *Trattato*.

Pareto divided the residues into six classes, in turn composed of numerous subclasses. In this chapter we will confine our attention to the first two, namely the class of combinations and the class of persistence of aggregates. The Class I residues are instincts that are to be seen in activities dedicated to the pursuit of novelty, which activate new combinations of facts or knowledge in the various spheres of human action. Entrepreneurial activity is a typical manifestation of this instinct for combinations. The persistence of aggregates, on the other hand, is the typically conservative residue of groups whose interest lies in stabilising the social order as in the case of rentiers, landowners, the military, peasants, etc. Unlike the Class I residues, which lead to change, the Class II residues tend to preserve the existing institutions and traditions (Tarascio 1991: 122–123).

Pareto's argumentation thus revolves around the conditions of social equilibrium, described as a situation in which the forces of stability and change balance out and prove to be complementary. It is, moreover, this equilibrium that favours economic and social progress. Breakdown of the equilibrium triggers chaotic processes which can lead to war. Neither of the two residues is in itself a direct cause of war (not even the Class II residues, although they relate to the pre-modern warlike aristocracies): it is alteration of the social equilibrium that can generate, as unintentional effect, 'movement of the war cycle' ([1916] 1935: §2225).

The élites in power in the various countries of the world show variable proportions of government leaders with the characteristics of the first or second class. The particular combination of government leaders is reflected directly in the ways of exercising power, and in particular in the use of force within the state and resort to war outside it.[28] While the Class II residues tend to the use of force, cultivate military values and a warlike spirit, the Class I residues tend to wither them. The aptitude for war shown by the various nations lies in this changeable proportion between the two classes of residues.

> If the combination-instincts are reinforced in a given country beyond a certain limit, as compared with the instincts of group-persistence, that country may be easily vanquished in war by another country in which that change in relative proportions has not occurred. [...] People who lose the habit of applying force, who acquire the habit of considering policy from a commercial standpoint and of judging it only in terms of profit and loss, can readily be induced to purchase peace; and it may well be that such a transaction taken by itself is a good one, for war might have cost more money than the price

of peace. Yet experience shows that in the long run [...] such practice leads a country to ruin.

(Pareto [1916] 1935: §2179, 1517–1518)

This aspect of Pareto's theory, too, rests on a cyclic, wave conception of human history, like the ebb and flow of historical occurrence and recurrence. Pareto abandoned the linear view of history of Spencerian inspiration that he had taken to in his youth, and on which he had developed his universalistic pacifism. He was now branding pacifism as baleful 'humanitarianism', bound to succumb to the recurrent flood bursting out from the latent warlike inclinations of human populations.

Also 'the movements of the war-cycle' are generated by manifold forces 'that tend to produce a movement in a direction counter to that of the cycle' ([1916] 1935: §2224, 1553). The Class II residues, which tend to preserve the military values in society, wear thin in the case of frequent wars.[29] Moreover, the Class I residues benefit from the fact that, 'as regard modern times, wars require not only men but also huge expenditures in money, which can be met only by intensive economic production, so that if wars in themselves increase the warrior element in governing class, preparations for war reduce it, drawing industrial and commercial elements into the seat of power' ([1916] 1935: §2224, 1553).

Thanks to the abstract, universal nature of this framework Pareto was able to adapt it and apply it as interpretative model to the various war cycles of history. The conflict between 'democratic' countries and 'aristocratic – military' countries – which, as we have seen, was one of the factors Pareto believed caused the World War – emerges quite logically from the schematic representation we have outlined. Adapting it to the European events of the early twentieth century, Pareto enhanced it at the lexical level with more specific references to the various countries, and with more detailed description of the social classes that can be characterised in terms of first and second class residues.

We will go into this class subdivision within the élites in full detail in the next section, discussing the speculators/rentiers dichotomy. Here we shall confine reference to some of the lexical peculiarities with which Pareto describes the political – social forms of the European states. It was, as we know, Pareto who defined as 'democratic – plutocratic', or even 'demagogic', the states in which Class I residues predominate. And in fact it was the States of the Entente that were characterised thus, on account of the use of public spending as a tool for consensus and power. In these States, the close symbiosis between politics and economics reduces the decision-making autonomy of the politicians, increasingly dependent upon the wishes of the plutocrats, the main funders of the extremely expensive election campaigns. It was precisely this dependence, as we shall see, that led to the perverse arms race which in fact neither the politicians nor the plutocrats meant to pursue to the point of war.

The situation was quite the reverse in the central Empires, where militarism was bound up with the aristocratic hegemony. In Germany, for example, the Emperor, the landed aristocracy of the Junkers and the military caste constituted a social block that kept the plutocrats out of the corridors of power. Essentially, the dichotomous logic proposed by Pareto contrasts the political systems on the basis of the capacity of the economic élites to dictate policy in each of the countries.[30] 'Plutocrats – Pareto wrote – are to be found in Germany as in these countries, but in Germany the government imposes its will on them, while in the other countries it is the plutocrats that impose their will upon the government' (Pareto [1915] 1980: 634).

Rentiers and speculators: war as unintentional outcome

Perhaps the most interesting aspect of Pareto's interpretative framework is that it evokes the dualism between rentiers and speculators. The dominant class, usually identified as the capitalist class, is by no means internally homogeneous; in fact, considerable social, anthropological and above all economic differences emerge which, however, do not always appear transparent at the phenomenological level. Pareto deemed it necessary to distinguish within the dominant class at least two socio-economic typologies – rentiers and speculators – which offer stylised representation of the various social inclinations of the ruling classes, and above all the various and often conflicting economic interests in play.[31]

In the *Trattato* Pareto formalised the distinction between speculators and rentiers, tracing it back to his theory of residues: in fact, the first two classes of residues – the instinct for combinations and the persistence of aggregates – serve as the basis for the classification Pareto proposes.[32]

The speculators represent those economic agents whose income is by its very nature variable and depends upon the personal impulse to pursue gain. This category is made up of a great variety of social figures including entrepreneurs, stock exchange speculators, bankers, notaries, lawyers, engineers, etc. (Pareto [1916] 1935: §2233), while the rentiers include economic agents whose incomes are prevalently fixed or almost fixed, and do not depend on intelligence, shrewdness or entrepreneurial vocation. This category embraces the holders of various typologies of capital (with sufficiently stable returns over time), such as government bonds, debentures, landed property or real estate and, in general, all forms of saving and investment that can generate an income ([1916] 1935: §2234).

Corresponding to the different sources of income and psychological differences, the rentiers show a greater propensity to save and the lesser propensity to consume, while the contrary applies to the speculators. Moreover, the latter's instinct for combinations, giving rise to incessant pursuit of new opportunities for profit, constitutes a powerful drive for change and economic progress. On the other hand, the persistence of aggregates residue prevalent among the rentiers has a contrary effect, generating social stability and offsetting the trend towards disaggregation that excess of speculative combinations may lead to.[33] Finally, contrasting with the cosmopolitan inclinations of the speculators we have the deeper national rootedness of the rentiers.

As mentioned above, Pareto defines as 'plutocratic governments' those states in which speculators predominate amongst the power elites. The predominance of a plutocratic rationale in the economically more advanced countries produces contrasting dynamics vis-à-vis war cycles. On the one hand, it contributes towards weakening the system of military values, while on the other hand it fuels the war economy value chain through economic and political mechanisms. The speculators/rentiers dialectic thus represents a crossroads where the two processes converge, neither of which is able to offer an exhaustive explanation of the causes unleashing wars in isolation. An uninterrupted concatenation of actions, carried out by actors independent of one another, may unintentionally lead to war (Tarascio 1991: 126). Thus there is actually no room for the fantasies of those who imagine the speculators working behind-the-scenes on plots to achieve domination hatched in secret meetings.[34]

Writing when global war had yet to loom on the horizon, Pareto stressed the point that speculators had no interest in the outbreak of a great war, despite the very considerable benefits they might stand to gain from the militarist policies. War had become essentially 'economic' (Tarascio 1991: 126), involving extensive industrial sectors. Military policies serve the interests of the speculators for two essential reasons: in virtue of the economic consequences of such policies, they stand to make handsome profits, while their ideological effects persuade the masses to nationalistic causes. The colonial wars offered rich pickings. So the speculators had everything to gain from increase in military spending, but the eventuality of the great war on the continent did not respond to their immediate interests. A full-scale war, fought with the involvement of the great masses of the population, would destabilise the equilibriums of power, favouring the classes characterised by predominantly military leanings (the Class II residues).

> When we say that at the present time our speculators are laying the foundations for a war by continually increasing public expenditures, we in no sense mean that they are doing that deliberately – quite the contrary! They are continually increasing public expenditures and fanning economic conflicts not in order to bring on a war, but in order to make a direct profit in each little case. But the cause, though an important one, is not the main cause. There is another of greater importance – their appeal to sentiments of patriotism in the masses at large, as a device for governing. [...] Not only that. Those men who are rich in Class I residues sense intuitively [...] that if a great and terrible war should occur, one of its possible consequences might be that they would have to give way to men who are rich in Class II residues. To such a war they are opposed in virtue of the same instinct that prompts the stag to run from the lion, though they are glad to take on little colonial wars, which they can superintend without any danger to themselves. [...] Some day the war they have made way for but not wanted may break out; and then it will be a consequence of the past activities of the speculators, but not of any intent they have had either at that time or ever.
>
> (Pareto [1916] 1935: §2254, 1577)

Pareto drew up the *Trattato* shortly before the outbreak of the First World War. Nevertheless, despite his explicit anticipations the eventuality of such a war seemed remote to him. The outbreak of war came as an abrupt surprise to Pareto, as it did to most of the observers. However, the theoretical framework he was formulating in the *Trattato* clearly included it among the possible events, and it was on the strength of this that he was able to assert the forecasting capacity of the scheme. And it was in fact this framework, formulated in abstract, general terms in the *Trattato*, that Pareto applied in the writings he published commenting on the tremendous historical cataclysm of the First World War.

The speculators certainly played a decisive role, and there was a degree of truth in the socialists' imputation of responsibility for war to the 'capitalists', but they did not grasp the real reasons that led to the outbreak of the war.[35] The speculators played their part in bringing on the war, but unwittingly. It was therefore erroneous to hold that the plutocrats had knowingly operated in such a way as to trigger hostilities.

> Neither the democrats nor the plutocrats among the Western peoples wanted the war, and if it had depended on their wishes, they would never have entered upon it. That they prepared for it unwittingly, pursuing their own immediate advantages in their disputes, without worrying too much about the future. [...] If the democrats and plutocrats had been less greedy, less lavish with public money for their own use and electoral purposes, it is quite possible that Germany would never have attacked them.
>
> (Pareto [1915] 1980: 637)

In this passage Pareto reasserts the paradoxical dynamics of the speculators/ rentiers dialectic. In the countries where the rentiers played a leading role, like Germany, for example, militarism was expressly pursued as political strategy while at the same time instilling warlike military values. On the other hand, in countries like France and England, where hegemony lay more with the speculators, the multiplication of military spending often saw warlike values tending to atrophy: this is what Pareto meant when he stated that France and England were not 'prepared' for war. The economic 'interests' of the speculators favoured increasing military expenditure, although the real aim was not to enhance the country's defensive or offensive capacities. Pareto had been pointing up this paradox since 1911, when prospects of a great European War were still distant:

> One of the most curious phenomena of our time is the arms race into which civilised peoples fling themselves, but without ever waging war against one another. They are forever preparing for it but never engaging in it. The interest of the speculators and entrepreneurs lies in the maximum expenditure on arms, for these transactions go through their hands. Nevertheless, they fear war in that it can shift the centre of political power. [...] It is truly fantastic to see that the very same people who dedicate increasingly great sums to arms then go on to seek to undermine the military spirit.
>
> (Pareto [1911] 1980: 423)

In this passage, I believe, lies the central point in Pareto's account of war. Written a few years before the outbreak of the World War, it delineates the main factors behind the arms race. In part the arms race was fuelled by political decisions, motivated by the pursuit of power and by the nationalisms, and in part by the economic interests of the war sector. Politicians, industrialists and entrepreneurs behaved like *sorcerer's apprentices*, fuelling processes that eventually they could no longer control.[36] The outbreak of hostilities simply bore out the validity of this conceptual framework.

The 1911 paper also holds an important position in the evolution of Pareto's reflections on war for another reason, for it represents a bridge between Pareto the economist and Pareto the sociologist. The rentiers/speculators framework – as we have seen, at the centre of Pareto's war sociology – took shape in his major economic work, the *Manuale di Economia Politica* (1906). Here Pareto had delineated the two complementary forces at work in society, the forces of 'stability' and 'selection',[37] and these forces translate respectively into the behaviours of the rentiers and speculators. The former is a force that conserves the social organism, the latter a force that brings about change. Social equilibrium is maintained by virtue of the way these two social forces balance out and offset one another. Nevertheless, it is rare for a society to find itself in a state of social equilibrium. Historical phases that see the element of changeability (or selection) prevailing – usually characterised by great ferment and dynamism – are followed by phases in which stability once again prevails. 'Human societies have a very strong tendency to give a certain rigidity to any new organization, to become crystallized in any new form. Therefore, it very often happens that the passage from one form to another is not by a continuous movement, but by jams; one form breaks up and is replaced by another, the latter in its turn will break up, and so it goes' ([1906] 1971: 314). These ground-shaking movements can be brought about by internal revolutionary uprisings, or by wars. In the *Manuale* Pareto points out that war can become a necessary outcome in societies characterised by the 'stability' factor, such as those in which the military values predominates. In such societies, Pareto wrote, 'it is not enough that law and custom permit a simple soldier to become general, it is a further necessary that war furnish him the opportunity' ([1906] 1971: 316). Thus war becomes a factor of change that eventually impinges on the social forms resting on the values of stability. In short, there is a common thread that binds Pareto's economics to his sociological reflections on war. The concepts of 'stability' and 'selection' expounded in the *Manuale* constitute the conceptual framework for the rentiers/speculators scheme upon which Pareto based his interpretation of war and its various manifestations.

In Pareto's view, then, war was one of the possible consequences, or occasionally the cause, of the alternation within society between the phases of change and stability – phases that in turn depend on the predominance of rentiers or speculators in the government élite. And in the 1911 text he added that the outcomes of war themselves are strongly affected by this demographic composition.

Increase in the second category [the speculators] has not come about in similar ways in the various countries, and consequently its proportion with respect to the first category changes from one country to another. A country where this proportion approaches the peak that endows it with the maximum power can, in the case of war, other circumstances being equally favourable, prove the victor, reducing to impotence and even taking control of the other countries, where the speculators, entrepreneurs and dwellers of *Cosmopolis* constitute a vast proportion. This, perhaps, is the gravest danger certain countries can find themselves facing.

(Pareto [1911] 1980: 424)

We also find a certain continuity with the arguments set out in the *Manuale* and the *Trattato* in the last writings dedicated to war, collected in the 1920 publication *Fatti e Teorie* (Facts and Theories). At the end of the war, when the macroscopic upheavals at the geopolitical level emerge in all their magnitude, Pareto returned to investigating its causes and, above all, its possible consequences. A striking aspect is the insistence with which he stressed the effectiveness of the interpretative scheme built on the rentiers/speculators categories, making just a few adjustments in the light of the subsequent events.

To begin with, there was an adjustment to be made regarding the outcome of the war. As we have seen, Pareto held that the predominance of Class II residues in the central Empires would make them militarily stronger, and thus the probable winners of the war. He saw his forecast being correctly borne out in the first phase of the war, but belied by the developments in the second phase.[38] Various factors, he held, had contributed to this reversal in the relations of power. First, through the serious diplomatic errors made by the Germans, which led among other things to Italy's entry alongside the Entente. Second, the exceptionally well-armed United States entered the arena. Finally, paradoxically, the excessive weight of the very same Class II residues, which had been transformed by the 'mystical William II [...] dominated by the Class II residues' from a factor of military force into the arrogant and stupid 'presumption' that the contribution of the Class I residues could be dispensed with ([1920] 1980: 883 [292]).

A further correction had to do with the intentionality of the processes that led to the outbreak of war. As we have seen, in various contexts Pareto stressed the fundamental contribution of the speculators in creating the conditions for war, but always pointing out that they had no intention of bringing it on. This appraisal was to some extent revised, pointing out the 'error' in the peremptory assertion that the speculators would 'never' have wanted the war. In the 'Epilogue' to *Fatti e Teoria* Pareto corrected his stance, observing that 'when a certain point was reached, a fraction of the "speculators" wanted the war' ([1920] 1980: 892).

The third correction, suggested by the consequences of the World War, concerned the future evolution of the Western States. From the very outbreak of hostilities, Pareto had aired the idea of a 'great transformation' underway in the Western world, accelerated by the cataclysm of war (Busino 1989: 681). However, initially his predictions did not include the prospect, then becoming reality, of a break up not only of the central Empires, but of all the world anchored to the Class II residues, or in other words the world of the rentiers and the aristocracy. The defeat was not only military, but also social: 'demagogic plutocracy has won, and won by a long way, destroying the military and bureaucratic plutocracy just as Rome conquered and destroyed Carthage and the Macedonian kings. Will our plutocracy continue to triumph, or, like Rome, will victory itself prepare for its overthrow?' ([1920] 1980: 780). Another factor contributing to the downfall of the rentier class lay in one of the principal economic consequences of the war, namely inflation, necessary to make the burden of public debt bearable. It was, according to Pareto, precisely post-war inflation that contributed to the increasing erosion of the rentiers' incomes.

Finally, there is a significant concluding observation penned when the war was over and done with, closely connected with the epoch-making transformation of the world élites mentioned above. Here, Pareto returns to the issue of the decline of the bourgeoisie which, as we have seen, had some influence on the budding Italian nationalism. Nearly twenty years later, he went back over the same ground, having also discussed it in the *Treatise*. How does the idea of the declining bourgeoisie relate to the rentiers/speculators dialectic? Pareto answers in a closely argued passage which to some extent serves to summarise the various issues addressed in this text, where attention dwells not only on the World War but also on the unresolved issue of the class war, possibly betraying a certain sympathy towards a class that was in decline.

> The decline of the bourgeoisie follows its course. Since the mid-century, the bourgeoisie has proved incapable of showing [...] resistance [...] to the socialists' declarations of war. [...] Its adversaries proclaim their will to destroy it, and it bows its head without even a minimum of intrepidity to cry death in the face of its enemies. The war to destroy the systems of the central Empires was logical for the demagogic plutocracy, illogical for the "conservative" bourgeoisie, if indeed such a bourgeoisie still exists. A sane approach for it could have been to weaken the military power of Germany, while destroying it completely was insane, and in doing so the bourgeoisie probably helped to dig its own grave.
>
> (Pareto [1920] 1980: 902)

This passage not only casts some light on certain key concepts which we have dwelt upon in this chapter, and which Pareto had frequent recourse to in interpreting the extraordinary convulsions of European society in the first two decades of the twentieth century, but it also looks ahead to the last stage in the evolution of Pareto's thought. In particular, it anticipates some of his contributions collected in the volume *Trasformazione della democrazia* (1921). In these writings the issue of the First World War clearly continues to represent the great watershed in European history, but by now it remains in the background. What does emerge, however, is a singular point of contact, not made explicit by Pareto, with his reflections on war over the previous two decades. In the *Manuale* in 1906 Pareto had insisted on the point that a great European War would have altered the social dynamics deducible from the normal operation of the economic, sociological and, indeed, political laws.[39] Among these alterations, he had added in his contributions to the nationalist journal *Il Regno*, there was also a shift in time of at least half a century for the conclusive confrontation with socialism. This prediction was not being borne out by the facts. The socialist 'peril' was more threatening than ever, and the war itself had left the nightmare of Bolshevism as a legacy. And in fact *Trasformazione della democrazia* evokes the new urgent need for the bourgeoisie to raise its head again, responding to the challenge thrown out by Bolshevism. 'As a result of the discords provoked by excessive stupidity and the consequent long drown-out war, demagogic plutocracy as a political form and the entire bourgeois system are reeling under the impact' ([1921] 1966: 306). If the bourgeoisie continues to show the 'cowardly', 'weak-kneed', 'stupid' and 'degenerate' attitudes typical of 'all decadent elites' it will not be able to stand up to the vigorous strength of 'the adherents of a leader like Lenin' ([1921] 1966: 312).

Final considerations

The interpretative key proposed in these pages aims to outline the varied aspects of Pareto's approach to war, and above all the changes it underwent in the course of time. At the political level, his initial pacifism gave way to a conception of war inspired by political realism, while at the theoretical level as from the beginning of the second decade of the twentieth century, war began to take the form of an object of scientific interest. This latter change occurred alongside the progressive shift from the field of economics to that of sociology, to some extent bearing out the idea that sociology of war is a more appropriate approach to the analysis of Pareto's thought on war.[40] As we have seen, however, in the conceptual framework formulated by Pareto it proves very difficult to pick out a clear-cut line separating the arguments of an economic and sociological nature, and the idea prevailing that the phenomena for can be understood only within the framework of a general social science. For this reason, we have sought Pareto's war sociology in the context of his intellectual biography, in an attempt to show the possible links with his economic thought.

In the *Cours* we find no specific attention to the subject of war, which appears as something alien to the universe of trade. There prevails a conception of the economy as an area governed by peaceful relations between the nations, and which sees in *laissez-faire* a powerful factor for keeping the peace. Pacifism thrives on the basis of a universalistic conception of liberalism, and at the political level this led Pareto to show explicit aversion to Italy's ambitions for power and to military expenditure.

In the *Manuale*, too, Pareto refrains from systematic treatment of the subject of war, but nevertheless here we find conceptual categories which were to be expressly utilised some years later. When Pareto came to incubate the idea of analysing the phenomenon of war scientifically, he did so from a position in close continuity with the *Manuale*. It would be wrong to say that Pareto viewed war in strictly economic terms, as did Pantaleoni, for example, like other economists of the time. But quite possibly the author of the *Cours*, the *Manuale* and the *Trattato* did not even make a problem of determining where the field of war economics ends and where that of war sociology begins. A seamless continuum leads from one to the other. What we have sought to demonstrate in these pages is precisely the intertwining of economic and sociological lines of argumentation about war, in turn inextricably bound up with Pareto's political biography.

Notes

1 I would like to thank Fabrizio Bientinesi and Luca Michelini for their assistance and helpful comments on earlier drafts of this chapter. None of them are, of course, responsible for any errors.
2 Cf. Fiorot (1969); Busino (1989).
3 Cf. Toscano (1995; 2015); Di Gobbicchi (2002).
4 Busino (1989: 69–116; 2002: 27–31).
5 On Teodoro Moneta and his position in the history of European pacifism, cf. Brock (1972); Gherardi (2007); Castelli (2012).
6 On Pareto journalistic activity in the *Secolo*, cf. Maccabelli (2016).
7 Cardini (1997: 36).
8 Busino (1989: 87); Mornati (2000: 266); Pareto to Pantaleoni, 12 august 1892, in Pareto (1960, I: 268): 'Militarism and protectionism are a company, and you will never have militarism with commercial freedom. [...] The protectionists and the military have always gone together and will always agree'.
9 Cf. Pareto ([1890] 1974a; [1891a] 1974a; [1891b] 1974a).
10 'Was it not better to remedy many of our ills, rather than set off in pursuit of military glory? What good has the money spent on the Triple Alliance brought to the Italian people?' (Pareto [1893] 1974a: 704).
11 If one accepts 'militarism', Pareto argued, one must 'undergo the consequences. Individual rights count for little on the battlefield, while the well-being of the army is and indeed must be priority' (Pareto [1892a] 1974a: 534).
12 Pareto ([1892b] 1974a: 562). The opening words of Pareto's booklet are equally significant: 'The main cause of the ills of our country *lies in the excessive burden of military expenditure*. The secondary causes, although related to the former, are: customs protection; the destruction of wealth for the sake of maintaining in Africa *a colony without settlers*, to build *electoral railroads*, to create *organisational entities*, and in general to fuel the *abuses* benefiting the *politicians* who approve of the *belligerent* and *protectionist* policy'.
13 The essay of 1901, *Un poco di fisiologia sociale* (A little social physiology), appears programmatic with respect to Pareto's pro-nationalist positions (Pareto [1901a] 1974b). The last chapter on the *Socialist Systems* (1901b) is also largely dedicated to the degeneration of the bourgeoisie, imputed to their inauspicious embracing of democratic faith. Again, the *Manuale* contains recurrent references to the theme of degeneration, all occurrences being in the context of the theory of the circulation of the élites (Pareto [1906] 1971: 94; 312–314; 356–358). Finally, in his correspondence the fullest evidence is to be found in the letters exchanged with Luigi Bodio, where Pareto repeatedly expresses his conviction of the ineluctable decline of the bourgeoisie (cf. Pareto 2001).
14 *Il Regno* was a political journal established in 1903 by Enrico Corradini. It 'immediately achieved a distinct identity [...] by developing a forceful and consistent radical right-wing critique of Giolittian Italy. Politically, the journal was an early voice, perhaps even the first audible voice, in a swelling chorus of Italian bourgeois lamentation over the peril of socialism and the impotence of liberalism' (Drake 1981: 221).

15 We owe masterly reconstruction of the crucial role taken on by pragmatism in economic and political discourse in the early twentieth century to Aurelio Macchioro. See in particular Macchioro 1991.

16 Prezzolini ([1903a] 1960: 131). See also ([1903b] 1960) where Prezzolini advocates Pareto's ideas as scientific and practical armies to fight the peril of degeneration: 'We do not need to borrow French or English ideas; […] we can turn to Gaetano Mosca and to Vilfredo Pareto who have given us in their works that which justifies scientifically and philosophically our practical work' (quoted in Drake 1981: 224).

17 'In Italy evolution is less advanced than in France and Switzerland, and so the bourgeoisie is somewhat healthier than in those two countries; but if it does not steady itself, it will continue slithering down to reach the state of the French and Swiss bourgeoisie. The same applies to the British bourgeoisie. Just see if the facts don't bear out this deduction' (V. Pareto to G. Prezzolini, 17 December 1903. In Pareto 1973, I: 508).

18 'The decisive success of the *Regno* came about in large part as a result of Vilfredo Pareto's […] collaboration. Pareto […] gave Corradini's enterprise a prestige that it never would have enjoyed otherwise'. (Drake 1981: 224).

19 Cf. Gentile ([1969] 2002: 131).

20 The new élite that 'arises from the people […] makes use of the intellectual proletariat, of the misfits who owe their origin in part to the public education stupidly brought in by the bourgeoisie, and is setting out in conquest of the State and, above all, the goods of that same bourgeoisie' (Pareto [1904d] 1974b: 438–439).

21 'There are so many societies serving to protect and favour the enemies of the bourgeoisie; why are then none intended to defend it?' (Pareto [1904b] 1974b: 414).

22 'The revolutionary socialist party probably will win because it is the only one, or almost the only one, that is not afraid to use force, which since the world began alone assures and conserves victory. And while the bourgeois humanitarians, like inept women, fall in a dither at the mention of bloodshed, the revolutionaries know that everything which presently exists has been produced by battles that certainly were not bloodless' (Pareto [1904c] 1974b: 435; Drake 1981: 225).

23 '*Il Regno*'s main themes were the exaltation of war, imperial Rome, dictatorship, high production and colonialism, and the negation of socialism, parliamentarism and humanitarianism'. (Marsella 2004: 206). They all reveals Pareto's influence.

24 Corradini ([1904] 1960: 477). Magnification of war became 'one of the recurrent themes in Corradini's apologetics, as well as anti-democracy and anti-socialism […] The Italian theoretician of nationalism sees in war the highest expression of industrial civilisation, and peremptorily asserts the "modernity" of war' (Bobbio [1969] 1986: 55–56). On the conception of war in the nationalistic culture, cf. D'Alfonso (2012).

25 In 1911, with the Libyan war, 'when, after the disastrous colonial expeditions at the end of the last century, Italy returns to a worldwide colonial policy with positive results, the Italian nationalists seize the opportunity for resurgence, and it is no coincidence that in the very same years the newborn "Nationalist Association" comes to life with birth of the National Idea and the Journal of the commercial companies' (Michelini 1999: 38–39). On the Italian Nationalist Association, cf. De Grand (1971).

26 'I'm sorry that my Sociology still awaits publication, for, in the part already published much that was prediction now seems to be deduction' (V. Pareto to L. Bodio, 2 September 1914, in Pareto 2001: 259).

27 'I did not want to change anything to the *Trattato*, which had been completely written before the war. This is a truly great experiment, as in a physics laboratory. In an Appendix I will examine the propositions which confirm and those that contradict the facts, and if so where can come the error' (V. Pareto to P. de Pietri-Tonelli, 21 May 1915, in Pareto 1973, II: 895). The Appendix was never published.

28 'If the governing elite is dominated by individuals strong in Class I residues, […] the use of force is avoided, and disputes are often resolved by pecuniary means or by

granting certain privileges to undermine discontent. [...] Governments strong in Class II residues tend to be [...] more authoritarian, and ready to use force to deal with discontent. Traditions are preserved, and social innovation is suspect' (Tarascio 1991: 123–124).

29 'We say, as regards ancient times, that wars cut swaths in warrior aristocracies. So on the one hand frequent wars draw men of bellicose instincts into the governing classes, but on the other hand they destroy them' (Pareto [1916] 1935: §2224, 1153).

30 The exception of Russia is accounted for in terms of affinity between the bureaucracy of the czarist Empire and the bureaucracy of the Anglo-French powers.

31 Pareto took his place in a long theoretical tradition of scholars who sought more complex representation of the ruling classes, without levelling them out in the category of *capitalists*. For a few limited references only, we may recall the dialectic proposed by Thorstein Veblen between the 'creative instinct', or 'workmanship', and 'predatory instinct', or 'sportsmanship', which does not offer a very close match with Pareto's but was prompted by the same need to delve into the groundwork of the motivations, inclinations and economic interests common to the ruling classes (cf. Veblen 1914). Again, Schumpeter's celebrated conception of the entrepreneur, as different from the capitalist, shows various features in common with Pareto's, starting from the use of the concept of 'combination' (Schumpeter [1911] 2008). Finally, taking a leap through time, the statistical representation recently proposed by Thomas Piketty underlines the presence in the decile in the upper centile of the range of incomes of two fundamental social typologies, namely those who owe their incomes to their skills, and those who owe them to capital and assets (cf. Piketty 2014).

32 Cf. Aspers (2001: 533–535); McLure (2001: 160–161); Garzia (2006).

33 'The *S* group [the *speculators*] is primarily responsible for change, for economic and social progress. The *R* group [the *rentiers*], instead, is a powerful element in stability, and in many cases counteracts the dangers attending the adventurous capers of the *S*'s. A society in which *R*'s almost exclusively predominant remains stationary and, as it were, crystallized. A society in which *S*'s predominate lacks stability, lives in a shaky equilibrium that may be upset by a slight accident from within or from without' (Pareto [1916] 1935: §2235, 1563).

34 'In speaking of "speculators", we must not think of the actors in a melodrama who administer and rule the world, executing wicked design by stratagem dark. Such a conception of them would be no more real than a fairy-story. Speculators are just people who keep their minds on their business, and being well supplied with Class I residues, take advantage of them to make money, following lines of least resistance, as after all everybody else does. [...] Fifty years ago "speculators" had no conception whatever of the state of affairs that prevails today and to which their activity has brought them' (Pareto [1916] 1935: §2254, 1576–1577).

35 'The socialists were well aware of the fact, but, as usual, they conveyed it badly, saying that it was a war of 'capitalists'. [...] In general, considerations of the sort made by the intransigent Socialists on the European war has some basis in the real fact that the plutocrats of the various countries quarrel among themselves, just as the Roman *mercatores* and Punic negotiators used to' (Pareto [1915] 1980: 38).

36 A few years after the end of the war, Pareto was to write: 'Involuntarily, with the Libyan war and the war of the Balkans the plutocrats prepared the way for the present war. The plutocrats play with fire; and they got burnt. Now they are trying to turn events to their own profit' (Pareto [1920] 1980: 708).

37 On the concepts of 'stability' and 'selection', which Pareto drew from the late nineteenth century literature on social anthropology, cf. Maccabelli (2008). It is worth noting that Pareto subsequently abandoned the concept of 'selection', replacing it with 'change'.

38 'The defeat of the Central Powers is a phenomenon of great significance. In the first phase of the war, Germany's armies were successful. [...] But this phase was followed

by another which eventually terminated in the total victory of Germany's enemies. [...] The first phase is easily explained: it is the natural consequence of the particular character of demagogic plutocracies. But how do we explain the second phase?' (Pareto [1920] 1980: 875).

39 'Great European wars and other events of the sort can halt the course of evolution that is now underway' ([1906] 1971: 366).

40 See, for example, Coulomb (2004: 71–72): 'Isolating "political issues" from his theoretical analysis, Pareto presents a theory of war which is more sociological than economic, notably because of its emphasis on the evolutionary law of selection of "superior" societies'.

References

Angelini, G. (ed.) (2012) *Nazione democrazia e pace. Tra Ottocento e Novecento*, Angeli, Milan.

Aspers, P. (2001) 'Crossing the Boundary of Economics and Sociology: The Case of Vilfredo Pareto', *The American Journal of Economics and Sociology*, 60(2), 519–545.

Bobbio, N. ([1969] 1986) *Profilo ideologico del Novecento italiano*, Einaudi, Turin.

Brock, P. (1972) *Pacifism in Europe to 1914*, Princeton University Press, Princeton, NJ.

Busino, G. (1989) *L'Italia di Vilfredo Pareto. Economia e società in un carteggio del 1873–1923*, Banca Commerciale Italiana, Milan.

— (2002) 'Introduzione alla lettura dell'opera di Vilfredo Pareto', In Manca (2002: 19–68).

Cardini, A. (1997) 'Libera concorrenza e teoria delle "élites"'. Le contraddizioni di Pareto e il centenario del *Cours d'économie politique* (1896–1897)', *Studi e note di economia*, 1, 35–58.

Castelli, A. (2012) 'Il pacifismo alla prova. Ernesto Teodoro Moneta e il conflitto italo-turco', in Angelini (2012, 111–141).

Corradini, E. ([1904] 1960) 'La conferma del cannone', *Il Regno*, 1(12), in Frigessi (1960).

— ([1904] 1960) 'La guerra', *Il Regno*, 1(14), in Frigessi (1960).

Coulomb, F. (2004) *Economic Theories of War and Peace*, Routledge, London.

D'Alfonso, R. (2012) 'La nazione dei nazionalisti', in Angelini (2012, 89–100).

De Grand, A.J. (1971) 'The Italian Nationalist Association in the Period of Italian Neutrality, August 1914–May 1915', *The Journal of Modern History*, 43(3), 394–412.

Di Gobbicchi, A. (2002) *I meandri della ragione. La guerra nel pensiero sociale del XIX e XX secolo*, Angeli, Milan.

Drake, R. (1981) 'The Theory and Practice of Italian Nationalism, 1900–1906', *The Journal of Modern History*, 53(2), 213–241.

Finer, S.E. (1968) 'Pareto and pluto-democracy: the retreat to Galapagos'. *The American Political Science Review*, 62(2): 440–450.

Fiorot, D. (1969) *Il realismo politico di Vilfredo Pareto*, Edizioni di Comunità, Milan.

Frigessi, D. (ed.) (1960) *La Cultura italiana del '900 attraverso le riviste*, Vol. 1, 'Leonardo', 'Hermes', 'Il Regno', Einaudi, Turin.

Garzia, M.B.C. (2006) *Metodologia Paretiana*, Tomo I, *Differenziazione, non linearità equilibrio*, Peter Lang, Oxford.

Gentile, E. ([1969] 2002) 'Papini, Prezzolini, Pareto e le origini del nazionalismo italiano', *Clio*, 7(1), in Id., *Il mito dello Stato nuovo*, Laterza, Rome-Bari, 83–104.

Gherardi, R. (2007) *Il futuro, la pace, la guerra*, Carocci, Rome.

Maccabelli, T. (2008) 'Social Anthropology in Economic Literature at the End of Nineteenth Century: Eugenic and Racial Explanations of Inequality', *American Journal of Economics and Sociology*, 67(3), 481–527.

— (2016) '"Campo politico, campo giornalistico e campo delle scienze sociali": l'itinerario di Vilfredo Pareto', in M.E.L. Guidi and G. Pavanelli (ed.) *Gli economisti italiani e la formazione dello Stato unitario (1850–1900)*, Angel, Milan, 57–94.

Macchioro, A. (1991) 'Pragmatismo ed economia politica nella svolta primonovecento', in Id. *Il momento attuale. Saggi etico-politico*, Il Poligrafo, Padova, 19–46.

Manca, G. (ed.) (2002) *Vilfredo Pareto (1848–1923) L'uomo e lo scienziato*, Scheiwiller, Milan.

Marsella, M. (2004) 'Enrico Corradini's Italian Nationalism: The "Right Wing" of the Fascist Synthesis', *Journal of Political Ideologies*, 9(2), 203–224.

McLure, M. (2001) *Pareto, Economics and Society. The Mechanical Analogy*, Routledge: London.

Michelini, L. (1999) 'Il pensiero economico del nazionalismo italiano. 1900–1923', in L. Michelini (ed.) *Liberalismo, Nazionalismo, Fascismo*, M&B Publishing, Milan.

— (1997) 'La modernizzazione secondo Pantaleoni e Pareto (1887–1905)', *Il Pensiero Economico Italiano*, 5(2), 81–118.

Mornati, F. (2000) 'Gustave de Molinari e Yves Guyot nella formazione del pensiero paretiano fino al *Cours d'Economique Politique*', in C. Malandrino, R. Marchionatti (ed.) *Economia, sociologia e politica nell'opera di Vilfredo Pareto*, Olschki, Florence, 247–271.

Pareto, V. ([1889] 1974a) *Dell'Unione doganale od altri sistemi di rapporti commerciali fra le nazioni come mezzo inteso a migliorare le relazioni politiche ed a renderle pacifiche*, in *Relazioni al Congresso di Roma per la pace*, Lapi, Città di Castello, in Pareto (1974a, 289–297).

— ([1890] 1974a) 'Avevamo ragione', *Il Secolo*, 13–14 November, in Pareto (1974a, 349–351).

— ([1891a] 1974a) 'Finanza e politica', *Il Secolo*, 11–12 January, in Pareto (1974a, 361–363).

— ([1891b] 1974a) 'Statistica dolorosa', *Il Secolo*, 22–23 April, in Pareto (1974a, 419).

— ([1892a] 1974a) 'Liberalismo transigente e intransigente', *L'idea liberale*, 24 July, in Pareto (1974a, 532–535).

— ([1892b] 1974a) *Le spese Militari e i mali dell'Italia*, Tipografia Alessandro Gattinoni, Milan, in Pareto (1974a, 562–567).

— (1893) 'The Parliamentary Regime in Italy', *Political Science Quarterly*, 8(4), 677–721.

— ([1893] 1974a) 'Triplice… cara!' *Giù le armi. Almanacco illustrato della Pace*, 4, 14–15, in Pareto (1974a, 704).

— ([1896a] 1974b) 'Cronaca', *Giornale degli economisti*, 12(5), in Pareto (1974b, 78–85).

— ([1896b] 1974b) 'Cronaca', *Giornale degli economisti*, 13(9), in Pareto (1974b, 122–129).

— ([1897] 1974b) 'Cronaca', *Giornale degli economisti* 14(6), in Pareto (1974b, 198–202).

— (1896–97) Cours d'économie politique, Vol. I–II, Lausanne, F. Rouge.

— ([1901a] 1974b) 'Un poco di fisiologia sociale', *La vita internazionale*, 5 settembre, 529–532, in Pareto (1974b, 365–373).

— (1901b) *Les systèmes socialistes*, Voll. I–II, Giard et Brière, Paris.

— ([1904a] 1974b) 'La borghesia può risorgere?' *Il Regno*, 1(7), in Pareto (1974b, 396–398).

— ([1904b] 1974b) 'Perché?' *Il Regno* 1(13), in Pareto (1974b, 414–416).

— ([1904c] 1974b) 'Umanitari e rivoluzionari', *Il Regno* 1(49), in Pareto (1974b, 433–436).

— ([1904d] 1974b) 'Memento homo', *Il Regno* 1(55), in Pareto (1974b, 437–439).

— ([1905a] 1974b) 'Logica umanitaria', *Il Regno* June 1905, in Pareto (1974b, 457–460).

— ([1905b] 1974b) 'Di tutto un poco', *Il Regno*, 16 December 1905, in Pareto (1974b, 461–465).
— ([1906] 1971), *Manual of Political Economy*, M. Kelley, New York.
— ([1911] 1980) 'Rentiers et spéculateurs', *L'Indipendence*, 1 May, in Pareto (1980, 416–424).
— ([1914] 1974b) 'Conflitto di razze, di religioni e di nazioni', *Il Giornale d'Italia*, 2 september, in Pareto (1974b, 523–528).
— ([1915] 1980) 'La guerra ed i suoi principali fattori sociologici', *Scientia*, marzo, 257–275, in Pareto (1980, 624–643).
— ([1916] 1935) *Trattato di sociologia generale*. Florence, Barbera, English translation: *The Mind and Society*, Edited by Arthur Livingston, Voll. I–IV, Harcourt Brace and Company, New York.
— ([1920] 1980) *Fatti e teorie*, in Pareto (1980, 593–915).
— ([1921] 1966) *La trasformazione della democrazia*, Partial English translation in *Sociological Writings*, Selected and introduced by S.S. Finer, Praeger, London.
— (1960) *Lettere a Maffeo Pantaleoni*, Voll. I–III, Banca Nazionale del Lavoro, Rome.
— (1973) *Epistolario*, Edited by G. Busino, Voll. I–II, Accademia dei Lincei, Rome.
— (1974a) *Scritti Politici*, Vol. I, *Lo sviluppo del capitalismo (1872–1895)*, Utet, Turin.
— (1974b) *Scritti Politici*, Vol. II, *Reazione, libertà, fascismo (1896–1923)*, Utet, Turin.
— (1980) *Scritti sociologi minori*, Utet, Turin.
— (2001) *Œuvres Complètes*, vol. XXXI, *Nouvelles Lettres (1870–1923)*, Textes, rassemblés, prefaces et annotés par F. Mornati et publiés sous la direction de G. Busino, Geneve, Droz.
Piketty, T. (2014) *Capital in the Twenty-First Century*, Harvard University Press, Cambridge, MA.
Prezzolini, G. ([1903a] 1960) 'Decadenza borghese', *Leonardo* 1(5), in Frigessi 1960, 129–131.
— ([1903b] 1960) 'L'aristocrazia dei briganti', *Il Regno* 1(3), in Frigessi 1960, 455–460.
Schumpeter, J.A. ([1911] 2008) *The Theory of Economic Development: An Inquiry into Profits, Capital, Credit, Interest and the Business Cycle*, Transaction Publishers, New Brunswick (NJ) and London.
Tarascio, V.J. (1991) 'Pareto on Conflict Resolution and National Security', in C.D. Goodwin (ed.) *Economics and National Security: A History of their Interaction*, History of political economy, Annual supplement v. 23, Duke University, Durham, London.
Toscano, M.A. (1995) *Trittico sulla guerra. Durkheim. Weber. Pareto*, Laterza, Rome-Bari.
— (2015) 'Durkheim, Weber, Pareto e la guerra. Prospettive da opposti fronti', in D. Pacelli (ed.) *Le guerre e i sociologi. Dal primo conflitto totale alle crisi contemporanee*, Angeli, Milan, 32–49.
Veblen, T. (1914) *The Instinct of Workmanship*, Macmillan, New York.

5   The Economics of Peace in the History of Political Economy

Fabio Masini

Introduction

There are plenty of volumes in the academic literature on the *economics of war*, at least since the well-known contributions by Arthur Cecil Pigou (1916, 1920, 1921) through the notorious *How to pay for the war* (Keynes 1940) until more recent works on the relationships between economics and military power, for example within the realm of *international political economy* (e.g. Cooper 1972). There are also authoritative studies that have reconstructed the historical evolution of such field of research, since mercantilism (e.g. Goodwin 1991; Coulomb and Fontanel 2001; Allio 2014).

It is more difficult to recall examples of contributions dealing with the *economics of peace*, i.e. how to design an economic order best suited to guarantee a long-lasting condition where war is banished. Keynes's (1919) *The Economic Consequences of the Peace* has of course something to do with it, tackling the long-term consequences of choices that would presumably threaten the perspective of peaceful relations worldwide. Nevertheless, in Keynes 'peace' is merely a truce, a temporary condition of absence of war, an unstable situation that is bound to last only for a while, however long this might be.

Most liberal thinkers from the eighteenth century onwards have repeatedly suggested that the provision of some crucial public goods – such as free trade and the adherence to a stable international monetary system – in *each nation* of the world would *naturally* lead to a peaceful system of international relations. Free trade and a stable international monetary standard would guarantee durable welfare and peace. During the twentieth century, especially after WWI, peace becomes an object of wide study, even within the liberal thought. Some influential subjects, such as the *Rockefeller Foundation*, the *Carnegie Endowment for International Peace*, the *Graduate Institute of International Studies*, devote specific and systematic studies to enquire into the conditions for a stable peaceful international system (De Marchi 1991).

Between the two world wars, some economists challenge the current approach and start thinking massively of *peace in Kantian terms*: a long-term, viable and permanent condition where conflicts in the world are not conducive to war but to a judiciary settlement (Lucht 2009). Peace appears no longer as the natural outcome of international public goods to be provided nationally – such as freedom, democracy, equity, etc. – but as the product of a meta-economic system of supranational institutions. These enquiries try to approach peace from a different perspective, namely to study the conditions for a durable peace, *from an international point of view*. As we shall see, nevertheless, most of them rely on *internationalism*, as though international institutions *per se* could guarantee peace in a world of fully sovereign states.

Within this debate, contributions emerged where economists wondered and challenged the structure and nature of State power. In these discussions, both economics and politics come in, forging reflections in *supranational constitutional economics* that stretch the conventional boundaries of economic science. The aim of this chapter is to highlight some of the thoughts of these authors, comparing them to *internationalism*, and illustrate the key features that were singled out as conditions to achieve a stable peaceful international system.

In order to illustrate this, two key questions are to be tackled. The first is: what is *peace* and what is the *economics of peace*? In the first section we shall discuss different ideas of peace emerging from economic literature in the last two centuries.

The second question we will try to address is: why should economists have something to say about a concept that apparently has not much to do with economics, like *peace*? To provide a tentative answer to this, in sections two and three we concentrate on two different attitudes towards the economics of peace – *internationalism* (section two) and *constitutional federalism* (section three). In section four we explore some more recent contributions to constitutional federalism, before we provide some concluding remarks.

Economists and peace-making

The literature on *economics and the war* has until the first world war provided interesting contributions, although spoiled by a 'complementary' conception of war and peace (Barber 1991): to speak of *economics and the war* was supposed to speak also of *economics and the peace*, as the two terms were considered antithetic. Of course, they are not, as the absence of war is not necessarily a stable peaceful condition but may be just a temporary truce. This solution of course helped solving the question of enquiring into a concept, peace, which was considered outside the domain of economic categories. War may be seen to have an economic relevance, as it is associated to transaction costs, resource scarcity, financing questions. This is particularly true if one shares a notion of wealth as connected to material welfare (e.g. Cannan 1914), that war destroys. War breaks the economic equilibrium, therefore challenging the core subject of economic analysis. Peace can more easily be tackled as an economic category if associated to war, if simply labelled as its negation (Dunne 1990; Goodwin 1991; Shaffer 1996).

The dominant view in economics considered war as the product of an inefficient relationship between the State and the market, both at a national and at an international level. According to this idea, the market could best work if left to operate with its virtuous automatic adjusting mechanisms and the intervention of the State would only cause malfunctioning. When war breaks out, the resources necessary for production are no longer provided on the global market and the very demand for final products becomes fragmented, further worsening the relations among states – which eventually become less and less sustainable and degenerate into a conflict.

The economist gives advice to the government suggesting to refrain from influencing the functioning of the market as a preventive cure against the risk of war. If and when a conflict bursts out, economists advise on how to substitute imports and design a production and consumption system coherent with the needs of war, also suggesting the adoption of financial principles coherent with the war.

According to this vision, in order to achieve a peaceful world, it is necessary to reduce the weight of the State in the economy, leaving its intervention only to the pathological situation of war.

International institutions may help this, creating a system of rules and organisms that make it more difficult or even forbid a public (national) intervention on fundamental questions like money, free circulation of goods, workers and capitals; for the smooth functioning of the global market requires no international conflict.

In brief, the market is the victim of wars, which are a matter of political choices that have nothing to share with economics. Economics can only try to adjust itself to a pathological situation of exogenous nature. Hence the birth of a wide literature on how to gather and direct the greatest possible amount of resources towards defence, how to finance the costs of war, etc.

These theses – which are linked to a concept of economics as a natural order that should not be harmed and should actively be (re)established – are widely debated in Europe in the nineteenth and the early twentieth centuries. In particular, they would find a fertile ground in the British culture before and between the two World Wars. It is not difficult to imagine why. Until the outbursts of the First World War, Britain had been the engine of the international economy and finance, with the role of hegemonic power. A role that had to be restored in a completely modified geopolitical scenery. Britain had also, traditionally, the most important and advanced theoretical reflection in economics, with active research centres also devoted to assist economic policy. Finally, Britain in the inter-wars years had remained free from the cultural and political influences that affected most countries in Europe, where the scientific research had been often addressed towards 'regime' objectives. And, more than that, Britain lived the years between 1919 and 1941 in fright, worried not to regain the central role it had beforehand, but also with a growing awareness of the precariousness of the situation that had followed the first conflict and the ineluctability of a new tragedy. It is not a surprise, then, if the most advanced reflection on peace is to be found among British economists between the two world wars.

As Kant recalled, *peace* is different in nature from *truce*; it is a permanent and structural condition that characterizes the relations among states, which has to be built and guaranteed with adequate juridical, political, institutional and economic instruments. It is with this awareness, with a concept of peace as a complex architecture of the international relations, as a radically and permanently different scenario in which economics is rooted, that some economists introduce in the British theoretical debate innovative thoughts on the relationship between economics and peace.

The first point is to understand in which way they provided such a different solution to the question of peace, in respect to their predecessors. A key point is that early liberal philosophers and economists thought that international peace was to be achieved through what Sally calls 'liberalism from below' (Sally 1998: 39), meaning that once the liberal principles are implemented in each and every State, the causes of war would naturally disappear. The adherence of each State to a stable international monetary standard and free trade would guarantee peace to be a lasting condition of international relations. This approach would be first challenged by some thinkers, such as Edwin Cannan (1914, 1927), in the early twentieth century, followed during WWI by others, such as Veblen's (1917) *Inquiry into the Nature of Peace* and Hobson's (1917) *Democracy after the War*.

Two main directions were taken, the first is *internationalism*, the second is what we might call *constitutional supra-nationalism*. The core of the latter, most innovative and radical approach that followed some of Cannan's reflections, calls for the foundation of a supranational federation, where sovereignty is disentangled from State loyalty and becomes a matter of multilayer sharing of needs and collective choices. But before we illustrate this in details, let us concentrate on the first of the two different strands that economists took concerning peace.

Economists and internationalism

The First World War showed that western civilization had an inherent tendency towards conflict and that this could be so devastating as to threaten the whole humankind. The war had cancelled out all the positive effects of the first wave of globalization of the last few decades (Keynes 1919: 7–23). The global market had become fragmented into national or imperial trades. Intellectuals were appalled by the war; the literature on the ways to avoid war grew immensely. Economists were among them.

Most of them dreamt of re-establishing pre-war conditions, with a new effort for free trade and the abandonment of tariffs, the return to the gold standard. These were, once again, the global public goods that, according to most economists, it was necessary to restore to have peaceful international relations.

Nevertheless, some were aware that those global public goods existed already in the pre-war era and had already disappeared as the war burst out. The problem was then how to avoid wars, with a different approach from the one followed earlier, where the production of such international public goods *from below* had proved ineffective. But economists found it difficult to abandon this perspective. In this respect, a huge literature flourished in different political orientations.

Marxists still believed that war was inherent to capitalism and that *socialism from below* would provide peaceful international relations. Mostly along the line of Rosa Luxemburg, capitalism requires pre-capitalistic countries to demand their products. Hence the imperialistic nature of capitalism (and of colonial wars). In order to have peace each country shall change its social and political structure. Once every country will have established a socialist State, peace will be the natural outcome.

Democratic internationalism shows different degrees of innovation. Wilson's *14 points* were the testimony of a dramatic naiveté among most democrats. The same naiveté affects the institutionalist Thorstein Veblen, who claims: 'the cause of peace and its perpetuation might be materially advanced if precautions were taken beforehand to put out of the way as much as may be of those discrepancies of interest and sentiment between nations and between classes which make for dissension and eventual hostilities' (Veblen 1917: 367).

An interesting exception is John Atkinson Hobson, social democrat who would later join the *Union of Democratic Control*. His book, *Towards International Government* (1914) was an example of his position towards the active construction of peace. But a more mature and interesting contribution is Hobson's (1917) *Democracy after the war*.

A section of Hobson (1917) is devoted to 'The close State *versus* Internationalism', where he claims that citizens have a common interest in promoting peace and abhorring war. Only a small section of the national population is interested in making war, so that there is a systematic 'struggle between the forces of democracy and those of the capitalist oligarchy' (Hobson 1917: 192).

The economic and political elite aims to 'conserve their own political and economic supremacy within the nation by every sort of concession, economic, social and political, consistent with the maintenance of that supremacy' (Hobson 1917: 192). This is the crucial factor affecting peaceful international relations, and the construction of apt international institutions is the key to weaken these interests:

> The notion of the League turning into a new Holy Alliance of the capitalist bureaucracy within each State for the concerted repression of all democratic movements can hardly be a serious apprehension in face of the divergences of interest between the ruling groups within the several states. But even if such a danger were latent in the formation of an international Government, it would be better for democracy to confront it than to lapse into the pre-war situation definitely worsened by the new powers wielded by reaction within each State.
>
> (Hobson 1917: 208)

The insistence on national (although common) causes of war, due to sectorial interests, prevents him from looking at the longer-run implication of interdependence worldwide. Nevertheless, he is rather clear on the potential risks of nationalism and protectionism:

> While, therefore, a closed State, national or imperial, might be socialistic in economic structure, it could not be democratic in government. For it is not

only actual war that is seen to be incompatible with democracy. Potential war is seen to be likewise incompatible. Now the nationalism, imperialism, militarism, protectionism of a 'closed State' are potential war.

(Hobson 1917: 201)

Hence the critique to socialism, due to the incapability to understand that a true democratic process, given the high level of interdependence at the global level, requires international institutions:

Even Socialism, though international in theory, has seldom set itself to any realization of the necessity of a concerted movement towards a mastery of the national State by the workers of the respective nations, with the object of building up an international democracy. Yet this is precisely the work that must be done, if democracy is to survive.

(Hobson 1917: 206)

Hobson (1920) speaks of *The Morals of Economic Internationalism*, although in the last page he makes it clear that the major powers (US and UK) had the responsibility to change the course of events thorough 'political cooperation':

If these countries in close concerted action were prepared to place at the service of the new world order their exclusive or superior resources of foods, materials, transport and finance – the economic pillars of civilization – the stronger pooling their resources with the weaker for the rescue work in this dire emergency, this political cooperation would supply that mutual confidence and goodwill without which no governmental machinery of a League of Nations, however skilfully contrived, can begin to work.

(Hobson 1920: 61)

He is even ready to give up the principles of democracy, if effectiveness in collective decision-making is at stake:

It is not true that the formation of a League of Nations, binding themselves to enforce by common action the fulfilment of their treaty obligations, places a new weapon in the hands of the ruling classes and constitutes a new danger to the workers. If such a League, however undemocratically controlled, is effective in its main object, it reduces the aggregate of military and naval force in the world and lessens the likelihood of its use.

(Hobson 1917: 208)

Although very close to understanding the importance of a top-down approach to peace-making, he still remains anchored to a *weak* conception of international organizations, without daring to go further as to claim in favour of *coercive power*, if legitimate institutions are built worldwide. If we exclude Hobson and the few examples we are going to show in the following pages, all that economists apparently had to say, even when not in the ivory tower of scientific analysis but charged with governmental roles, was to demonstrate that self-sufficiency (implied in the economics of war) was a Pareto sub-optimal solution compared to international cooperation. The Van Zeeland Report was one of the most typical examples of this. Paul Van Zeeland, economist, financier and at that time Prime Minister of Belgium, was asked in April 1937 by the governments of France and Great Britain to enquire 'into the possibility of obtaining a general reduction of quotas and other obstacles to international trade' (Bartlett 1938: 4). As Van Zeeland himself claimed: 'international trade is not an end in itself, it is only a means directed towards an end' (quoted in Bartlett 1938: 2). But again, the only practical proposal is a League of Nations committed to the establishment of free trade through the progressive reduction of tariffs. The League of Nations and other international institutions of similar kind flourished during the inter-wars period thanks to this ideology.

The third channel through which internationalism spread, was liberalism. Liberal internationalism was divided into two main approaches. The first is Keynesian liberalism that, in the second phase, i.e. after the outbreak of WWII, committed to global cooperation in order to reflate the economy, leaving room for manoeuvre at home for expansionary policies. Durbin (1942), Meade, Beveridge, and Keynes himself, of course, were among the leading figures of this approach. For example, Durbin points at worldwide domestic expansions: 'Bearing in mind the lesson of the catastrophic depression of 1929, if depression is not to spread so as to make action all over the world imperative at the same time, the country suffering the depression should take steps to offset it' (Durbin *et al.* 1942: 24). But this, in turn, requires benevolent international institutions to avoid expansionary policies to be unilateral and therefore offset their positive effects. What is needed is international cooperation, the enforcement of which hardly any author dwells upon.

The second, which can be attributed to *neoliberal thinking*, had two urgencies: (a) to build liberal institutions at home, so that state intervention should be kept at a minimum; and (b) to build international institutions that could guarantee the smooth functioning of the global market and of a stable monetary standard.

Mainstream economics has usually assumed peace to be the normal state of affairs when no political intervention in the market is made by the State. The best contribution one could make towards peace-making was to struggle for the liberal values in each country. No liberal State would ever engage in conflicts, this was the assumption, because in a free market where no influence from politics or lobbies can hinder the circulation of capitals, goods, people the market can achieve the maximum welfare for the whole humankind.

Nevertheless, the pursuit of *liberalism from below* was becoming harder and harder. It was necessary to pursue liberalism from above, through international institutions that would deprive states from authority over the free circulation of resources worldwide. Hayek's claims in favour of a supranational federation were but a means to avoid national public intervention in the economy, especially in the monetary field, to avoid the damages of 'monetary nationalism' (Hayek, 1937).

This was clearly instrumental to diminish the room for manoeuvre for public policies, not as a means to create a public collective democratic body at the level where it is most necessary. Hayek's proposals for a European federation (1937; 1944) were clearly aiming at a negative-sum game concerning public intervention in the economy: a supranational federation was to be a technical institution to avoid that political pressures could interfere with the functioning of the global market. Peace was again, as in classical liberalism, the outcome of both national liberal institutions and a soft power at the international level.

Economists and supranational constitutional federalism

We have seen that peace has been seen as the by-product of *liberalism from below* (but also of *socialism from below*, or *democracy from below*) or as an international construction relying on very loose international institutions (*internationalism*).

A radically different attitude is provided by those who believe that both approaches miss the crucial point: national exclusive sovereignty is inherently conducive to war and peace can produced only though a multilayer system of shared sovereignties. This line of reflections, that can be attributed first to Luigi Einaudi, Attilio Cabiati, Edwin Cannan, would later become more mature with Lionel Robbins, although also Jacques Rueff, Wilhelm Röpke and others have sympathized with this view. More recently Robert Triffin, Robert Marjolin, Tommaso Padoa-Schioppa, Mario Draghi have occasionally expressed similar claims. Let us now try to understand the nature of such idea and its role in the history of economics.

Rooted in the British debate between the end of the nineteenth and the beginning of the twentieth centuries, the main point of Einaudi (1918a, b, c; 1919; 1947) and Robbins (1937a, b; 1939a, b; 1940), who are the most advanced thinkers along these lines, is that peace is a global public good that is very difficult to provide because it requires a radical change in the juridical structure of human constitutions. Sovereignty cannot lay in the hands of monopolies like the nation states, because this intrinsically implies that conflicts will ultimately result in wars. The only possible solution is to share sovereignty in a way that different, concentric (i.e., from local to global) governmental bodies are assigned to shared needs of individuals.

In 1897, in the newspaper La Stampa of Turin, appears an article, *Un sacerdote della stampa e gli Stati Uniti europei*, in which Einaudi shares the view of a renown British journalist, William Thomas Stead, who had considered the joint intervention of the six major European powers to defend peace in Crete (after the outbreak of a violent anti-Turkish revolt) as 'the birth of the United states of Europe' (quoted in Cressati 1992: 35). The most interesting part of Einaudi's article is the reason why such an opinion could be agreed upon: the fact that the six powers had agreed not to decide 'according to the rule of the *liberum veto*' (Einaudi 1897: 37).

Although certainly a classical liberal, Einaudi claims that freedom, at the international level, does not depend on the possibility to act according only to national sovereign choices but on a set of rules where international decisions are taken by majority principle; in short, 'State sovereignty has to be limited' (Morelli 1990: 21). The crucial point is that the absolute and exclusive sovereignty of each national State, embodied in the veto rule at the international diplomatic level, makes it impossible to pursue any collective action and therefore to provide a collective public good such as international peace. Hence the way out:

> From this imperfect phase when even only one of the six powers, with its opposition, could make any plan accepted by all the others inapplicable, we will slowly come to a point when the majority will be able to impose decisions on the minority without making recourse to the *ultima ratio* of the war.
>
> (Einaudi 1897: 37–38)

Einaudi clearly identifies the nature of the critical point in the method to agree on collective choices: from an intergovernmental (or confederative) method based on the adoption of a veto rule, to a federal system based on majority voting. He would later explore in more details the question in his further contributions soon after the first world war (1918a; b; 1919; 1920).

Robbins, who is active mostly in the thirties on these matters, makes a step further. The first point is that peace is not a mere and temporary absence of conflicts but a permanent condition that requires a specific institutional structure. The causes of war are to be found both in inefficient institutions and in market failures depending on a perverse concept of *sovereignty*, which is exclusively attributed to nation-states: 'The ultimate condition giving rise to those clashes of national economic interest which lead to international war is the existence of independent national sovereignties' (Robbins 1939b: 99).

In this respect, Robbins maintains that classical liberalism is 'anarchic', as international relations are only tackled through national diplomatic efforts, without any superior coercive institution. But the existence of systems of power with an exclusive and absolute sovereignty is not coherent with the necessity to safeguard peaceful international relations nor with economic efficiency. The economy is in fact founded on the production and consumption of private and public goods. As concerns the former, they need to be produced and exchanged in a plurality of territorially concentric markets because each good and service is provided to satisfy the needs of more or less wide groups of individuals. Each market (for each good) needs to be backed and guaranteed by specific rules and juridical systems. Similarly, there are collective and shared needs that require the production of public goods which are not to be provided necessarily at the national level. In both cases, the economy needs an institutional, political and juridical system that has to be structured from the local to the global dimension, following a principle that we would now call *subsidiarity*.

According to Robbins (1937a, b; 1939a, b; 1940) the most adequate constitutional framework coherent with these urges is the federal one. Federalism provides an optimal constitutional equilibrium between decentralization and centralization, between local and global; 'Independent Sovereignty must be limited'

(Robbins 1939b: 104) and 'the national states must learn to regard themselves as the functions of international local government' (Robbins 1939a: 105).

A mere confederative agreement among national states, as those who had characterized the several international conferences in the Thirties, would be unable to provide the collective public goods that are necessary for the constructive operation of global market forces. What is required is a constitutional architecture based on a multilevel federal system which allows decentralized choices and, at the same time, central strategic unity: in Robbins's own words: 'There must be neither alliance nor complete unification, but Federation; neither *Staatenbund*, nor *Einheitsstaat*, but *Bundesstaat*' (Robbins 1937a: 245, italics in the original).

For Robbins, the federal structure does not necessarily imply less government, in a negative-sum game as for Hayek. Federal authorities may decide whether or not to intervene in economics and to what extent (Robbins 1940: 240–241). Of course, we are not suggesting that Robbins would have argued in favour of socialist policies, but simply that this kind of political struggle was to be framed within an appropriate constitutional set of rules and institutions such that supra-national decisions are made in a democratic way and not left to the law of the strongest which usually governs diplomatic conferences. A federal structure is therefore a constitutional architecture where different ideological approaches can politically confront each other, not necessarily a means to reduce public intervention in the economy. Robbins's *constitutional federalism*, is therefore the opposite of Hayek's *instrumental federalism*.

More recent approaches

This approach to supranational institutions as a premise to peaceful international relations would later become a much more complex question. Supranational constitutional federalism, which seemed a viable solution to international conflicts before the end of WWII, suddenly appeared to be unrealistic and utopian soon after the war, when concrete steps were taken to supranational integration in a 'peaceful' context.

The end of the war diminished the ability to design innovative plans for international peace. Economists devoted less and less lines to peace, or concentrated again their studies on conflicts (mainly based on game theory). Only a few, during the Seventies, tried to combine political and economic reflections, around a new topic called *International Political Economy* (e.g. Cooper 1972).

Some authors, nevertheless, still approached peace from the point of view of supranational constitutional federalism, applying this to European integration, where the conditions for such a project were at the same time more likely and more challenging. Jean Monnet, Robert Triffin, Robert Marjolin and – generally speaking – most founding fathers of European Union (Adenauer, De Gasperi, Schuman, Spaak, Spinelli) had something similar in mind when struggling for European integration. The intellectual influence of Einaudi and Robbins did not disappear with them. We will nevertheless skip these authors, to concentrate on two more recent and more surprising (because very influential economists in key international institutions) contributors to this idea: Tommaso Padoa-Schioppa and Mario Draghi.

Padoa-Schioppa, co-rapporteur of the *Delors Report* on *Economic and Monetary Union* in 1989, member of the influential *Group of Thirty*, key figure in international macroeconomic supervision, recently member of the Board of the ECB and *Minister of Treasury* in Italy, contributed much on the question of peace. Just to recall his main arguments, Padoa-Schioppa wondered whether Europe is a successful project and, although underlining its shortcomings and its unfinished nature, he claimed:

> In fifty years it has realized something that we had never seen in history: a group of countries has organized itself in a pacific and transparent way to exercise, in common, sovereignty in the fields where states have remained only virtually sovereign, because they face problems greater than their ability to tackle them individually.
>
> (Padoa-Schioppa 2006: 52)

Padoa-Schioppa stresses the link between exclusive sovereignty and peace, underlining the importance of sharing sovereignty if conflicts have to be reduced. He explicitly talked about this in the speech he gave as Minister of Economics and Finances at the inaugural lecture of the 'Politecnico of Milan', in November 2007:

> Today, in the world, we count about two hundred nation-states; almost all of them tenaciously hanging on the illusion of unlimited sovereignty. [But ...] *the identity of each individual is multiple.* There is no incoherence between being from Milan, Lombardy, Italy, Europe and, lastly, citizens of the world. [...] Recognizing this principle must make us aware that when one belongs to a community that we now call *national*, this does not contradict nor diminishes our belonging to other communities, both more restricted – around the municipality or region – and more ample, on a continental or world scale.
>
> (Padoa-Schioppa 2007: 2)

This concept of multiple (or multi-layered) identities must be reflected in the structure of power allocated to the satisfaction of the needs of each collective body. This is of course threatened by a competitive human nature, when this is unfettered by rules conducive to judiciary conflicts instead of war:

> The relationships among human communities are based on two extreme models: conflict and union. At one end we have war; on the other we have competition. On one side conflict, war, the lack of any law different from the law of force: the force of weapons, of deception, of money, of intimidation. Competition, in its multiple forms, is somehow in the middle: it is a

contest where commercial struggles are a means to affirm the supremacy of a competitor on the other. [...] Peace is not to be attained dampening in people and human communities the impulse to excel, to perform better than others, to win. It can be attained establishing a condition, an order in which those impulses keep on emerging but bound to rules.

(Padoa-Schioppa 2007: 4–5)

And a few lines afterwards:

The economic order implies a political order. Peace cannot be built dampening, among individuals and human communities, the impulse to excel, to perform better than the others, to win. It can be built through a condition, an order where those impulses are free to be expressed but under a set of rules. [...] Such condition is competition. But in order not to degenerate into war, it needs strong rules, and those rules can be provided only by politics, by a strong political power. [...] Europe is the only place where, for the first time in history, international competition has been really shaped in a pacific way.

(Padoa-Schioppa 2007: 5)

Competition as a peaceful proxy for conflicts among human beings is certainly a public good that should be provided internationally, but it is not the only one. There are needs and wants that we all share as human beings, which require legitimate democratic global institutions to provide:

Sometimes the "generality" of interests is not planetary, but trespasses the boundaries of nation states. But we possess neither representativeness nor democracy to pursue general interests that trespass national borders. When it was formed, the nation State had such a wide perimeter as to represent, for its citizens, an almost unlimited universe as concerns culture and material conditions of existence. [...] But today, the vital interest of mankind to physical and civil survival has no representativeness; there is no place where human beings are represented as such. International cooperation does not imply democracy; and the European one only achieves it in an incomplete way.

(Padoa-Schioppa 1999)

More recently, similar concepts were expressed by Mario Draghi, former *Governor of the Bank of Italy*, now *President of the European Central Bank* and member of the *Group of Thirty*. Arguing about the nature of sovereignty, in relation to the reforms of the European Union, Draghi makes interesting claims that I think worth quoting at length:

One way to look at sovereignty is normative, and was historically favoured by absolutists such as Jean Bodin in the sixteenth century. Sovereignty here is defined in relation to rights: the right to declare war and treat the conditions of the peace, to raise taxes, to mint money and to judge in last resort.

Another way to look at it is positive. Sovereignty relates to the ability to deliver in practice the essential services that people expect from government. A sovereign that is not capable of effectively discharging its mandate would be sovereign only in name. This second approach is more consistent with the writings of the political philosophers who most influenced our modern democracies. John Locke, in his second treatise of government, affirms that the sovereign exists only as a fiduciary power to act for certain ends. It is the ability to achieve those ends that defines, and legitimizes, sovereignty. The same argument is made by James Madison in federalist paper 45, in which he states that "no form of government whatever has any other value than as it may be fitted for the attainment of [the public good]".

(Draghi 2013)

Sovereignty is therefore not an abstract right to impose power over citizens but depends on the ability to satisfy their needs. From this point of view, a different perspective opens up for the concept of sovereignty, as it is no longer *a given amount of power*, but a varying ability to satisfy the wants of human beings:

I see this positive view as essentially the right way to think about sovereignty. And I think it needs to be the guiding principle when deciding which powers should be at national or European levels. We need to look at effectiveness, not at abstract principles that may be empty in today's world. Such an approach moves us away from a zero-sum view of sovereignty as power, where one body loses sovereignty and another gains it. Instead, by placing the needs of citizens at the center, it allows us to view sovereignty in terms of outcomes – and this can be positive-sum.

(Draghi 2013)

This is the nature of shared sovereignty. And it is the key to conflict resolution, as it implies that the power to make war is allocated only at the supranational level (and this in turn implies that conflicts can only be a *domestic* matter, manageable through judiciary power and police).

European integration has, in effect, been a process of progressively applying this principle: governments have pooled sovereignty every time it has proved necessary so that they could continue to deliver on their duties towards their people. At the start of the process, the objective was to prevent continental war. Two world wars had demonstrated the inability of European governments, acting alone, to provide physical security for their citizens. Thus, they established common institutions, such as the Coal and Steel Authority, that could guarantee peace more effectively.

(Draghi 2014)

It is important to stress that both Padoa-Schioppa and Draghi called for shared sovereignty and constitutional federalism as *economists*, not as *something else*.

If economics is to understand and ease the satisfaction of human needs and wants, and if this is effectively accomplished only through a multi-layered system of governments, then a constitutional design that accepts this and models human society accordingly, is the most relevant economic challenge.

Concluding remarks

Notwithstanding the recent increase of *places* where apparently peace is studied and debated in connection with economics (e.g. journals like *The Economics of Peace and Security Journal* and *Journal of Peace Research*, or associations like *Peace Science Society International* and *Economists for Peace and Security*) they are all connected with the reduction of armaments and the management of conflicts. No mention is done to peace unless in contraposition to war. The object of these studies is not peace: it is war. This approach has a long history. Economists have always dealt peace as a residual concept, where the absence of conflicts allows for the best functioning of the market. Mercantilism considered conflicts as inevitable, and peace as mere truce. Socialists and Marxists would suggest a conflict-ridden development process of capitalism, with some arguing for tendencies to armed conflict through attempts to overcome inherent contradictions and crisis, including new forms of imperialism. Institutionalists considered vested interests creating arms spending in economies, though it would not necessarily be in anyone's interest to go to war. Democrats were too much concerned with the national framework of democracy, without understanding the crucial role of supranational democracy. Liberal and neoclassical perspectives would see peace merely as the best situation for accumulation, underestimating the importance of rule enforcement.

Two main approaches emerge in the way peace is considered in political economy: *internationalism* and *constitutional supranational federalism*. The former is the one shared by all those who believe international peace is attainable *from below*, considering peace as the product of the implementation in each and every country of the principles of liberalism, democracy or socialism. From this point of view, peace-making is still basically a national problem, although supranational institutions are required to provide a place for cooperation: Hayek and Keynes are, from this perspective, on the same side. The former advocated the need to avoid State intervention in the economy and instrumentally claimed in favour of a European (or world) institution providing a stable monetary framework where money supply is not under the discretional control of any political body: he only meant to reduce sovereignty, not to redistribute it. The latter was convinced that only growing economies with the full utilization of their resources could contribute to an international peaceful framework and called for international institutions only to promote reflationary policies worldwide; he did not ultimately challenge national sovereignty.

The second approach is founded on the idea that peace is only sustainable when sovereignty is no longer a monopoly of nation States but is shared by a concentric system of multilayer governments, each providing collective goods, therefore requiring a binding and enforceable supranational juridical agreement. This testifies of the constitutional nature of this approach to the economics of peace, posing questions related to the kind of competences that each governmental level should have. Along this line of reflection, we can find diverse people such as Einaudi, Robbins, Padoa-Schioppa, Draghi and others.

Unfortunately, only a minor quota of economists in the history of economics has overcome the internationalist approach, thus paving the way to what Ulrich Beck called methodological nationalism (meaning that the only juridical framework that implicitly or explicitly is considered as legitimate is the national one) in social sciences. This short review of the economic literature testifies of the fact that economics suffers heavily from this disease, so that it makes it unable to tackle problems of externalities and interdependence worldwide. From this point of view, the contribution concerning supranational constitutional federalism, provides the only perspective to face this challenge.

References

Allio, R. (2014) *Gli economisti e la Guerra*, Soveria Mannelli, Rubbettino.

Bartlett, P.W. (1938) *The Economic Approach to Peace. With a Summary of the Van Zeeland Report*, London, Embassies of Reconciliation.

Cannan, E. (1914) *Wealth*, London, P.S. King & Son.

— (1927) *An Economist's Protest*, London, P.S. King & Son.

Cooper, R.N. (1972) Economic Interdependence and Foreign Policy in the Seventies, *World Politics*, 24(2), 159–181.

Coulomb, F. and Fontanel, J. (2001) 'War, Peace, and Economists', in Brauer, J. and Webster, L.L. (eds.) *Economics of Peace and Security*, Encyclopaedia of Life Support Systems.

Cressati, C. (1992) *L'Europa necessaria. Il federalismo liberale di Luigi Einaudi*, Torino, Giappichelli.

De Marchi, N. (1991) 'League of Nations Economists and the Ideal of Peaceful Change in the Decade of the Thirties', in Goodwin (1991), 143–178.

Draghi, M. (2013) 'Europe's pursuit of 'a more perfect Union', Lecture at Harvard Kennedy School, Cambridge (MA), October 9; www.ecb.europa.eu/press/key/date/2013/html/sp131009_1.en.html.

— (2014) 'Memorial Lecture in Honour of Tommaso Padoa-Schioppa', London, July 9, www.ecb.europa.eu/press/key/date/2014/html/ sp140709_2.en.html.

Dunne, P. (1990) 'The Political Economy of Military Expenditure: An Introduction', *Cambridge Journal of Economics*, 14(4), 395–404.

Durbin, E.F.M., Evans A.A., Benson W., Bentwich N., Balogh T. and Joseph M.F.W. (1942) *The Economic Basis of Peace*, Peace Aims Pamphlet, n° 16, London, National Peace Council.

Einaudi, L. (1897) Un sacerdote della stampa e gli Stati Uniti europei [A Priest of the Press and the United States of Europe], *La Stampa*, August 20, 1–2.

— (1947) 'La unificazione del mercato europeo', in *La guerra e l'unità europea*, Bologna, Il Mulino, 1986, 163–169.

[Einaudi, L.] Junius (1918a) La Società delle Nazioni è un ideale possibile? [Is the Society of Nations still a viable goal?], *Corriere della Sera*, January 5; in Ibid. (1920), 79–94.

— Junius (1918b) *Il dogma della sovranità e l'idea della Società delle Nazioni [The Dogma of Sovereignty and the Idea of the Society of Nations]*, Corriere della Sera, December 28; in Idem (1920), 143–156.

— Junius (1918c). 'Il dogma della sovranità e l'idea della Società delle Nazioni', *Corriere della Sera*, December 28; in *Lettere politiche di Junius*, Bari, Laterza, 1920, 143–156.

— Junius (1919) Fiume, la società delle nazioni ed il dogma della sovranità *[Fiume, the Society of Nations and the Dogma of Sovereignty]*, Corriere della Sera, May 6; in Ibid. (1920), 157–168.

— Junius (1920) *Lettere politiche di Junius [Junius's Political Letters]*. Bari, Laterza.

Goodwin, C.D. (ed.) (1991) *Economics and National Security. A History of their Interaction*, History of Political Economy, Annual Supplement to Vol. 23, Durham, Duke University Press.

Hayek, F.A. (1937) *Monetary Nationalism and International Stability*. London, Longmans Green.

— (1944) *The Road to Serfdom*, London, Routledge and Kegan.

Hobson, J.A. (1917) *Democracy After the War*, London, Allen & Unwin.

— (1920) *The Morals of Economic Internationalism*, Boston and New York, Houghton Mifflin.

Keynes, J.M. (1940) *How to Pay for the War. A Radical Plan for the Chancellor of the Exchequer*, London, Macmillan.

Lucht, M. (2009) 'Toward Lasting Peace. Kant on Law, Public Reason, and Culture', *American Journal of Economics and Sociology*, 68(1), 303–352.

Morelli, U. (1990) *Contro il mito dello stato sovrano. Luigi Einaudi e l'unità europea*, Milano, Franco Angeli.

Padoa Schioppa T. (1999) 'Gli Stati votano, le persone no', *Corriere della Sera*, October 17, www.tommasopadoaschioppa.eu/mondo/gli-stati-votano-le-persone-no.

— (2006) 'L'Europa fra malinconia e riscatto, Intervista', *Giornale di Brescia*, 20 maggio, 62.

— (2007) *Pensare l'internazionalizzazione*, Intervento alla cerimonia di inaugurazione del Politecnico di Milano, Milano, 12 novembre.

Petricioli, M. and Cherubini, D. (eds) (2007) *Pour la Paix en Europe. Institutions et société civile dans l'entre-deux-guerres – For Peace in Europe. Institutions and Civil Society between the World Wars*, Bruxelles, Peter Lang.

Pigou, A.C. (1916) *The Economy and Finance of War*, London, Dent.

— (1920) *Capital Levy and a Levy on War Wealth*, Oxford, Oxford University Press.

— (1921) *The Political Economy of War*, London, MacMillan.

Robbins, L.C. (1937a) *Economic Planning and International Order*, London, Macmillan.

— (1937b) 'The Economics of Territorial Sovereignty', in Woodward Manning, C.A. (ed.) *Peaceful Change*, London, Macmillan, 41–60.

— (1939a) *The Economic Basis of Class Conflicts*, London, Macmillan.

— (1939b) *The Economic Causes of War*, London, Jonathan Cape.

— (1940) 'Economic Aspects of Federation', in Chaning-Pearce, M. (ed.) *Federal Union. A Symposium*, London, Jonathan Cape, 167–186.

— (1947) *The Economic Problem in Peace and War*, London, Macmillan.

Sally, R. (1998) 'Classical Liberalism and International Economic Order: An Advance Sketch', *Constitutional Political Economy*, 9(1), 19–44.

Sandler, T. (2000) 'Economic Analysis of Conflict', *Journal of Conflict Resolution*, 44(6), 723–729.

Sforza, C. (1949) *Quelli che parlano di pace e quelli che vogliono la pace. Un discorso, dei documenti e delle postille*, Milano, Rizzoli.

Shaffer, E.H. (1996) 'Peace, war and the Market', *Canadian Journal of Economics*, 29(2), 639–643.

Veblen, T. (1917) *An Inquiry into the Nature of Peace and the terms of its perpetuation*, London, Macmillan.

6 Italian Economic Analyses of the First World War

'Historical Materialism' Versus 'Pure Economics'

Luca Michelini

Introduction

From the end of the nineteenth century through the first twenty years of the next, Italian economic theory was distinguished by two schools of thought: the 'historical materialism' of Achille Loria, the original interpreter of the classical school and Marx, and the 'pure economics' of Maffeo Pantaleoni, an equally originally interpreter and father of the marginalist theory. The aim of this essay is to compare how the two economists, who were also well-known outside of Italy, interpreted the causes of the First World War in economic terms.

Loria viewed the war as a manifestation of the laws of capitalism, based on the struggle between classes and between states for the distribution of wealth and for the codification of a national and international constitutional regime entirely suited to the economically strongest. The dialectic between growing populations, private appropriations of 'common land' and capitalist exploitation, was the source of the laws of distribution and he used it to explain the origins and consequences of the Great War according to a scientific perspective aimed at closely reconnecting theoretical analyses with social and political intent. Loria's view of Marx cannot be written off as totally positive: He criticized and rejected the German philosopher's theory of value, and the historical materialism he championed was the opposite of Marx's, since that of Loria centred on the tensions between population and private appropriation of lands with diminishing fertility. However, it is precisely on the basis of Marx that Loria viewed the war's outbreak, how it was conducted and its outcome as a sort of 'triumph' of historical materialism (Loria 1920: 1–2), as the definitive proof of the hermeneutic validity of the Marxist approach in which the capitalistic relationships in production condition all manifestations of human activity.

Pantaleoni's scientific perspective was entirely different. The champion of 'pure economics' sidestepped the pitfalls of the 'economic causes of the war', refuted the validity of a classist *economic* analysis of capitalist society, and relegated the matter of exploitation only to the political actions that prevent market mechanisms from developing. In the face of different, not only socialist but also nationalistic, currents of economic theory that viewed the conflict as the start of a new era characterized by increased government intervention on the economy,

Pantaleoni wanted to confirm the validity of 'pure' market laws even in wartime, in order to prevent 'war collectivism' from defining post-war economic and social development and leading to the birth of a true 'socialist system'.

It when dealing with the economic and social effects of the Great War that Pantaleoni came closer to Loria, because he brought social clashes between classes with opposing interests back to centre stage of historical development. However, the two economists had radically different theoretical and methodological approaches. As opposed to Pantaleoni's interpretation, for Loria history is not the arena of the dialectic between compartmentalized human actions – 'economic actions', 'political actions', 'moral actions' – nor is it the stage for a historical dialectic which can be reconstructed through totally *independent and distinct* disciplines that analyse those actions. For Loria, according to a cause – effect logic, exploitation that is the basis of the laws of wealth distribution is at the root of the birth, development and fall of all aspects – from the social and political – institutional to the ideological and moral – of 'social constitutions'.

Both Pantaleoni and Loria established an organic connection between theory and practice.

Pantaleoni fought for Italy's entrance into the war from nationalistic positions. The 'need for war', as he described Italy's decision to join the world conflict, was one of the few *collective* objectives that he defended constantly. He called for 'mobilization' to participate in an enormous war with consequences that could not easily be calculated – not only in terms of its immediate cost, and public finances, but also in terms of its economic, social and institutional costs. It is important to remember that Italy made the decision to enter the conflict during a period – the summer of 1915 – in which the 'stationary' nature of the war was as clearly evident as the destabilizing effects it could have on the nations that were directly involved.

It is also important to note that during and immediately after the war even though Pantaleoni reiterated his plans of presenting pure economics as politically 'neutral', they were totally aborted because he delegitimized all social change, from the most radical and revolutionary to the most reformist and gradual. And, he directed his attacks against both liberal and socialist reformisms in the most systematic and incessant manner. After the war, Pantaleoni was completely insensitive to the attempts at making Italy a more economically, socially and politically democratic society. Even after the murder of Giacomo Matteotti, he continued to support and encourage the nationalist and fascist 'reaction' in the name of a 'Manchester school' economic programme, making more than a secondary contribution to the collapse of the liberal Italian state and reaching theoretical – political conclusions that could not be attributable to the liberal tradition, as evident from the violent anti-Semitic press campaign in which played a key role.

Loria's outlook seems very different. Even though he sided with the 'democratic interventionism', according to his analyses the Great War was the proof of how capitalism had already run its course. The contradictions characterizing him created the prospects for a true change of regime moving towards socialism. While remaining anchored to a reformist – and not communist political stance, and thus criticizing Bolshevism, Loria maintained that the economic system which had generated the European conflict was historically ready for its end. And, unlike the economists who lengthily discussed the political and social neutrality of economic science, Loria did not become absorbed in intellectual and political militancy – either on the side of the nationalists or the fascists.

The comparison between the two economists' scientific approaches does not aim at reconstructing their political commitments. Rather it is a matter of showing how the first world war was the opportunity for the founders of the most important Italian schools of economic thought to reaffirm their respective points of view. For both men, the economic events of the Great War confirmed the laws of economics and, again for both, the war offered the opportunity for reinforcing the social and political prospects that those laws involve. A comparison of the two theoretical approaches can contribute to an understanding of their specifics.

Loria: a class war

In 1921, Loria devoted his book *Aspetti sociali ed economici della guerra mondiale* to the analysis of the causes and effects of the Great War.

The causes of the war were eminently economic[1] and referred back to the phenomenon of imperialism that grew and developed in a context of generalized economic stagnation: a slowdown in the growth of wealth and innovation; decreased profits, real wages and income of the many unproductive classes, whose fundamental role is to stabilize the power of the dominant classes by creating consensus. It was a set of circumstances that spurred nations throughout the world to adopt a systematic armament policy. The imperialistic clash centred on the differences between England and Germany. England was characterized by a social constitution dominated by the capitalist class and the profit motive. Germany, on the other hand, had a social constitution dominated by the alliance between land rent and banking interests, that were 'warlike par excellence' (Loria 1921: 20–21). The lines of economic expansion of the Central Powers, that were starved for new markets and raw materials, clashed with the interests of France, Russia and the United States of America. Furthermore, all the countries that took part in the war were driven by exquisitely economic reasons: for example, the Trentino, the Tyrol, Fiume and Trieste were of primary economic importance to Italy. It is 'always essentially economic reasons that that push nations to start a war' (Loria 1921: 30).

The shared need of the dominant classes in all the countries involved in the conflict to defeat the socialist movement was no less important as a cause of the war. Capitalism was pervaded by 'serious problem': 'it is the problem of centuries of antagonism between the few who own everything and the many who have nothing – it is the problem of ownership' (Loria 1921: 30).

Under the auspices of a military regime, the war made it possible to smother and repress both class conflict and normal political dialectic. The war was a 'safety valve' that destroyed socialist internationalism by steering it back towards obedience and nationalism, and it restored the bourgeois order. The war also struck the privileged classes by destroying their wealth and decreasing their incomes: but the losses these classes suffered were much less than what they would suffer from the birth of a socialist regime. That German socialism abdicated its historical role and came out in favour of the war was due to the fact that it was absorbed into the bourgeois system and abandoned all 'ideals of justice' (Loria 1921: 39).

The economic conduct of the war confirmed its class-based character. The war caused a decrease of the social product, even though there were some opposite results due to several factors: increased productivity (through innovations) in the industries that manufactured war materiel, intensified exploitation of labour facilitated by the recourse to female workers to replace the men who were called to arms. The decrease in produced wealth, both domestically and internationally, was caused by the change in the natural distribution of capital and labour brought about by the war. It was a change that 'lacerated' society (Loria 1921: 114) making the social conflict that characterized capitalism even more bitter. However, the loss of wealth caused by the war was not undifferentiated or uniform among either the social classes or the nations involved in the conflict.

Even though the scarcity of labour caused by the war led to improvements in the workers' condition, price increases outpaced salary raises; small and medium-sized businesses as well as the lower middle class and bourgeoisie were negatively impacted while large industries and banks profited because of the concentrations encouraged by the state. In the final analysis, according to Loria 'public loans and the most unbridled speculation' that characterized the war, 'increased the income from unproductive capital and the amount of this capital and the rise of agricultural and rents increased incomes from farming and construction; while income from productive capital (with the exception of investments in wartime industries) diminished along with the incomes of holders of fixed-interest loans and white collar workers' (Loria 1921: 259).

The war also furthered the redistribution of wealth through the manner in which the dominant classes divided the financial burden. There were three alternatives for meeting the financial needs of the war: taxes and specifically the capital levy that Loria favoured, public debt, printing of paper money at forced and the extension of banking credits (allowed by the public debt) without any concern for the amount of their deposits. Loans acquired 'clandestine character, that made them uniquely dangerous', because it allowed almost 'unlimited expansion' of the money supply (Loria 1921: 149). The economic policy choices made by all of the belligerents once again reveal their clearly class-oriented nature: it was precisely those 'who had wanted the war' and 'who largely profited from the war, [and] forced most of the costs of the war' to be paid by 'those who hadn't wanted war' and 'did not reap any advantage from it' (Loria 1921: 305).

The war caused a drastic redistribution of wealth not only domestically, but also internationally as borne out by the United States of America's rise to the status of a world power, as it transitioned from being a debtor nation to being a creditor nation. It was a geopolitical ascent that probably marked the end of the supremacy of the pound sterling that was edged out by the 'almighty dollar' (Loria 1921: 348).

Thus, the outcome of the war confirmed the economic analysis of its origins.

Loria insisted on stressing that the war was not – as nationalistic propaganda would have it – the clash between Middle European autocracy and Western democracy because a similar classification would have no room for a country such as Tsarist Russia with its social constitution that had absolutely nothing in common with systems described as democratic. The means for fighting the Great War and its effects were eminently economic. In other words, peace was not dictated by American democratic political ideals, such as the principle of self-determination of peoples so loudly proclaimed by President Woodrow Wilson, but by purely imperialistic appetites. Even the birth of the League of Nations involved clearly defined economic interests that show how the stronger winners tried to twist and bend the results to the detriment of the weaker allies such as Italy. It was the 'economically strong victors' who 'stipulated the greatest advantages for themselves' (Loria 1921: 81).

The conflict had momentous consequences on the post-war social and political order. Real revolutions broke out in the defeated nations (Russia, Bavaria, Hungary), but even a victor country such as Italy risked destabilization.

In the victorious countries, the war led to a popular push for the democratization of the economy and institutions precisely when society was undergoing a process of wealth concentration. The war, therefore, is at the root of a glaring contradiction. It triggered a social conflict that could not be resolved mainly politically: as long as 'economic relations remain on the old capitalist base' democracy 'is nothing other than the political model in which the government is in the hands of four financiers' and the alliance between unproductive capital and unearned income opened the way to power for the conservative faction as proved by the unexpected success of the clerical party in Italy's 1919 political elections. 'Just as the war of 1870 created socialism, the war of 1914 cleared its path to power' (Loria 1921: 432). For Loria 'the masses' real rise to power is incompatible with the persistence'; and even the institutional programmes aimed at stabilizing the post-conflict peace were totally utopian, because 'only a state governed by the workers [...] can necessarily be a pacifist state' (Loria 1921: 444). The ultimate result of the war was to spur the birth of an 'egalitarian economy of labour' (Loria 1921: 455–456).

What relationship did Loria establish between theory and practice? To grasp the meaning of this connection it is important to recall that for him unearned income could not be ascribed to any labour or service offered by the capitalists and in his eyes, rather than a scientific resolution, the marginalist theory represented a true counterrevolution: – 'a brand new metaphysics' (Loria 1904: 201–217) – with respect to the classical school that had established an organic relationship between theory and history and had studied the nature of capitalist ownership and profit. Loria had supported these theses when discussing marginalism in general and Pantaleoni's *Principii di economia pura* in particular (Michelini 1998: 86–89). Going beyond the conclusions of the classical school, which he did mention, Loria spoke of a capitalist economy characterized on the one hand by an improvement in the conditions of the working classes and, on the other by increasing wealth concentration and social differences. It was the law of profit maximization that determined both the quantity of the social product and how it was distributed among the several social classes. The growth of unproductive capital (bank and brokerage capital) and of unproductive labour (workers who do not produce material goods), the development of parasitical forms of monopolistic competition, economic – political imperialism, the inter-capitalist war and, finally, the opening of the possibility of going beyond capitalism were nothing other than the direct consequences of the profit law (Perri 2004). Loria maintained that 'the reduction of labour to one part of the product is not a natural and eternal phenomenon, but rather the result of essentially historical and contingent causes. And, actually, we can conceive of a state of things in which the entire product goes to the workers, without any part of it being the prerogative of the capitalists and owners' (Loria 1903: 534–535). In Loria, however, there is no direct and mechanistic connection between theory and practice. On the one hand the reality of exploitation outlines an ideal horizon that extends beyond capitalism where, like for the so-called 'Ricardian socialists' and, as opposed to Marx, the way is opened to a market society where the workers totally appropriate the product. On the other, the reality of exploitation did not at all lead Loria to a voluntaristic and aprioristic political revolutionism – which he wrongly attributed to Marx –, but rather the exact opposite, it opened the prospects for the gradual shift from one economic system to another. Not even dramatic events such as the Great War and the Bolshevik Revolution could make Loria change his political outlooks. Even if the war was a momentous episode for the fate of capitalism revealing all of its anti-historicism, it did not mean that the transition from theory to practice is not filled with complexities and nuances, nor did it mean that that the workers' movement should abandon the terrain of reforms.

Loria never was an active socialist militant and during the world war he politically distanced himself from the emerging communism, and repeatedly came under the fire of the young Antonio Gramsci. As we know, Loria was politically a democratic interventionist (Maccabelli 2010). In June 1915 he dusted off Mazzini, Cavour and the Risorgimento, pleading that the resolution of the 'social question' be *subordinated* to the resolution of the 'political question' that was based on the 'principle of nationality' (Loria 1915: 3). In any event, he did not rebuke Italian socialism for its initially neutral stance, but for the fact that when the war did break out, and especially in 1917 when the country was in greatest danger following the defeat at Caporetto, it did not openly and organically come out in favour of democratic – that is not nationalistic and imperialistic – interventionism (Loria 1921: 36).

All this notwithstanding, the proximity to socialist reformism was always constant in Loria's position. It was Gramsci himself who justified his consistent anti-Loria arguments on the basis of the acknowledgement that the economist's ideas were a reference point within the socialist cultural and political world (Gramsci 1918: 573). During and immediately after the war, Loria backed a series of 'qualitative' and 'quantitative' reforms as he described them in *I fondamenti scientifici della riforma economica* (Loria 1922). He wanted to flank the struggle against the typical forms of unearned income with a peaceful and gradual elimination of capitalism by combining forms of worker self-help with reform measures on the part of the government, a tool he believed *indispensable* for getting out of the clutches of capitalism. It was no accident that *Critica Sociale*, the journal of Italian reformist socialism looked favourably on Loria's book since, 'unlike all the supporters of romantic revolutionism', he has the 'great merit of authoritatively reconfirming some of the cardinal theses of socialism, especially of evolutionary socialism' (Marchioli 1923: 272).

During the war, and thanks to the government, the social factions reached a point of cooperation in the 'industrial mobilization': and yet, Loria suggested entrusting the establishment of forms of co-management between owners and workers to the lawmakers (Loria 1918), anticipating proposals which would characterize the harsh Italian debate on the so-called 'worker control' that developed following the occupation of the factories in the autumn of 1920. Positions comparable to Loria's, such as the 'control' project proposed by the Giolitti government to defuse the Italian revolutionary movement that developed during the autumn of 1920 would be rejected by opposing points of view, by Gramsci and by Pantaleoni – the former in the name of a political praxis that aspired to the revolutionary transfer of 'all powers' to the factory councils, according to the Soviet model, the latter in the name of a violent, Fascist action-squad return to the 'freedom of labour' (Pantaleoni 1922: 101–132).

During the war, Loria was in favour of price controls, an effective tool for wiping out increases in unearned income and for combating monopolistic forms of production. He was in favour of taxing the extra-profits of war and of loading the financial cost of the conflict onto the shoulders of the classes that were responsible for it through a capital levy. Loria was against inflation, a tool that reduces savings and the purchasing power of salaries and he was against recourse to public debt which he considered a manifestation of unproductive capital, that is a factor that produces unemployment and decreases both the total social product and the share due the salaried worker. *I fondamenti scientifici della riforma economica* contains a detailed list of what the state could do to reform capitalism under a production policy whose theoretical and historical basis is technical progress. In order to increase produced wealth, the state could promote cooperation, make landowners farm uncultivated lands or expropriate them, with indemnification, or hit them with taxes; it could grant low-interest loans or reward increased production. To increase labour productivity, the state could limit female and child labour and decrease working hours. The state could also take action on prices: decrease them by abolishing protectionism, limit the power of monopolies by setting prices, regulating the supply, promoting purchasing coalitions, or by becoming the producer. Still within the limits of economic growth characterized by technical progress, the scope and extents of an income policy were no less important with regulatory actions on wages, on interest rates on productive and unproductive capital, on profits, on unearned income, along with room for progressive taxation and for policies to help fight unemployment. The state could also take actions on productive factors, especially by alternating the distribution of land – redistributing it or transforming into government property. In more general terms, the aim of the book is to defend – while opposing collectivism – the tax that strikes 'profits from unproductive capital' (Loria 1922: 535) as a tool for proposing a free and gradual change, to arrive at a society based on a 'plurality of free associations of producers which will allow the state broad participation in business income and permit mutual exchange of their products on a level with their respective production costs' (Loria 1922: 542).

In his 1921 book Loria spoke favourably of the economic literature that emphasized the economic causes of the European war. His arguments, however, move on a much more radical level because they are meant to be a direct attack on the capitalist system and on those scientific approaches which, de facto support it. From the methodological standpoint it was not only a question of stressing the economic factor as a driver of history, but of questioning the analytical bases of 'bourgeois' economic theories. For Loria, there was an *organic* connection between structure and superstructure, between the 'economic' and non-economic factors of historical development: the superstructures are the indispensable tools for governing an economic system based on exploitation (Loria 1913: 563).

The difference between this and Pantaleoni's approach could not be more clear.

Starting from *Principii di economia pura*, (Pantaleoni 1889), and continuing with his many essays on economic theory collected in the two volumes of *Erotemi di economia* (Pantaleoni 1925), Pantaleoni defined pure economics as the discipline which within the scope of 'human actions' isolates 'economic actions' from 'predatory' or 'political' actions and from 'protective' or 'mutualistic' actions. Aside from a few exceptions, economic theory or 'pure economics' is the 'science of voluntary and therefore pacific order' and it concerns the 'contractual relationships' that can be established 'only in those cases in which there is either parity of strength or in which – and it is the same thing – there is no awareness of an existing disparity, or the consequences that would result from recourse to violence are unknown' (Pantaleoni 1925: 358). Contractual relationships are formed where there is a 'presumption of equality between the parties, a presumption that also exists when the initial positions, the starts, were not equal' (Pantaleoni 1925a: 187). In his view, all definitions and all analyses of 'strength' and 'weakness' refer to a science other than economics. He calls it 'history' or 'sociological' disciplines and they encompass all the social sciences – including the science of finances – that are distinct from economics. According to Pantaleone, therefore, the difference between weak and strong, involves 'a theory of social struggles and the equilibriums to which these struggles lead' This theory is the domain of 'sociology' and, more generally, of all the disciplines that analyse the different types of past and present 'social selection': struggles between individuals, tribes, nations, races, social classes, sexes', and struggles between 'supra-organic structures' such as 'languages, customs, laws, religions, ideas, etc.' (Pantaleoni 1925: 329–330).

The error many economists made was that of wanting to carry the main theoretical discourse on economics which centred on the economic action, towards a discourse pertinent to other social sciences as proposed by all those who included concepts of strength and weakness in economics and who study the 'strengths and causes' that govern the 'social constitutions' (Pantaleoni 1925: 330). Pantaleoni was fully aware that the inclusion or exclusion of these 'non-' or 'extra-economic' left its mark on entire epochs in economic science. For example, there were 'optimistic' periods when circumstances under the heading of 'legal acquisitions' of wealth actually concealed predatory or parasitical relationships were overlooked, and these were followed by other periods that were more concerned with illustrating this aspect of the historical events, as in the writings of D. Ricardo, J. S. Mill, A. Wagner, W. Roscher and A. Marshall (Pantaleoni 1925: 335, 342–346).

Furthermore, it was a working method used in particular by the socialism's theorists, such as Marx and Loria, who – wrongly – yearned to go beyond a 'particularly narrow' *but no less well-grounded* conception of economics. As fascinating as that may be, it means leaving the field of economics and the economist 'speaking of distribution of wealth', dwelling on 'inheritance', on 'laws of ownership' and on 'transfers [of property]', analysing the 'longstanding and newly created status relationships', studying 'war, taxation, thefts and frauds' (Pantaleoni 1925: 330–331); And the work of those who study the production of wealth taking into account 'oppression and plundering' is equally different from the economist's task (Pantaleoni 1925: 330–331). In brief, Pantaleoni's stance was totally different from that of the socialist and Marxist theoreticians: he did not at all believe that 'an economist can explain historical phenomena, not even in the *final analysis,* or detail each complex and concrete manifestation only with the aid of his science' (Pantaleoni 1925: 185).

On the methodological level, Pantaleoni's view was the exact opposite of Loria's: what Marx called superstructures have an evolutionary logic that is totally different from and independent of the logic that governs the structure of society. History, naturally, sees the interaction between these logics, but that interaction does not raise even the slightest doubts about the theoretical and practical soundness of these logics. Furthermore, for Pantaleoni, economics was not the arena for the clash between social classes with opposing interests and it did not involve any relationship in which one exploits the other to its detriment. In this theoretical and methodological context war is considered the result of purely 'non-economic' actions and the scientific discipline that has to concern itself with it – no matter which – cannot be economics because, as we shall see shortly, economics can only study some, detailed aspects of wars. The only exploitation relationship that can occur on the economic level is driven by 'politics' which, like a parasite, uses the economic system to pursue its own chief goals.

Pantaleoni: war as an 'economic necessity'

Pantaleoni's works dedicated to the world war confirm the approach he had proposed in the above-mentioned essays texts. The author collected the most important of these in the following volumes published by Laterza: *Tra le incognite* (Pantaleoni 1917b), *Note in margine della guerra* (1917a), *Politica: criteri ed eventi* (Pantaleoni 1918), *La fine provvisoria di un'epopea* (Pantaleoni 1919). These books contain a variety of writings: literary output: newspaper editorials (published for the most part in *Il Giornale d'Italia*), essays that appeared in the nationalistic magazines *Politica* and *La Vita italiana*. The two truly theoretical essays in the collections are: 'Considerazioni sulle proprietà di un sistema di prezzi politici' (1911) and 'Gli insegnamenti economici della guerra', written in 1916.

The most useful essay for analysing how Pantaleoni dealt with the war is the last one, in which he wrote: 'The arrival of war, in the economist's mind, *is like the arrival of a new style or need, in the series of styles or needs that had previously been satisfied or gratified*' (Pantaleoni 1917: 15). The economist's task is to analyse the specifics of this new need, the best tools for fulfilling it, and finally the consequences that the birth of the need and the cost of its fulfilment produce on the economic level. And this is precisely what Pantaleoni's essay proposed.

The need for war is intense and its arrival – which according to Spencer translates into the temporary rebirth of a 'military society' (Pantaleoni 1917b: 11) – is a form of shock, profoundly altering the peacetime division of labour and equally profoundly changing the pre-war system of prices, with marked increases in the costs of the (many) goods essential to the pursuit of the war and decreases in the prices of other goods. The economic cost of war can be determined through a complex calculation: the social product suffers a loss due to the sudden dual change from peacetime to wartime economy and back again. Furthermore, war destroys wealth, even if we cannot rule out the fact that technological progress can work in the opposite direction: in 1916 he predicted that technological progress could 'compensate us, with interest, for the destruction of wealth caused by the war' (Pantaleoni 1917b: 2–4).

On the financial level, the alternatives were taxes, debts and paper money; the redistributive effects of the forced circulation were considerable. In all the victorious warring countries, recourse to debt and printing of paper money prevailed due to the 'scope' of the war and their 'unpreparedness' for it (Pantaleoni 1917b: 56). Even the efficient Germany that had planned the war for four years could not but turn to debts and paper money. In general, and unlike private parties, governments can 'contract almost unlimited debts' by using forced circulation (Pantaleoni 1917b: 120), and especially if – as was the case – they limit the free circulation of goods by prohibiting exports thus blocking currency revaluation which is the only mechanism that can limit or halt public debt.

As opposed to Loria, Pantaleoni aimed at protecting the extra-profits of war, that were considered essential for satisfying impelling military needs, but maintained that the extra income be punished fiscally by 'egalitarian envy' (Pantaleoni 1917b: 79–80). He also condemned all forms of price controls, which he viewed as a tool that depressed industrial output. As to the workers, it was important on the one hand to consider the decreased purchasing power of their salaries, and on the other the series of extra income the workers enjoyed because of their debtor status. Unlike Loria, he did not even mention the capital levy, but did plead for reform of the tax system in the context of a definite return to free enterprise.

For Pantaleoni, any measure that could get in the way of a technical need for maximum productivity was particularly bad for the increase in wealth and hence for the contributory potential. Many of those measures were the so-called 'working conditions' demanded by socialists and labour unionists (Pantaleoni 1917b: 110).

The reform of the tax system had to be based on the following provisions: 'abolition of taxes and levies that hampered business'; creation of the 'share-holder state' where necessary (overseas transport of emigrants, businesses based on water-power licenses); creation of some new monopolies (alcohol, along with the nationalization of sugar production and underground Resources), greater recourse to existing monopolies (tobacco), relinquishing of others (insurance and telephone services); radical reform of taxes on movable assets (which bourgeois professionals systematically evade); taxation should only affect corporate profits; radical downsizing of the costs and number of bureaucrats and civil servants; balancing the public budget. On the international level, Pantaleoni was pragmatically in favour of a customs tariff system that was the simplest possible while awaiting the creation of new free trade areas (Pantaleoni 1917b: 120–129).

Pantaleoni had a dual attitude towards the increased public intervention brought about by the war. On the one hand, he could not but acknowledge the impelling and essential need for it to the point that he proposed that, when indispensable, the state become a shareholder of the involved industries, with the creation of government monopolies and nationalizations when *technically* indispensable. On the other, however, he heatedly opposed the state's increasing and *undifferentiated* meddling in the economy.

We can now try to compare Pantaleoni's and Loria's writings on war.

In the first place, Pantaleoni did not analyse the need for war: he did not analyse either how it was constructed starting from individual needs or the political and state mechanisms of how it actually came about. The mechanism through which this need is constructed is, by definition, foreign to the scientific *corpus* of pure economics which takes it as a given datum, we could say, exogenously. As we have seen, its cause, being the fruit of political and social struggles can be analysed by recourse to disciplines other than economics. The economist is a technician who examines the economic features of any need, thus providing the characteristics of the 'military need' without wondering about any *economic* origins and without making any statement about the historical (non-economic) consequences of its many effects.

Second, the analysis of the need for, and the economic and financial cost of the war, even though highlighting the redistributions of wealth that war involves, tends to put the class-characteristic of this redistribution into the background. Marginalist economic logic tends to highlight *individual* actions, not the actions and conflicts of social classes. So it should come as no surprise that when he discussed impact of the war and inflation on salaries, Pantaleoni tended to consider the workers not as a class but as individuals, with each involved in his own way, in a redistribution of income not only in terms of wages, but also, as creditors or debtors or holders of contracts or belonging to certain industries that may or may not have been protected for political reasons. Nor should it be surprising that while Loria considered recourse to debt as a financial instrument to cover the cost of the war as a class decision since public debt is one of the privileged forms that unproductive capital can take, Pantaleoni explained it in very different terms. That is, he justified recourse to debt as an inevitable decision dictated by the suddenness and intensity of the military need and by the lack of preparation on the part of the belligerent parties, Germany included. And lastly, we should not be surprised by the fact that unlike Loria, Pantaleoni criticized both the taxation of the extra-profits of war and price-controls.

Third, we can see that according to Pantaleoni, the causes of the war become a subject of study completely extraneous to the scientific *corpus* of economic science. Indeed, in Pantaleoni's text the main concern is to confirm the validity of economic laws against the opinion of all those who, from different political positions – from protectionist nationalists, to some liberal currents to socialists and communists – saw the beginnings of a new economic era in wartime collectivism.

Pantaleoni's opinion of these expectations of scientific and social renewal was terse and dismissive:

> Now, if there is any confirmation of economic doctrine – as old as the hills – provided the recent activities of the government, it is this: that it is entirely incapable of exercising commercial and industrial functions. In all the parliaments of the warring countries, the same men who had most loudly called for the state to purchase grains and coal, to regulate prices, to prohibit certain imports and exports, see to others, encourage certain agricultural and industrial production, close the stock markets, declare moratoriums, cancel contracts, regulate exchange rates, freights charges, see to unemployment, outlaw excessive profits, requisition, expropriate, punish and reward, help credit, increase the supply of paper money, those same men, in particular every

school of socialists and radicals, have heaped their respective governments with accusations of incompetence, of inertia, of slowness, of incomprehension, of ignorance and have made the workings of their governments seem like financial disasters.

(Pantaleoni 1917b: 75–76)

The second theoretical cornerstone on which Pantaleoni built his conception of the European war was the *Considerazioni sulle proprietà di un sistema di prezzi politici* (Pantaleoni 1911). It is a fundamental text because it is the theoretical background used to refute any, not only socialist, governmental or political doctrine or proposal that wanted to seize the opportunity of the expanding public intervention during the world war to present the overcoming of capitalism which Pantaleoni called 'Manchesterian'.

The aim of the *Considerazioni* was to show what the objectives of socialism are, what it instruments it uses to achieve those goals and the consequences of the economic and political system once established. By setting political prices, that is selling the same goods at a different price to individuals differentiated on the basis of ethical – political criteria; using political coercion and hence creating a liberticidal system which, in addition to having a cost, is indispensable for preventing individuals from escaping that differentiation; creating a system that is egalitarian in the starting and end-points and in the fulfilled needs; triggering a process of gradually nationalizing the means of production – by pursuing these goals and using these instruments socialism ends up by building an economic system that is incapable of feeding itself and hence needs a system of economic prices based on freedom of negotiation, on the difference in the beginning and endpoints and the inequality of fulfilled needs to exploit parasitically. By developing and applying the methodologies we have analysed above, Pantaleoni showed how the 'economic actions' of the market are victims of 'predatory actions' on the part of socialism. When it lacks a victim to 'strip', socialism is destined for economic implosion (Pantaleoni 1919: 1–53).

This is a theoretical argument that we find on every page of the four Laterza volumes dedicated to the economic, social and political events caused by the World War.

However, we must not forget that Pantaleoni was critical not only of socialist parasitism, but also of the 'bourgeois' variety. In fact, it is the modern capitalist economies that are characterized by a more or less vast extension of the system of political prices and not only because of the actions of the anti-system parties. It is essential to remember one of the classic texts that glows with the theoretical criticism that Pantaleoni launched against the bourgeois system and where the analysis of the Italian capitalist system is more precise: that is his essay *La caduta della Società Generale di Credito Mobiliare* (Pantaleoni 1895). This essay presents an analysis that also implies reflections on the Banca Commerciale Italiana and, more in general, the entire Italian financial system to which Pantaleoni dedicated considerable attention during the war.

The long analysis in the 1895 essay focuses on several phenomena: a generalized industrial revolution (in transportation, energy sources, in all industrial areas involved in the phenomenon of movement to towns and the construction that was transforming the cities) that were followed by decreasing yields. The government intervention which, based on forced circulation, facilitated borrowing and hence industrial investment even when those investments were yielding less; a gigantic system of moral risk and informative asymmetries where expansion of credit was based on the awareness on the part of the banks – the so-called mixed banks – and the businesses they financed, created a situation in which an eventual collapse could not but force the government to intervene with a rescue through the issuing institution. The author showed the earnings and losses caused by the collapse of Italy's biggest mixed bank. The profits of the founders and administrators were 'surprising', especially since 'the majority of the board members did not deserve anything because they did not contribute to the company in any serious or appreciable manner' (Pantaleoni 1936: 432), everything was due to the entrepreneur – innovator who steered it, alone at the helm. The amount of the destroyed wealth and the losses was enormous – around one billion lire.

The essay concludes with a detailed analysis of the subject of bank rescues, and the viewpoints of two opposing sides, those for and those against. While not siding openly with one or the other, the Pantaleoni focused on a series of important critical issues of public rescues, to conclude by calling for the birth of a new kind of law that would be capable of distinguishing degrees in the economic guilt to punish through bankruptcy (shareholders, long-term savers, administrators, etc.), allowing a glimpse of an intent to build a 'regulatory state' rather than an 'entrepreneurial state'. On the other hand, those in favour of the rescue were those directly involved in the crisis and were trying to make those who had behaved more prudently pay for the cost of their gambles. Therefore, it was a matter of 'some entirely personal motive, which those reasons dress up to look decent' (Pantaleoni 1936: 474). The slogans that were used to promote the rescue – patriotism, defence of employment or landed property, etc., – and were anything but socialist slogans, all hid very specific appetites. In Italy, the 'inflationists' prevailed, saying that the reason the government had to intervene with the rescue operations was because it was the government that was behind the expansion of credit and the growth of the businesses connected with it. It is obvious that all private interests try to pass themselves off as public interests. In the final analysis, those in favour of government rescues maintain that it is the issuing institution that must be called to 'judge which failed businesses should be socialized' thereby distributing the cost among the community in a clandestine or hidden manner (Pantaleoni 1936: 476–477). According to Pantaleoni, however, the decision for a public rescue must be backed by a careful, case-by-case analysis. And it should be fully clear that the body called to affect the rescue, that is the political power that controls the issuing institution is one of the social actors, the one that is congenitally less capable than the others of reasoning appropriately and impartially.

Aside from Pantaleoni's regulatory intentions, the importance of his analysis of Italian capitalism is evident. Not only is capitalism characterized by an ineliminable dialectic between economic and non-economic actions, it is also governed by social forces which, through capillary control of the state and the issuing institution systematically practice real parasitical 'class politics' – the economist's words.

It is an analysis that Pantaleoni developed systematically during the twentieth century and was proposed again after the world war when the power system centred on the Banca Commerciale became an object of criticism – the bank in his opinion was the true meeting point between bourgeois and socialist parasitism. The press campaign that Pantaleoni promoted in 1915, supporting the Italianization of the Banca Commerciale, that was viewed as a vanguard of German power in Italy, went hand-in-hand with his approach to the Italian nationalist movement that translated into a definite interventionist stance. The clump of power that crystallized around the Banca Commerciale pulled the threads of all those political factions, the Giolitti liberals and the socialist reformers who sucked the country dry like parasites and who with the war could and must be routed from politics and economics (Michelini 2011).

There are three comments we can make about Pantaleoni's analysis of 'bourgeois parasitism' and, more generally, of the relationship between economics and politics that he defined in his analyses.

First, we must emphasize how the criticism that Pantaleoni directed toward the Italian government was similar to, but *must not* be confused criticism of the Marxist and Loria's traditions: In Pantaleoni, the Italian state is in fact the 'business committee' of the bourgeoisie, but only of *part* of the bourgeoisies that invites a *part* of the proletariat to the banquet thereby demonstrating a guilty lack of awareness that they are actually preparing the tools that the proletariat will use to install a real socialist system, and in due time tear down the alliance with the 'reformist bourgeoisie'. These are the theoretical bases for Pantaleoni's initially nationalistic and later Fascist militancy. As opposed to Loria, for Pantaleoni there was no innate exploitation or parasitism in the market laws and the state is not the necessary and indispensable tool for guaranteeing the survival of an intrinsically unfair and conflicted economic system as it is in Loria. For Pantaleoni the actions of the State become 'class-related' when it is monopolistically and parasitically dominated by one part of society, bourgeoisie and proletariat included, to the detriment of another part of society or other bourgeois and/ or proletariat groups.

Second, it is obvious that, insofar as it is possible to identify different and multiform politically-based and sociological criteria for defining the 'part' of the civil consortium that organized to conquer the state and live as parasites to the detriment of the other 'part' of society, i.e. the part excluded from political power, the four volumes published by Laterza reveal an Italian state and society that is profoundly characterized by strictly 'class' aimed at controlling and twisting market mechanisms in any possible way. Even though 'proletariat' and 'bourgeoisie', are not part of the reasoning in pure economics, and comprise only *one* of the possible criteria for defining the 'part' of society that aspires to power, they are obsessively present in the country's history during and after the war. In other words, for Pantaleoni history is the realm of 'political prices' and of the social forces that fuel them, and in final analysis, there are two 'parts' of society that confront each other for power: the proletariat and the bourgeoisie not matter how they are divided into different vanguards or rearguards. In Pantaleoni's eyes, Mussolini's rise to power also had a specific and explicit class characteristic: 'the bourgeoisie was ready to give' Mussolini 'as the leader, a great part of the credit for the victory over the proletariat' (Pantaleoni 1922: 207–219). There can be doubts about the fact that Pantaleoni interpreted the *Biennio Rosso* – or 'two red years', when Italy was just one step from a socialist revolution, and fascism's rise to power, as a class struggle, a clash that involved the political vanguards of the 'proletariat' and of the 'bourgeoisie'.

The pervasive character that the class struggle acquires in Pantaleoni's reasoning also comes across in his considerations on the geopolitical aftermath of the Great War.

Totally silent on the economic causes of the war, when faced with Allies' 'betrayal' of what Pantaleoni considered Italy's legitimate imperialistic aspirations, he repeatedly emphasized the brutally imperialistic nature of the Peace of Versailles and the intentions of the League of Nations. His criticism of American foreign policy, in particular, concludes overlapping the anti-Semitic press. In the United States, England and Bolshevik Russia Pantaleoni saw the concrete manifestations the ideas of a shadowy Jewish international conspiracy dedicated to destroying the Christian and bourgeois order. The dangerous link between bourgeois and socialist parasitism that he saw at the national level was being replicated internationally as well. And in this geopolitical context Pantaleoni wanted Italy, relying on an organic but virtuous bank – business – state relationship, to develop its own expansionist imperialistic policy (Michelini 2011).

Third, we have to note that it would have been logical to expect that the analysis of bourgeois and socialist parasitism be the basis for an explanation of the Great War as a parasitical phenomenon. By creating the framework for political prices and concrete historical developments, classes and their struggles, party interests, the struggle between elites and between nations could, and should, have been at the centre of his considerations on the origins of the world war. (Robbins 1939). In fact, Pantaleoni's entire analysis dedicated to the pro-German role of the Banca Commerciale Italiana can be read in this sense and it *indirectly* refers a theoretical framework that aims at tracing the origins of the war to national – state power politics (of Germany in particular) and of the Italian social groups hegemonised by that policy (Giolittians and socialist reformists). Actually, however, Pantaleoni's analysis did not aim at discussing the causes of the war – that is German imperialism. Rather, he wanted to show the nation the *traitors* (who fought for Italian neutrality) to be eliminated, and the invitation he extended to the 'healthy forces' of the country was to get rid of them in any way possible. To use Schmitt's word, they were '*hostes*' (Pantaleoni 1917b: XII).

Conclusions

The economic analyses of the First World War proposed by Loria and Pantaleoni are radically different.

For Loria, the war was the manifestation of an economic system, the capitalist system, which was based on exploitation and on profound social and economic conflicts on the national and international levels that were destined to be resolved in a change of system. A tool used by capital and by unearned income to reiterate its dominance over the proletariat, the war only helps accelerate the breakdown of capitalism itself.

For Pantaleoni, too, the war was the opportunity for finding confirmations of economic laws: laws that carefully avoid questioning the origins of profits, of the social conflict and of the Great War and which all aim at rejecting socialism, and more in general, all forms of social and institutional democratization of the country. If, for Loria, the war had to mark the end of capitalism, for Pantaleoni, on the opposite side, it had to mark the end of all forms of economic parasitism, that is, of socialism.

In the final analysis, Loria and Pantaleoni presented two opposing definitions of 'economic parasitism' and two diametrically opposed formulas for eliminating it. For Loria it was a matter of going beyond distinction between the state and civil society which to him seemed unfair, to arrive not at a planned society that no longer revolves around markets and money like the one Marx envisioned, but a market society where the worker's product will be 'completely' attributed to him. For Pantaleoni, on the other hand, it was a matter of finding a new and synergic relationship between the state and the market without raising the slightest questions about laws of production and capitalist distribution, but indeed, by reinforcing their most reactionary historical versions. While Loria fought for the birth of a more democratic, in terms of opportunity, capitalist system, for Pantaleoni it was a matter of proving the legitimacy of a society that was radically unequal in terms of political, civil and social rights, and he did so on the basis of political, institutional and economic-policy ideas that made him one of the economists closest to fascism between 1921 and 1924.

In the history of Italian economic thought and therefore, leaving aside all the other schools, I believe we cannot and must not underestimate the importance of Loria's considerations on the war. His voice disputed the scientific approaches that deliberately did not raise the question of recognizing the causes, and in particular the economic causes, of the Great War or which, even they focused on the issue tended to lead it back to the *natural and uneliminable* conflict between economics and politics, between the reign of peace and harmony and the criminal realm of clashes between elites and nations in their struggle for power. Loria's contribution is important because he made it possible to recognize the social philosophy underlying the philosophies that come across as neutral thought techniques. By showing the community the most rational (economic) way of achieving certain social goals (for example 'the need for war'), those techniques actually aim at concealing the radically conflicted nature of the capitalist *economic* system, of the 'rationality' of its laws and of the *economic* processes beneath the definition of 'social needs'.

Note

1　'The thesis that wars are wholly due to economic causes has one of its ablest advocates in Professor Loria' (Edgeworth 1918: 318). See also Gide (1922: 383).

References

Edgeworth, F.Y. (1918) 'The Economic Causes of War. By Achille Loria'. Translated by John Leslie Garner, Chicago, Kerr, 1918, *The Economic Journal*, vol. 28, 1918, n. 111, p. 318.

Gide, C. (1922) 'A. Loria, Aspetti sociali ed economici della guerra mondiale (1921)', in *Revue d'Économie Politique*, 1922, vol. 36, p. 383.

Gramsci, A. (1918) 'Achille Loria', *Il Grido del Popolo*, 19 January, in Gramsci 1982.

— (1982) *La città futura, 1917–1918*, Einaudi, Turin.

Loria, A. (1903) 'La scienza economica e i problemi sociali del nostro tempo', *Giornale degli economisti*, vol. XXVII, 1903, pp. 534–535.

— (1904) *Verso la giustizia sociale*, Società editrice libraria, Milan.

— (1913) *Le basi economiche della costituzione sociale*, Bocca, Turin.

— (1915) 'Perché i socialisti italiani devono essere fautori della guerra', *Gazzetta del Popolo*, 20 June, p. 3.

— (1918) 'Per la democrazia industriale', *Minerva*, 1 November, pp. 697–699.

— (1920) 'Il trionfo del materialismo storico', *Minerva*, 1 January, pp. 1–2.

— (1921) *Aspetti sociali ed economici della guerra mondiale*, Milano, Vallardi.

— (1922) *I fondamenti scientifici della riforma economica*, Bocca, Turin.

Maccabelli, T. (2010) 'Tra politica ed economia: gli scritti di Achille Loria sui quotidiani', *Il Pensiero economico italiano*, n. 1, pp. 167–182.

Marchioli, E. (1923) 'Le basi scientifiche del riformismo economico', *Critica Sociale*, 1–15 September, n. 17, p. 272.

Michelini, L. (1998) *Marginalismo e socialismo: Maffeo Pantaleoni, 1882–1904*, FrancoAngeli, Milan.

— (2011) *Alle origini dell'antisemitismo nazional-fascista. Maffeo Pantaleoni e* La Vita italiana *di Giovanni Preziosi, 1915–1924*, Marsilio, Venice.

Pantaleoni, M. (1889) *Principii di economia pura*, Firenze, Barbera.

— (1895) 'La caduta della Società Generale di Credito mobiliare italiano', *Giornale degli Economisti*, s. II, Vol. 10, April, pp. 357–429, Vol. 11, November, pp. 437–503.

— (1911) 'Considerazioni sulle proprietà di un sistema di prezzi politici', *Giornale degli Economisti e Rivista di Statistica*, s. III, Vol. 42, February, pp. 114–138, republished in Pantaleoni (1919).

— (1917a) *Note in margine alla guerra*, Laterza, Bari.

— (1917b) *Tra le incognite. Problemi suggeriti dalla guerra*, Laterza, Bari.

— (1918) *Politica: criteri ed eventi*, Laterza, Bari.

— (1919) *La fine provvisoria di un'epopea*, Laterza, Bari.

— (1922) *Bolcevismo italiano*, Laterza, Bari.

— (1925) *Erotemi di economia*, Laterza, Bari, vol. 1.

— (1936) *Studi storici di economia*, Zanichelli, Bologna.

Perri, S. (2004) 'La 'solitudine' di Achille Loria: positivismo, questione sociale e distribuzione', *Il Pensiero economico italiano*, 205–223.

Robbins, L. (1939) *The Economic Causes of War*, Jonathan Cape, London.

7 Changes in the Pacifism of Akamatsu Kaname from the Interwar Period to WWII

Tadashi Ohtsuki[1]

Introduction

This chapter investigates the changes in the attitudes towards WWII of a Japanese economist, Akamatsu Kaname (1896–1974) of Tokyo University of Commerce (former Tokyo Higher Commercial School)—currently known as Hitotsubashi University.

As the term 'Total War' literally suggests, many economists in Europe, the USA and other parts of the world found themselves involved in World War II directly or indirectly, regardless of their intentions. The Japanese economists, including Akamatsu, were no exception.

When the economists were faced with the issues of the war in Japan, two research groups found particular distinction.[2] One was '*Akimaru Kikan*' (Akimaru Agency[3]), in which a number of Japanese economists analyzed the capability of some of the important countries involved to sustain the effort of WWII.[4] The other carried out the research activities in Southeast Asia under the leadership of Akamatsu as from the end of 1942.

Akamatsu is internationally known for his 'Wild Geese Flying Pattern theory',[5] or '*Gankou Keitai Ron*' in Japanese, presented in the first half of the 1930s,[6] which explains the patterns of industrial development in developing countries. Between 1921 and 1939 he taught economics and also took part in economic research activities at Nagoya Higher Commercial School, now known as the 'School of Economics, Nagoya University'. In April 1939, he moved to Tokyo University of Commerce and started research activities as chief of the research department of the Institute of Economic Research of East Asia ('*Toua Keizai Kenkyusho*') attached to this university.[7] From the end of 1942 to the end of WWII, when Japan had been overwhelmed by the war, under the command of the Japanese military administration, he led researches on natural resources in Southeast Asia as its head, and clearly changed his attitude towards the war through this experience.

As pointed by Akashi (2006a, 7), until recently Fukami (1988) has offered the only detailed overview of the research activities by the Japanese military administration in Southeast Asia. In fact, researchers were not allowed free access to the relevant documents preserved in the Military Archives attached to the National Institute for Defense Studies until the end of the 1970s. After Fukami's publication,

Akashi (2006a), Akashi and Yoshimura ed. (2008) and Ohtsuki (2010) also came out based on newly available historical material.

Recently the first biography of Akamatsuby Ikeo (2008),[8] together with review of this biography by Hirakawa (2009), and Hirakawa (2013), were published, Hirakawa in particular questioning Ikeo's opinion that Akamatsu was a supporter of democracy in wartime. The changes of his pacifist attitude have not been studied in sufficient detail.

Japan played a decidedly major role in WWII, when a number of Japanese economists had direct connection with the military government, like many other economists in their respective countries. Studies on the research activities of Japanese economists or their thought in wartime Japan have been scant even in Japan, although some 70 years have passed since the end of WWII, and this has led to the gaps in studies on the history of Japanese economic thought. This study seeks to fill some of the gaps, and also to draw some comparisons with other cases in the world.

Higher commercial schools in Japan: correlations between education and research

This chapter illustrates the economic research activities conducted in higher commercial schools (here in after HCS), including the ones which would be transformed later in commercial universities, which are little known in English literatures. In Japan the teaching of economics began in such imperial universities as Tokyo in 1878 and Kyoto in 1899 after the introduction of the so-called 'Western Economics' with the end of the national seclusion in 1854[9] and the beginning of the Meiji Restoration in 1868.However, the imperial universities offered lectures on economics simply as one of the subject sunder the faculty of law, until a faculty of economics was formed in 1919.Nor was there any specific research institute. In this respect the HCS played very significant roles in research as well as education.

From practical education to research

In 1884, modelled on the 'Institut Supérieur de Commerce d'Anvers'[10] in Belgium, the first government-run HCS in Japan was attached to the 'Tokyo School of Foreign Languages' ('*Tokyo Gaikokugo Gakko*', present Tokyo University of Foreign Studies). In the following year this commercial school was merged with the '*Tokyo Shogyo Gakko*' ('Tokyo School of Commerce'), which in 1887 became the '*Koto Syogyo Gakko*' ('Higher Commercial School'), and in 1902 was subsequently renamed the '*Tokyo Koto Shogyo Gakko*' or 'Tokyo Higher Commercial School'.

Following this school, two higher commercial schools were established in Osaka[11] (1901) and Kobe (1902). In 1903, commercial education, which aimed at training engineers at the elementary or secondary level to form new engineers as from the Meiji Restoration in 1868, came to be regarded as a part of higher education. These first three commercial schools, which were located in—then, and indeed still today—important commercial and industrial cities in Japan, later became universities.[12] With the end of the Russo-Japanese war in 1904–1905, which created the demand for workers with advanced commercial education in such fields as economics, bookkeeping and foreign languages to work overseas, three higher commercial schools were established additionally: Nagasaki and Yamaguchi in 1905, and Otaru in 1910.

Furthermore, in the first half of the 1920s eight higher commercial schools[13] were also founded. In the first place, this was because he prosperity that came with WWI demanded further graduates from higher commercial education, and secondly this prosperity enabled the then Prime Minister Takashi Hara (1856–1921) to implement the 'positive policy'.[14]

With regard to the education in these higher commercial schools, two features in particular distinguished it from that in the imperial universities. First, as stated above, the commercial schools primarily aimed at developing expert knowledge in commercial studies, and then putting it into practice through simulation classes. On the other hand, the imperial universities aimed to groom human resources for the posts of government officials necessary in the process of modernization of Japan, so the emphasis came on academic education. Second, the most important foreign language studied in commercial schools was English for convenience in international business, while the imperial universities favoured German (Yagi 1999: 17), Japan's academic and social systems being modelled on those of Germany in many cases during this period. In the higher commercial schools, however, in addition to English some other foreign languages were also taught. For example, in Otaru HCS, French, Spanish, German, Chinese and Russian were taught. This clearly reflected the geographical location, Otaru being in Hokkaido, near China and Russia. Such a diversity of foreign languages was created by both foreign lecturers and Japanese teachers who had studied abroad. Furthermore, both foreign and some Japanese lecturers also taught economics and commercial studies using texts not translated from the original language.

Such an academic environment also stimulated the Japanese teachers, again favouring the development of economic researches. One of the most important examples can be found in Nagoya HCS, at which Akamatsu worked from 1921 to 1939 before leaving for Tokyo University of Commerce (previously Tokyo HCS).

Soon after his graduation from Kobe HCS in 1919, and then the two-year specialized course at Tokyo HCS in 1921, he began work as a lecturer at Nagoya HCS. In Kobe HCS Akamatsu had studied Marx because of his interest in the labor movement, but in Tokyo HCS he came up with some critical studies on Marx after taking part in the seminar of Fukuda Tokuzo,[15] then one of Japan's leading economists. From 1924 to 1926, he had the opportunity to study abroad: in Berlin for about a year from 1924 and Heidelberg from April 1925 to January 1926, and subsequently Harvard Business School from March to June 1926[16] (Akamatsu 1975: 24–34).

In Heidelberg, he attended the lectures and the seminars of H. Rickert (1863–1936), H. Glockner (1896–1979) and K. Jaspers (1883–1969). In Glockner's class he studied the *Phänomenologie des Geistes* (1807) by Hegel, which gave Akamatsu the idea of critical studies on the school of the new Kantists from the standpoint of Hegel, and also the idea of his synthetic dialectics. Moving to the USA in 1926, he was especially interested in the case method education system and empirical studies by the Harvard University of Committee on Economic Research, the latter of which eventually formed the basis of his 'Wild Geese Pattern theory' in the 1930s. On his return to Nagoya, he established the industrial research bureau called '*Sangyo Chousa Shitsu*'—'the Bureau of Business Research'[17]—on the basis of the results of his study abroad, and subsequently the first empirical analysis in Japan began under his leadership.[18] Shortly before this establishment E. F. Penrose (1895–1984) had arrived at Nagoya HCS as a lecturer in late 1925[19] and also advanced in his research on quantitative index of products with the help of Japanese lecturers and students during his stay at Nagoya from 1925–1930,[20] which also attracted Japanese lecturers. Later on, Akamatsu's research at Nagoya came to the knowledge of the professors at Tokyo UC. In 1939 he moved to this university, and applied his research approach to 'Asia studies', responding to the demand at that time in Japan.

'Asia studies' in the HCSs

Research activities developed in the HCSs also had another important feature. Like Nagoya HCS, some other commercial schools also established research bureau. One of their most important characteristics was 'Asia studies', which Akamatsu's research in Southeast Asia in the first half of the 1940s also formed part of.

With the spread of Japanese territories resulting from the wars in Asia, providing business persons with higher commercial knowledge and skills of foreign languages, the HCSs also began to research native customs and markets in the new colonial areas of Japan for further commercial and industrial development. In fact, Nagasaki, Yamaguchi, Otaru and Takaoka HCSs, located in important provincial port cities in Japan and also with easy access to the Japanese colonial areas on the continental part of Asia, opened the new courses specializing in practical studies on trade between East Asia, especially China and Japan. Thus the HCSs came to establish research bureau to further both education and researches regarding this area.

Taking Yamaguchi HCS as an example, being located near the Korean Peninsula and China, it established a course on Chinese trade and a society for the study of East Asia's economy in 1916. This society developed into a research institute in 1933, which consisted of the department of general affairs, research, resources, and an editorial department. The new curriculums evidently included visits to areas in East Asia for practical studies, but in many cases they did not necessarily produce such good results as had been expected because of their short duration. Moreover, the teachers had insufficient opportunities for researches overseas or made little effort to engage in them. Instead, they concentrated mainly on collecting material and conducting the relevant research. They also produced her publication entitled '*Toua Kenkyu*' (which means '*Studies on East Asia*'), but the articles presented there were in most cases based not on field surveys but on collected references (Matsushige 2006: 241–250).[21] In short, Asian studies in this HCS could be regarded as essentially academic.[22]

These kinds of research institutes also came to be established in other HCSs—Kobe University of Commerce in 1919 and Osaka University of Commerce in 1928, Tokyo UC being an exception, building on the former Tokyo HCS.

'*Asia studies*' *in Tokyo University of Commerce before Akamatsu*

Tokyo HCS became the first commercial university in Japan in 1920 and was renamed 'Tokyo University of Commerce', but it could not establish a research institute until 1940 because the Ministry of Education would not approve the budget. It only had an economic research department in 1909, which concentrated mainly on collecting material or data published by banks, companies, exchanges and so on, like the other bureaus attached to HCSs (Maruyama 1989: 67).

This does not mean, however, that Tokyo HCS or Tokyo UC did not get involved in 'Asia studies'. Given the increase of interest in the continental regions in Asia after the First Sino-Japanese War and the Russo-Japanese war, some lectures concerning this area had already started in Tokyo HCS, such as 'economic conditions in East Asia', 'colonization policy', and 'Manchurian and Mongolian Affairs'.[23]

Among them, for instance, 'economic conditions in East Asia' was held as early as 1904, 35 years before Akamatsu's arrival. The aim of this course was to teach the 'practical knowledge necessary for business or commerce in China'. This was first given by Ishida Kiyosada,[24] second by Professor Negishi Tadashi from 1908 to 1939 and third by Muramatsu Yuji from 1940. The former two lecturers actually went to China for business (Ishida), and for research (Negishi), while Muramatsu engaged in researches focusing mainly on material and data, like the researchers in the other higher commercial schools (Suehiro 2006a: 47–48).

However, President Ueda Teijiro (1879–1940) of Tokyo UC, dissatisfied with the situation, observed:

> It will be important to cultivate human resources to work in China. Tokyo UC also has to make a contribution. What is most important is to pay attention also to East Asia, while we are now paying attention only to the Western world. To do so we—both teachers and students—need to have many more opportunities for study visits to China. We also need a research institute.
>
> (Ueda 1963: 315)

Fortunately, in October 1938 he heard from Murata Syozo (1878–1957)[25] that Kagami Kenkichi (1879–1940),[26] a graduate of Tokyo HCS and the then president of Tokyo–Kaijyou Fire Insurance Company,[27] had the idea of contributing money for the purpose of training human resources fit to address the coming of age of East Asia (ibid.). Ueda was keen to secure the contribution of Kagami.

At the same time, Ueda 'keenly felt that [Tokyo UC] needs more staff for further development of research' (Ueda 1963, 322), so he requested Akamatsu to move from Nagoya HCS to Tokyo UC.[28] Ueda knew from Ota Tetsuzou (1889–1970), who was professor at Tokyo UC, of the empirical researches by Akamatsu at Nagoya, the details of which were explained in the above section 'From Practical Education to Research'.

At first, the then President of Nagoya HCS, Kunimatsu Yutaka (1880–1965) disapproved of Ueda's request, but some days later Kunimatsu consented (ibid.). Akamatsu accepted Ueda's request and started work at Tokyo as from April 1939.

Soon after Akamatsu''the s arrival at Tokyo UC, President Ueda went on a tour of academic inspection in Manchuria and China from April to May 1939. On returning from this inspection, he recognized 'the necessity of those who directly research on racial characteristics, social systems etc. in China, and further investigate the recent trends there' (Ueda 1939, 172). As Akamatsu pointed out, President Ueda seemed to 'have an idea for the establishment of the research institute' (Akamatsu 1941a: 112).

Unfortunately, Kagami passed away soon after Ueda's inspections, but his donation was made in accordance with his dying wishes. In June 1939 Ueda's plan for this institute was made public, and in April 1940 the institute named '*Toua Keizai Kenkyusho*' (the Institute of East Asian Economic Research) was established in the library of Tokyo UC, which had four departments: research, resources, statistics and general affairs. Akamatsu was appointed as director of the research department.[29] Following the researches in industrial bureau at Nagoya HCS, Akamastu intended to establish the second research bureau.

The outbreak of WWII and Akamatsu's pacifism

Establishment of the research bureau was accomplished in April 1940, but the researches originally intended had inevitably to change because of the new needs of WWII.

In May 1940, only a month after the establishment, president Ueda died suddenly, and Takase Sotaro (1892–1966) became the next president. He made special efforts to have this institute government-run.[30] Finally, on February 5th 1942, it became a government-run organization, covering general researches on economies in East Asia. This, however, soon led to an ironic upshot, and also gave rise to complications for Akamatsu's pacifism.

Akamatsu's pacifism before the nationalization of the research institute

During his Nagoya period, as mentioned in the above section 'From Practical Education to Research', Akamatsu was able to advance his researches, using both synthetic dialectics and empirical studies, especially up until the middle of the 1930s. However, in July 1937 'the Marco Polo Bridge Incidence' occurred, and in December 'the Second Sino-Japanese War' broke out, inevitably creating an atmosphere of fascism in the HCSs. We can find some changes in his works as from this period.

In 1936, recognizing Japan's colonial expansion and controls by the government, he wrote:

> The formation of Manchuria has surely created demand for the intelligent-sia and mental workers, and has played a significant role in brightening up all the schools in our country. *When the new land for youth develops, the age is always brightening all aspects.* [...] Government control needs to be enhanced more thoroughly.[31]
>
> (Akamatsu 1936: 98–99)

At the same time, he also pointed out the risks entailed by government control:

> What we are worry about [...] is the fact that government control often has possibility to deprive the people or students of spontaneity and progressiveness.
>
> (Akamatsu 1936: 99)

According to Akamatsu, at that time he 'developed to totalitarianism utilizing synthetic dialectics' (Akamatsu 1938a, 2). This means the developments in his thought had veered from Marxism to totalitarianism over the twelve years since 1925[32] (Akamatsu 1937: 2). He further noted in his article presented in December 1938:

> The totality of our nation is incarnated, as the Emperor, in the significance of the foundational principle or the absolute spirit, while the whole life of our nation [the totality of our nation] lies in the significance of intuitive existence.
>
> (Akamatsu 1938b: 15)

Akamatsu, regarding the Emperor as the absolute spirit of Japan, judged the Japanese invasion positively. At the same time, however, he also hoped for the situation would not worsen. In fact, after moving to Tokyo UC, he presented an article in June 1939, when research had yet to come under way, still hoping that WWII would not break out:

> If WWII broke out within some ten years ... it would not be such an easy problem for human beings. It would be fortunate if what I am writing now were to prove mere fallacy and purely theoretical discussion.[33]
>
> (Akamatsu 1939a: 60)

We can also find another article by Akamatsu in November 1941, when Japan and the US were negotiating for a peaceful settlement, just one month before the Attack on Pearl Harbor in December:

The bold Prime Minister must not urge [to the war]. First of all, he must bring down the rising wave. Then, what should the great politician do other than that?

(Akamatsu 1941b: 1)

Unfortunately, on December 8th 1941, Pearl Harbor was attacked, and members of the institute had a meeting. One of the members, Yamada Isam (1909–1986), later looked back on the meeting, observing:

We were to work for the military administration, but the purpose was thoroughly academic research in the Southeast [Asian] areas. So our position did not change. That was very important … We went there and cooperated with the military administration, but in fact we did not really want to do so. We did want to go on with our academic researches.

(Tokyo-daigaku Kyouyou-gakubu Kokusai-kankeiron Kenkyu-shitsu ed. 1981: 121)

According to other members, Itagaki Yoichi and Yamada Hideo, 'We were told that our status would be higher if we became military governors. But Professor Yamanaka and Professor Sugimoto did not want to accept this condition. Rather we preferred [to go on with the research] as Professors of Tokyo UC'[34] (Hitotsubashi-daigaku Gakuenshi Hensanjigyou Iinkai ed. 1983: 45).

The members of Tokyo UC agreed among themselves that they would assist the military, focusing mainly on academic researches, and also retaining their status as professors (Fukami 1988, 120). With regard to this point Akamatsu later stated, 'I would have been forced to write various things [against my will] if I had not been to Southeast Asia then' (Akamatsu 1975: 48).

Two aspects of Akamatsu clearly emerge here, which are difficult to reconcile with one another: on the one hand, his pacifism is reflected in the fact that he hoped there would be no worsening of the war; on the other hand, his acceptance of Japanese colonial expansion, and totalitarianism.

Cooperation with the Japanese military administration and changes in Akamatsu's pacifism

In September 1942, the then President Takase of Tokyo UC was asked by his younger brother Takase Keijiro (1905–1982), who was then Lieutenant Colonel of the Imperial Headquarters, to cooperate with the General Army in Southeast Asia through his research activities. This was because the Japanese 25th Army had no researchers and scant references or information about the occupied area at the beginning of Japan's military administration (Akashi 2006a: 8). Seven months before this request, when the research institute was founded, president Takase had already written:

Since this Great East Asian War, Japan has developed in Southeast Asia very vigorously, so our country needs new economic research in this area as soon

as possible .... Our institute wants to advance our activities positively so as not
to miss this golden opportunity ... And we would also like to contribute to the
national policy sufficiently. [...] We are going to send our staff there as soon as
possible, and to collect materials on the economy and important problems there.

(Takase 1942: 1)

Takase agreed with his brother on the need for the researches in Southeast Asia,
so he accepted the request from the military administration (Akamatsu 1975: 44).
According to Akamatsu's autobiography, however, on being informed of Takase's
acceptance, Akamatsu stated that he would like to dispatch as few members as
possible because the institute was in its early stages. However, Professor Sugimoto
Eiichi (1901–1952) said that 'we should cooperate with the army thoroughly', and
also 'asked Akamatsu to go to Southeast Asia as a leader'[35] (ibid.).

At the same time, Akamatsu's view point also came to show some changes.
In Akamatsu (1942a),[36] for instance, he wrote:

> This war has enabled expansion in the East Asia area. To be government-run
> is a good opportunity for this institute. In particular, establishing this area
> is now clearly becoming the national policy. [...] our purpose is now also
> clear and vast. But our researches should not be those for the current policy.
> Such researches will be done by the government and our institute should
> advance our research more purely. It will take forever for Japan to estab-
> lish the Great East Asia area. The research institutes in universities aim to
> advance researches which will give directions for this long-run policy. [...]
> I would like to make this institute part of this scheme.

(Akamatsu 1942a: 1)

We find that he asserted the importance of the difference between the researches
by this institute and those by the government, while showing his satisfaction with
the nationalization of the institute. At the same time, he also decided to approve
the foundation of the Great East Asia Co-Prosperity Sphere. He further continued
to state his opinion on this point in June 1942.

> The Great East Asia Co-Prosperity Sphere is close to being gloriously
> achieved by the Imperial Military ... But we still lack India, Australia and the
> Chiang Kai-shek government in Burma. [...] To gain these areas we take both
> military and economic war yet further.

(Akamatsu 1942b: 18)

Evidently, by this time Akamatsu was supporting widespread invasion by the
Japanese military. He added:

> All our intelligence has been invested in forming the economy of the Great
> East Asia Co-Prosperity Sphere.

(Akamatsu 1942b: 19)

Akamatsu himself was conscious of his role in participating in this Japanese invasion even though he was not a military. In September 1942, three months after the publication quoted above (Akamatsu 1942b), he further stated:

> Now the Imperial Military has absorbed all the inner part of the Great East Asia Co-Prosperity sphere, and the victories of our military in the continental part of China are developing rapidly, and finally this Co-Prosperity sphere is now preparing for the stabilization of the undefeated empire.
>
> (Akamastu 1942c: 1)

In this period, he came to advocate 'the historical inevitability of the construction of the sphere economy in the Great East Asia Co-Prosperity' (Akamatsu1942a: 2). That is, he thought that the war would eventually cease, and peace would reign. But he clearly acquiesced with the expansion of the Great East Asia Co-Prosperity through war.

In the next month Akamatsu (1942d) was published. Here he discussed the need for highly developed industries differentiated on the basis of rationalization, increased efficiency and new technologies, to which end 'all the energies of our nation must be channelled' (Akamatsu 1942d: 125), and also the need to create an extensive bloc to ensure the greatest possible degree defence of the state. Akamatsu thought that this was also 'the immediate goal for Japan then' (ibid.: 124), towards which 'our nation should strive' (ibid.: 127).

In this article he stated as:

> Our spirit of founding a nation, or *Hattukou Ichiu*, has come to be realized as the concrete idea of creating a new world order through the Great East Asia War. [...] The new idea of the emancipation of the Great East Asia from colonization, the foundation of Asia for [by] the Asian peoples, [...] and the new world order without any exploitation has been settled on the basis of the essential trend of Asia centring in Japan.[37]
>
> (ibid.: 52–53)

In this period, he emphasized the importance of developing of the Great East Asia Co-Prosperity through the war with concerted efforts by the entire nation. Additionally, his doctoral thesis submitted in the end of 1942 was entitled '*Keizai Shin-Chitsujyo no Keisei Genri*', which meant '*The Principle of the Formation of the New Economic Order*'[38] brought about with the structural changes through the world war.

Finally, on December 18th 1942 the research group commanded by Akamatsu left Kobe port for Singapore, where the headquarters of the Japanese Military Administration in Southeast Asia was then situated (Akamatsu 1975, 44; Fukami 1988: 122–123). According to Akamatsu, more than forty people attended this research. At first he aimed to establish the third bureau in Southeast Asia, followed by that in Nagoya and Tokyo, and endeavoured to advance research activities academically.

The Japanese military administration, however, demanded not academic researches but practical research for the development of natural resources because by then Japan's fortunes in the war were deteriorating seriously.[39] Akamatsu made efforts to change their research styles and contents, but in vain. Within a year he was writing, 'our academic research is not a main issue' (Akamatsu 1975: 46), and his idea of establishing the third bureau completely disappeared.

At last, in the middle of 1944, the research activities were completely abandoned. Instead, Akamatsu and the other members, especially Itagaki Yoichi, made efforts to grasp the mentality of the indigenous population of Malaya.[40]

Akamatu thought it important to permit Malaya to gain its independence because this would help Japan's army in that the native people there would resist the British Armed Forces. But this idea was ruled out by the Imperial Conference. Thus, he 'decided to conduct a movement for the independence of Malaya by himself' and called upon 'the leaders of the natives there to take part in it', explaining that 'Malaya would be governed by Britain again [after the end of WWII]'. Thereafter, the movement found the approval of the Japan army, regardless of the Imperial Conference. Finally, through this movement Indonesia became decolonized from the Netherlands before the end of the war, while Malaysia gained independence after the war (ibid.: 46–47).

As the evidence presented in this chapter shows, Akamatsu's pacifism clearly changed in the course of events with, first, the outbreak of the war, second the nationalization of the bureau, and lastly his actual participation in research with the Japanese Military.

Conclusion

When Akamatsu was endeavoring to forge ahead with his research in Tokyo based on that in Nagoya, he never expected the outbreak of the war, while judging the spread of the territory of Japan positively. But inevitably, and all too soon, things changed, an eventually he found himself cooperating with the Japanese Military in Southeast Asia. After the end of WWII, he wrote in his autobiography:

> The cooperation of research with the Japanese military administration was ordered by the President [of the university], so I am not responsible for that.
>
> (Akamatsu 1975: 48)

But he also recognized that:

> Some of my works or articles during the war entailed considerable problems [...] especially my article.
>
> (Akamatsu 1942d: ibid.)

Akamatsu is one of the few economists who admitted to their wartime experience, while some kept it secret or cancelled that part of their lives from their curriculum. After the war he was reinstated as professor of Hitotsubashi University under the new educational system and in 1971 Akamatsu declined the decoration of the Order of the Sacred Treasure, Gold and Silver Star from Japan in reward for his 50-year career as a lecturer, about which he actually never talked. To know the truth is no longer possible. But considering that his wife did not agree with this decoration because of its significance in wartime Japan (Akamatsu *et al*. ed. and written by Akamatsu Yoshiko 1973: 48–49), his rejection might indicate the 'complete' disappearance of his pacifism from the latter half of 1942 to its reappearance as he played a positive role in the independence of the Southeast Asian region, promptly recognizing the defeat of Japan.

Notes

1 I would like to acknowledge financial support from the JSHET (Japan Society for the History of Economic Thought), which enabled me to present the original version of this chapter at the XIII AISPE (Associazione Italiana per la Storia del Pensiero Economico) Conference at University of Pisa.
2 Recent studies on economists or economics in wartime Japan are Komine (2005), Makino (2010), Ohtsuki (2010, chapter 9), Yagi (1999, chapter 8), Yanagisawa (2008).
3 Akimaru Jiro (1898–1992) was then Lieutenant Colonel of the Japan Army.
4 It is now known that Arisawa Hiromi (1896–1988), Miyakawa Minoru (1896–1985), TakemuraTadao (1905–1987), and Nakayama Ichiro (1898–1980) took part in this agency. For the details, see Makino (2010, chapter 1).
5 This English name was first translated by Shinohara Miyohei (1919–2012).
6 The first version of this study was Akamatsu (1935), which was later developed utilizing the framework of the major cycle (long wave) theory by N.D. Kondratiev (1892–1938). For the details, see Ozawa (2005); Ohtsuki (2011).
7 This institute is the present 'Institute of Economic Research' attached to Hitotsubashi University.
8 See also Ohtsuki (2010).
9 After the exclusion of the Portuguese in 1639, Japan implemented a policy of isolation from all foreign countries except for China and the Netherlands for more than two hundred years. The first 'Western Economics' in Japan was *Grondtrekken der Staatshuishoudkunde* written in Dutch, the original version of which was *Outlines of Social Economy* (1846) by William Ellis (1800–1881). This Dutch version was translated into Japanese by Kanda Takahira (1830–1898) in 1867, and it became the first textbook of economics in Japan. Following this stage, the German historical school and then Classical Economics were introduced by the end of the nineteenth century (Tamanoi 1971, 18).
10 This was established in 1852.
11 This was not government-run, but municipal.
12 They were called the 'Big Three Commercial Universities'.
13 They are Nagoya (1920), Fukushima and Oita (1921), Hikone and Wakayama (1922), Yokohama and Takamastu (1923), and Takaoka (1924), all of which became the faculties of economics of universities when the new education system was organized in 1949.
14 It included the enhancement of national defence, the expansion of higher education, the promotion of industry, and the development of transportation.
15 This was because Fukuda considered critical studies to be important for further academic development (Akamatsu 1975: 13–18).
16 The details of his study abroad, see Akamatsu (1975: 24–37), Hirakawa (2013, 28–30) and Koide (1975, 275–280).
17 This translation can be found in Akamatsu (1975, 38). We can also find another translation 'The Industrial Research Bureau' on the back cover of Sakai and Akamatsu (1935). This bureau is now known as the Economic Centre, School of Economics Nagoya University.

18 According to Akamatsu, empirical analysis had not yet begun even in imperial universities, Tokyo University of Commerce or Kobe HCS. They had a research bureau or department, but their research style was that of German bureaus, which aimed mainly at gathering articles from newspapers (Akamatsu 1975: 37).

19 With a handwritten recommendation from A.C. Pigou, and on the advice of D.H. Robertson and A. Robinson he came to teach at Nagoya HCS in 1925 after his graduation from the Economics Tripos of the University of Cambridge (Penrose 1975, 323; 1987, 6). Other than Penrose, such as G. C. Allen and A. Ashton also belonged to this HCS as a government employee. Regarding Allen's stay in Japan, see Allen (1983).

20 After Penrose left for the Food Research Institute of Stanford University in 1930, this work was taken up by Koide Yasuji (1907–1985). Later Penrose introduced this work thorough his work (Penrose 1940). For the details, see Ohtsuki (2011: 310).

21 For detailed research on this publication, see Matsushige (2006: 245–250).

22 As Matsushige (2006: 245–250) also pointed out, many teachers or professors of HCS were likely to prefer academic research to field research. This was because most of them graduated from imperial universities or Tokyo University of Commerce whose professors also engaged in academic researches. In the case of Yamaguchi HCS, only a few teachers preferred field research.

23 According to Hitotsubashi-daigaku Gakuenshi Kankou Iinkai (1991: 55, 98), the former was given by Hori Mitsuki (1875–1940), and the latter was by Negishi Tadashi (1874–1971).

24 He was then a branch manager of Mitsui Bussan in Zhifu, China.

25 He graduated from Tokyo HC in 1900.

26 Regarding Kagami Kenkichi, see Suzuki ed. (1949).

27 Now the 'Tokio Marine & Nichido Fire Insurance Co., Ltd'.

28 Another reason for this request was that Itani Zenichi (1899–1980), who then taught commercial policy and economic policy in Tokyo UC, transferred to Osaka Chamber of Commerce and Industry as its executive director in 1939 (Ueda 1963: 322; Akamatsu 1975: 91).

29 The directors of the other departments were: statistics—Sugimoto Eiichi (1901–1952), resources—Odabashi Sadajyu (1904–1984), and general affairs—vacant.

30 For the details, see Maruyama (1989: 153–159) and Ohtsuki (2010: 75).

31 The words in italics originally had dots over them.

32 According to Akamatsu, 'to explain this change in my thoughts is not easy now'. But he also added that '[such a change] was consistent' (Akamatsu 1938a: 2). It is at present hard to pinpoint the decisive factor in this change. As Hirakawa (2013: 43) pointed out, it could be at least said that his study at Heidelberg was of importance to him.

33 Akamatsu (1939c) also discussed this issue.

34 We have no way of telling which of the three members stated this.

35 Akamatsu was surprised at the changes in Sugimoto's thinking towards the right, because he had studied Marx. According to Akamatsu, the change came as a sensitive response to Japan's crisis (Akamatsu 1975: 44).

36 This was presented in the same school paper, in which the above quoted Takase (1942) was also included.

37 This part was included also in Akamatsu (1943: 12; 1944a: 80). The former was partly reprinted from Akamatsu (1940).

38 This was later published as Akamatsu (1944b) after the author received a doctorate degree in economics from Tokyo UC in September 1944.

39 For the details of the research activities in Southeast Asia, see Akamatsu (1975: 43–47) and Ohtsuki (2010, chapter 9).

40 For the details, see also Itagaki (1988) and Itagaki and Yamada (1998).

References

Titles in [ ] are abridged English translation of the Japanese title by the author.

Akamatsu Kaname (1935) 'Wagakuni Youmou Kougyouhin no Boueki Susei', *Syougyou Keizai Ronsou*, Nagoya HCS, 13(1), 129–212 [Trend of the Trade of Woollen Products of Japan].
— (1936) 'Kyoudan Zuisousono 2', *Kenryou*, The Literary Club of Nagoya HCS, 38, 96–103 [Occasional Thoughts of Akamatsu 2].
— (1937) *Sangyoutousei Ron*, Chikura Syobou, Tokyo [*Theory of Industrial Control*].
— (1938a) 'Kyoudan Zuisousono 3', *Kenryou*, 42, 2–5 [Occasional Thoughts of Akamatsu 3].
— (1938b) 'Keizai-tetsugaku no Nihon-teki Jikaku', *Risou*, Risou-sha, Tokyo, 91, 5–21 [Japanese Sense of Economic Philosophy].
— (1939a) 'Sensou to Cyouki Buttka Hadou', *Bungeishunjyu*, Bungeishunjyu-sha, Tokyo, 17(11), 60–68 [Wars and Long Waves].
— (1939c) 'Oushu Senran no Tenbou: Keizaigaku to Gensyou Yosoku no Mondai', *IttukyouShinbun*, Tokyo   Shouka Daigaku Hitotsubashi-kai, 294 (Sep. 25th), 8 [Perspectives on the European War: Problems of economics and forecasting phenomenon].
— (1940) *Senji Keizai Tousei-ron*, Nihon Hyoron-sya, Tokyo [*Theories on the Control of War Economics*].
— (1941a) 'Ueda-Sensei to Syou-dai Touakeizai Kenkyusho', *HitotsubashiRonsou*, Tokyo University of Commerce, 7(1), 112 [Professor Ueda and the Institute of Economic Research of East Asia attached to Tokyo University of Commerce].
— (1941b) 'Kyouran wo Syouhukuseyo', *Nagoya Shinbun*, November 8th, Evening paper (November 9th), 1 [Bringing down the Rising Waves].
— (1942a) 'Daitoua Kensetsu no Cyouki-teki Shishin he'. *IttukyouShinbun*, 342 (February 10th), 1 [Towards Long-term Guidelines for the establishment of the Greater East Asia Co-Prosperity Sphere].
— ed. (1942b) 'Daitoua Keizai Senryaku', *Koron*, Dai-ichiKoron-sya, Tokyo, 5(6), 16–20 [Economic Strategies for the Great East Asia].
— ed. (1942c) *Shin-sekai Keizai Nenpou* vol. 9, Shokougyousei-sha [*Annual Report of the New World Economy*].
— (1942d) 'Kokuboukeizaigaku no Sougou Bensyouhou', in Akamatsu Kaname, Nakayama Ichiro and Okuma Nobuyuki *Kokuboukeizai Souron*, Ganshodou, Tokyo, 1–128 [Synthetic Dialectic of Defense Economics].
— (1943) *Sensou no Keizaiteki Ki-in nitsuite. Taisen Gen-in Kenkyu Shiryou*. The Research Department of Ministry of Foreign Affairs of Japan, Tokyo [*On Economic Causes of the War*].
— (1944a) 'Kokubou Keizaigaku', in Kobe Shodai Shinbun-bu (ed.) *Keizai oyobi Keizai-gaku no Sai-syuttupatsu*, Nihon Hyoron Sya, Tokyo, 63–80 [Defense Economics].
— (1944b) *Keizai Shin-Chitsujyo no Keisei Genri*, Risou-sha, Tokyo [*The Principle of the Formation of the New Economic Order*].
— *et al.* ed. and written by Akamatsu Yoshiko (1973) *Yoshiko no Tsuisou*, private edition [*Recollection of Akamatsu's Wife, Yoshiko*].
— (1975) 'Gakumon Henro', in Kojima ed. (1975), 9–68 [Autobiography of Akamatsu].
Akashi Youji (2006a) 'Kaisetsu', in Akashi Youji ed. and annotation (2006b, vol. 1, 7–17 [Comments on Akashi Youji ed. and annotation (2006b)].
— ed. and annotation (2006b) *Nanpou Gunseki Kankei Shiryou* 35(22 vols.), Ryuukei-shosya, Tokyo [*Historical Material of the Japanese Military Administration in Southeast Asia. Reprinted Edition*].

— and Yoshimura Mako ed. (2008) *New Perspectives on the Japanese Occupation in Malaya and Singapore, 1941–1945*, NUS Press, Singapore.

Allen, G.C. (1983) *Appointment in Japan: Memories of sixty years*, Athlone Press, London.

Fukami Sumio (1988) 'Tounan-Asia niokeru Nihon Gunsei no Cyousa', *Nampo Bunka*, Tenri Nampou Bunka Kyoukai, 15, 119–151 [Researches by the Japanese Military Administration in Southeast Asia].

Hirakawa Hitoshi (2009) 'Book Review of Ikeo (2008)', *SyakaiKeizaishi-gaku*, Shakai-Keizaishi Gattukai, 74(5), 95–97.

— (2013) 'Akamatsu Kaname to Nagoya Koto Syougyou Gakko', *Keizai Kagaku*, Nagoya University, 60(4), 13–64 [Akamatsu Kaname and Nagoya HCS].

Hitotsubashi-daigaku Gakuenshi Kankoulinkai (1991) *HitotsubashiDaigakuGakuseishiShiryou Hoi Bettusatsu vol.12*, Hitotsubashi-daigaku Gakuenshi Kankoulinkai [*Resources of the History of Education System of Hitotsubashi University* Vol.12].

Hitotsubashi-daigaku Gakuenshi Hensanjigyou Iinkai ed. (1983) *Dainiji-taisen to Hitotsubashi*, Hitotsubashidaigaku Gakuenshi Hensanjigyou Iinkai [*WWII and Hitotsubashi University*].

Ikeo Aiko (2008) *AkamatsuKaname*, Nihon Keizai Hyoron-sha, Tokyo [*Biography of Akamatsu*].

Itagaki Yoichi (1988) *Asia tonoTaiwa* (new edition), Ronsou-sha, Tokyo [*Dialogues with Asia*].

— and Yamada Hideo (1998) 'Nanpou-gun Gunsei-soukanbu (Nochidai 7 houmen gun) Cyousa-bu Nihon Gunseika Malaya Singapore niokeru Cyousa', in 'Nihon no Eiryou Malaya Singapore Senryou-ki Shiryou Cyousa' Forum (ed.) *Interview Kiroku Nihon no Eiryou Malaya Singapore Senryou (1941–1945)*, Ryukei-shosha, Tokyo, 19–57 [Researches in Malaya and Singapore under the Japanese Military Administration].

Koide Yasuji (1975) 'Akamatsu-sensei no Gakumon to Nagoya Jidai', in Kojima ed. (1975), 265–313 [Akamatsu at Nagoya].

Kojima Kiyoshi ed. (1975) *Gakumon Henro*, Sekai Keizai Kenkyukai, Tokyo [*Akamatsu: His Life and Works*].

Komine Atsushi (2005) 'Senkan-ki Nihon no Keizai Sanbou Ron, *Ryukoku-daigaku Keizaigaku Ronsyu*, Ryukoku-daigaku, Kyoto, 45(2), 109–123 [Economic General Staff in Interwar Japan].

Makino Kuniaki (2010) *Senjika no Keizaigakusya*, Cyuou Kouron-sha, Tokyo [*Economists in Wartime*].

Maruyama Yasuo (1989) *Sensou-no Jidai to Hitotsubashi*, Jyosuikai, Tokyo [*Wartime and Hitotsubashi*].

Matsushige Mitsuhiro (2006) Senzen Sencyu-ki Koutou Syougyou-gattko no Asia Cyousa, in Suehiro responsible ed. (2006b), 239–282 [Research Activities by Higher Commercial Schools in Asia before and during the Wars, with a Main Focus on Those in China].

Ohtsuki Tadashi (2010) *Akamatsu Kaname no Gankou Keitai Ron to Sono Tenkai*. Ph.D Theses of Tokyo University of Foreign Studies [*AKAMATSU Kaname's 'Gankou Keitai Ron' and its Development—His Nagoya period and the perspectives of a stage theory of economic development*].

— (2011) 'The Background of K. AKAMATSU's '*Gankou Keitai Ron*' and its Development: Early empirical analysis at Nagoya', in H. Kurz, T. Nishizawa and K. Tribe (eds.) *The Dissemination of Economic Ideas*, Edward Elgar, Cheltenham, 292–314.

Ozawa, T. (2005) *Institutions, Industrial Upgrading, and Economic Performance in Japan—The flying-geese paradigm of catch-up growth*, Edward Elgar Publishing, Northampton, Massachusetts.

Penrose, E.F. (1940) 'Japan, 1920–1936', in E.B. Schumpeter (ed.) *The Industrialization of Japan and Manchukuo, 1930–1940*, Macmillan, New York, 80–270.

— (1975) 'My Nagoya Era and Professor Akamatsu', in Kojima ed. (1975), 323–327.

— (1987) 'Memoirs of Japan, 1925–1930', in R. Dore and R. Sinha (eds.) *Japan and World Depression*, St Martin's Press, New York, 6–13.

Sakai Syouzaburou and Akamatsu Kaname (1935) *Cyousa Houkoku 17th*, The Industrial Research Bureau, Nagoya HCS [*Researches of Woolen Industries in Japan 3*].

Suehiro Akira (2006a) 'Ajia Cyousa no Keifu', in Suehiro responsible ed. (2006b), 21–66 [Genealogy of Researches in Asia].

— ed. (2006b) *Teikoku Nihon no Gakuchi* vol. 6, Iwanami Syoten, Tokyo [*Knowledge of Imperial Japan. Asia as Area Studies*].

Suzuki Sakae ed. (1949) *Kagami Kenkichi Kun wo Shinobu*, Kagami Kinen Zaidan, Tokyo [*In Memory of KagamiKenkichi*]

Takase Soutarou (1942) 'Nanpou Kenkyu no Kyumu. Shimeiiyo-iyo Kakudai', *Ittukyo-uShinbun*, 342 (Feb. 10th), 1 [Urgent Significance of Researches on Southeast Asia. The increase of the importance of missions].

Tamanoi Yoshirou (1971) *Nihon no Keizaigaku*, Cyuoukouron-sha, Tokyo [*Economics in Japan*].

Tokyo-daigaku Kyouyou-gakubu Kokusai-kankeiron Kenkyu-shitsu ed. (1981) *Interview Kiroku D. Nihon no Gunsei* 6, Tokyo-daigaku Kyouyougakubu Kokusai-kankeiron Kenkyu-shitsu [*Interview Records on the Japanese Military Administration (March 1978–March 1979, by Akashi Youji)*].

Ueda Teijiro (1939) 'Mansyu, Hokushi, Cyushi no Kyukou Shisatsu', *Bungeishunjyu Genchi Houkoku Jikyoku Zoukan*, Bungeishunjyu-sha, Tokyo, 21, 170–173 [Quick Inspections of Manchuria, and the North and the Central Part of China].

Ueda Teijiro (1963) *Ueda Teijiro Nittuki Bannen-hen*, Ueda Teijiro Nittuki Kankoukai, Tokyo [*Diary of Ueda Teijiro: In his later years*].

Yagi Kiichiro (1999) *Kindai Nihon no Syakai Keizai-gaku*, Chikuma Shobou, Tokyo [*Social Economics in Modern Japan*].

Yanagisawa Osamu (2008) *Senzen Senji Nihon no Keizaishisou to Nazism*, Iwanami-Shoten, Tokyo [*Economic Thought and Nazism Before and During the War*].

8 War in Sismondi's Interpretation of Modern Capitalism

Fresh Analytical Perspectives

Letizia Pagliai[1]

The reception with which an author meets over time necessarily depends on alternative and, at times, antithetical interpretative approaches and changes of perspective. Not so in the case of Jean Charles Léonard Sismondi's closely-argued analysis of war, which scholars have never addressed with the attention it merits, either in his writings on the economy or in his historical and institutional works. And yet it escapes no one that Sismondi was writing during one of the most conflict-ridden periods in European history,[2] when political economy had been raised in the parlance of the *philosophes* to one of the most exalted positions among the sciences, because it addressed the immediate, practical problems facing the state, and when the close conjunction between the notions of 'war' and 'market'[3] persisted at length, both notions indicating engagement in a contest setting out to resolve conflicts of interest. Around the time that *The Wealth of Nations* was coming out, Condillac summed up that view, in which the prime 'trigger' in every conflict was envy of wealth among the nations, in other words, jealousy of trade: 'European trade is not an exchange of works in which all nations will each find their advantage; it is a state of war in which they only think of how to plunder each other' (Condillac 1997 [1776]: 202).

So such a lack of attention for a topic of such broad scope may seem paradoxical in many respects, considering that the late eighteenth and early nineteenth centuries constituted an epoch-making turning point in the ongoing dialectic between economy and war, and between economy and peace.

Armaments, armed forces provisioning, taxation, finance and the demographic consequences of wars all became pressing issues when war radicalised as a phenomenon in Europe post-1790 (Crouzet 1964), first with the French Revolution, then with the Napoleonic Wars, and lastly with the long war between Greece and Turkey. Sismondi's direct involvement in these events brought him up against three periods in which freedom 'fell sick': first the revolutionary Terror, then the regression that the Napoleonic empire constituted, and lastly the authoritarianism of the Restoration. On the one hand, he delivered a reading of them as a chronicler of events, anxious to build up a liberal public opinion on current political topics;[4] on the other, however, he set himself to solving the problems posed by social evolution and, to that end, addressed the issue of civil liberties in relation to forms of government. A comparison between absolute and free governments based on an analysis (1796–1798) of the various countries' constitutions was the initial upshot (Di Reda 1998). He extended his studies into monumental histories, one of the *Italian Republics in the Middle Ages* (1809–1818) and one of the French (1821–1844), in which, like other empirical historians – such as Leopold von Ranke, Thomas Babington Macaulay and Jules Michelet – he included wars of conquest, civil wars[5] and religious wars[6] in his accounts. However, it was the science of government, with its pointers to the institutions that allowed and enhanced social progress, tempered selfish impulses and satisfied needs, that drew him towards economics, leading him to lay the foundations for the grandiose edifice of a system of social sciences.

This gradual course pursued in his studies, with several interests occupying him at the same time, gave Sismondi a not exclusively economic approach to war, which was inevitably side-lined by historiographical interests chiefly focusing on the analysis of the mechanisms according to which business activities operated within the social structures.

The pages that follow, prefaced by the theoretical and historiographical context, are an attempt to retrace his thinking on the idea of war in both the main avenues of his writings, in the awareness that Sismondi always regarded the key factor – both in economic theory and in his chronicling of constitutional history, albeit in different situations of time and place – as the relationship between economics and politics, and between society and state.

Sismondi's image as the first prober of the relationship between the production cycle as a whole and a complete theory of society has – as I have just mentioned – eclipsed other equally interesting factors crucial to an understanding of the theoretical concatenation of his thinking on war. The fertile eccentricity of Sismondi's thinking on war lies, indeed, in its unorthodox disciplinary positioning, on the borderline between different fields of knowledge (history, economics and constitutionalism), as he states in his early writings: 'Political economy is based on the study of man and of men; one must know human nature, the condition and fate of societies in various periods and in different places; one must consult historians and travellers; one must see for oneself' (Sismondi 1803: i, XV). The atypical nature of his modus operandi explains better than any other factor the widespread aversion or indifference[7] he encountered in that specific sphere, and it also explains the greater sympathy with which other authors in his set were interpreted, setting out as they did to rationalize the phenomenon in more linear economic terms than his own: first and foremost Malthus' demo-economic arguments and Say's principle that founded a new conception of international relations (honed in the 2nd edition of the *Traité*) on the *loi des débouchés*.[8]

The failure to read Sismondi's work as a coherent whole has thus left us hostage to generalizations. On looking into the *Nouveaux Principes*, some people have thought they saw in it a Malthusian-type demographic line of argument to the effect that war was a factor for evening out economic unbalances (Silberner 1946: 14n), whereas Sismondi did not link population variations to variations in overall subsistence, but to those in each social class's income. In particular, there was a tendency to heed a single statement made in the work, the one bestowing on war the power to balance out overproduction:

> It seems that frightful calamities are called to the task of returning human societies to order, just as lightning, hail, and storms purify the air; as plague, war, and famine maintain equilibrium between coming generations and the food the earth can provide.
>
> (Sismondi 1827a: 503)

Others suggested instead that Sismondi was a pacifist, capable of waiving interventionism in the event of the state adopting a defensive strategy (Coulomb 2004).

The slow evolution of the 'economic perception' of war, a century and a half on from the Congress of Westphalia and the resulting peace treaties (1648), held out various interpretative models. The first 20 years of the nineteenth century, when the whole of Europe's political and social structures were subverted, saw an intensification of the debate on the way to fund war, on the impact of its funding, and on the changes in production to which war gave rise, no less than of the one on conflicts among states, both from the theoretical point of view and from that of government strategies, producing results that often differed greatly from one another.[9] However, the roots on which economic science had been able to draw hitherto formed just two major branches, which were more compatible with economic policy than with a theory systematically thought through. One was the wane in warmongering for mercantile ends,[10] which regarded war as an indispensable tool of might (Marchal 1931; Heckscher 1935), and the other the thinking of the French physiocrats and the liberals.

There was also a third major stance recurrent in the political thinking of the late Enlightenment and early Romanticism, to the effect that progress (*civilization*) would be capable of curbing – if not of eliminating – violence. For the sake of brevity – given that an in-depth examination of the topic exceeds our brief – we merely mention the fact that this stance subscribed to the doctrine of the peaceful development of international relations prompted by the great expansion in international trade. It was first formulated by Montesquieu (1748), who saw peace as the natural effect of trade (Pii 1998).[11] J. Mill subsequently adapted it to suit Napoleonic circumstances (1808), and a progressive philosophy of history was finally built on it by Benjamin Constant, a member of the Coppet Group and a close friend of Sismondi, arguing that peoples would acknowledge that trade brought greater advantages than war (Constant 1997 [1819]).

No one can fail to see how much this approach to international relations owes to both Enlightenment and liberal thinking. By offering competitive trade a change of tack enabling it to cast aside the prohibitive system, the optimism of economic liberalism had stylised a growth model alternative to the modern era's more traditional model of conquest and/or plunder and featuring incentives to trade of greater mutual satisfaction for the nations.[12] It would, however, be misleading to think in terms of an overwhelming pacifist attitude at the end of the eighteenth century, with a complete reversal of the mercantilist[13] tack, as the economic facts prove that it existed side by side with the long-standing legacy of said practices. What is more, the free-trade thesis itself envisaged an exception to the economic utility of international trade, when the country was being defended, with the introduction of a sanctions policy, and that meant that one advantage (*utility*) could be subordinated to a far greater one (*defence*).

The depoliticising limit lurking in the idyllic identification of free trade with universal pacifism was a very obvious element, above and beyond any rhetorical formula. If the typical form in which the tendency towards domination materialises is force, it may manifest itself as violence (war) or as coercion or the imposition of rules by the state (political deeds). This is what happened, under the pressure of embargo policies,[14] to the Republic of Geneva, which had already been stripped of its independence by annexation to France. Sismondi perceived the continental blockade (1807–1812) as an act of war and an irrational attack on the most undisputed free-trade certainties:

> "An enormous void is to be seen among the people", he wrote from Geneva in 1809, The number of marriages has declined alarmingly; there is a lack of farm labourers; no buyers are to be found for foodstuffs; the leases on the farms are being left to lapse, and work in the countryside is being abandoned; trade and manufacturing collapsed long ago; everything is running out, everything is ending, and yet, with all this wretchedness and all this depopulation, war is breaking out again from north to south.
>
> (Sismondi 1933: 289–290)

The end of the Napoleonic Wars did away with any vestige of belief in the automatic process whereby any possible war (*esprit de conquête*) would be foiled by the expansion of the free market (*esprit de commerce*). The line of reasoning focused rather on the war economy, on the voluntary and involuntary changes that the spread of war throughout Europe thrust upon the countries involved and marked their mutual relations. For instance, there was a tendency to place marked emphasis on the impact that exorbitant military spending made on the debt,[15] on the way the financial circuits operated, on the enormous demand for capital and on the rise in the interest rate.[16] Sismondi himself, who had already addressed the repercussions of the French revolutionary *assignats* in the *Essais* (Di Reda 1998), turned the sights of his invective onto war finance (*Du papier-monnaie* 1810), accusing governments of taking advantage of the public's trust. Emphasising the stability of the intrinsic value of currency, he warned governments against their habit of printing money to fund the public debt.

So it was not so much the long 'all-embracing' war that prompted a change of tack in the debate on wars among states, but rather the major economic and financial crisis that ensued, extending at least until the days of the Reform Bill, and throwing economic thinking's traditional, pre-revolutionary approaches into disarray. It was precisely this European crisis, the first in the modern era to be statistically appraised with an, albeit partial, series of data (Moreau 1824), that engendered the organic analysis of economic fluctuations: an in-depth study of economic activity's various phases decade by decade, dividing them into stages of *prosperity, crisis* and, lastly, *liquidation*, to be seen in financial crashes, bankruptcies and unemployment (Juglar 1862: 140). Post-War Britain already looked locked into this latter condition, weighed down as it was by its public debt and reduced to printing money, as reported by J.-B. Say, who was sufficiently alarmed to fear it would go bankrupt (see Forget 1999: 17). Reviewing Say's *De l'Angleterre et des Anglais* in France's official gazette, Sismondi contemptuously recounted Britain's administrative conduct, which had shamelessly impoverished the middle class: 'Behold the banker without whom the continent is not in a position to arm or to meet the cost of war!' (Sismondi 1815).

Whereas studies of the economic consequences of war and systemic crises predominated during the Restoration, the more traditional topic of 'economic warfare' was addressed by shifting the Enlightenment's long philosophical and political debate into satirical and moralistic mode, breaking free of the constraints its authority imposed with a liberating bound. *The Eclectic Review*, which lavished sarcasm on universal peace, pacifist associations, and the meek religious approach to war, was a glaring example. 'No: The Public must not be led away by the declamations of Jacobin orators, or the sentimental philanthropists', its self-made, anti-conformist publisher, Josiah Conder, asserted. 'Wars ever have been, and Wars ever will be. The business of empires cannot be carried on without them. A nation must have its arm of iron as well as its arm of gold' (Conder 1817: 2).

Flaunting scepticism as to the *philosophes*' good intentions and faulting the philanthropic line's lack of scientific foundations and the naivety of certain universalistic propositions were thus the hallmark of the ousting from a Garden of Eden situation, from the ethereal condition that had marked the watchwords of the Enlightenment, where peace was the purpose and outcome of the progress achieved by the human race or, to put it better, was the condition for the full respect of equality and natural rights. Chords of this tenor are struck in the early Sismondi (1803: i, 263) as well, when he brands the notions of 'universal peace', abolishing ignorance and barbarity worldwide, as voiced by the Abbé de Saint-Pierre, as ingenuous. According to some studies (Mitrany 1933: 33), this reaction highlighted the flimsiness and weakness of supranational political thinking, which – despite the combined efforts of the many liberal thinkers who addressed the moral and political issues inherent in international relations in the eighteenth century – had come up against the reality principle determined by constant war among the nations, whereas others (Ashworth 2003: 110–111) saw it as springing from governments' double moral standards, as manifest in the incompatibility between their domestic policies and those they pursued on their borders.

Post-Napoleonic Europe set the seal once and for all on the glaring rift between the theory and practice of the Enlightenment, torn as it was between the ideals of peace propounded by writers and philosophers – from Kantian non-interventionism to the Abbé de Saint-Pierre's scheme for perpetual peace – and the reality of war that had formed the constant backdrop to the century's events. However, for people who, like Sismondi, had recognised liberty in its truest and most valid terms in the eighteenth century, meaning in its relationship with historical, social, political and economic laws, that rift between the world of events and the world of values could not be bridged and, indeed, continued to make itself manifest to fluctuating degrees in its theoretical formulation.

Suffice it to consider that Sismondi regarded war as an art (*science militaire*) with its own rules and principles, and hence with its own theory and practice (Sismondi 1836: 2). There are two aspects to be stressed on this head. The first is the fact that he regarded the art of war as one of the social sciences, alongside education, religion and history, and as forming a pair with jurisprudence: one teaches society to defend the collective interest of the state against external threats, while the other teaches it to defend individual rights.

The second is that the reference to the art of war is part and parcel of the wide-ranging philosophical scheme of the Enlightenment, which included the science of war among the headings of its most representative undertaking, l'*Encyclopédie* (1757). Be that as it may, it is not so much the context of the encyclopaedia entry that is worth noting, but the content, the whole of which followed Grotius's *De jure belli et pacis* (1625), and which thus placed it firmly in the perspective of natural and political law. Although Grotius was not one of the contributors to Sismondi's intellectual grounding, he pointed the way to the formalisation of the more strictly legal disciplines (natural law, law of peoples) focusing on war and peace that consolidated over the eighteenth century. Smith had been unable to avoid taking on Grotius[17] and Hobbes[18] for the purpose of defining the state of war.

Grotius featured in Sismondi's library (Sofia 1983), alongside other writers associated, in the political scheme of the Enlightenment, with ideals of peace and cosmopolitanism, and, although they arrived at a consequent irenicism on grounds, to extents, and with results that often differ widely, they laid those rich foundations for Sismondi's thought that seem, instead, to have been lacking on the economic front, where they boil down to Smith and the lesser-known Nicolas-François Canard (Sismondi 1803: i, *passim*).

The range of authors who had addressed the political and legal theory of war and from whom Sismondi drew inspiration sets out from the topic's historiographic debut in Greek civilization (Thucydides), takes in Hume, continues to have a place in 'politics' as the art of dispute mediation in Hobbes and Montesquieu,[19] and extends to Rousseau. Sismondi grants a place in his personal pantheon to Geneva-born Rousseau as well (Paulet-Grandguillot 2012), who, in his *State of War*, had already pinpointed the philosophers' failure to supply a universally accepted political system for the sovereignty of states in the international context:

> I open the books on Right and on ethics; I listen to the professors and jurists; and, my mind full of their seductive doctrines [...] Thoroughly instructed as to my duties and my happiness, I close the book, step out of the lecture room, and look around me. I see wretched nations groaning beneath a yoke of iron. I see mankind ground down by a handful of oppressors. ... I see on every side the strong armed with the terrible powers of the Law against the weak.
>
> (Rousseau 1997: 162)

So Sismondi's attitude, with regard to 'war and the formation of the state' and 'war and society', falls within Rousseau's conceptual reference framework, whereby war is an intrinsically political phenomenon (see Williams 2014: 205). Albeit setting states one against the other, and putting peoples at loggerheads, the real purpose of war is more to destroy the body politic than to exterminate (Galice and Miqueu 2012: 38).

This long preamble enables us to introduce the topic of 'necessary' war, albeit with the negative repercussions that come about when the social contract is loosened, in Sismondi and that of the 'law of nations', as set out by Vattel (1995 [1758]), and of which Rousseau makes fairly frequent use. Sismondi's assertion that 'war is always a crime when it is not necessary'[20] is closely linked to another in which he states: 'In my eyes, setting out to alter the status of the East with weapons is a violation of international law. Friendly nations may intervene only with peaceful mediation'.[21] Political economy, a still recent science, was prepared – in Sismondi's interpretation – to stand comparison with other systems of thought, such as political philosophy and public law, whose various, and interrelated, lines of reasoning gravitate around 'foreign' relations'.[22] In this respect, they harked back to the thinking of the School of Salamanca, no less (Melé 1999), which – as the chief forerunner of economic analysis – had raised major questions concerning which law governed relations among sovereign states, which wars were legitimate, and the theories of contractualism regarding the right forms of government. In particular, the Enlightenment had highlighted a legal issue (Rousseau 2008 [1755–1761]) relating to state sovereignty's habit of undermining international law, and Smith himself had put forward observations on the fragility that aggressiveness in foreign policy created in the system of relations among states[23] and stigmatised the uncontrollable spending on the defence of the colonies.[24]

Sismondi regarded war primarily as a natural phenomenon: 'the calamities of war, either civil or foreign, are evils tied to our nature, much as floods and earthquakes are part of our living on this planet' (Sismondi 1991 [1827]: 147). It is nonetheless also a sovereign right that moulds government and production practice when it is exercised; indeed, a state defines itself by 'the right to obey its own laws alone, to govern with its own magistrates, to sign alliances, to make peace or war and, lastly, to administer its finances' (Sismondi 1832: i, 86). But what exactly did Sismondi mean by social evolution? Primitive man existed in an untamed state of universal war; before civilization (understood as a doctrine of tolerance) came, man was incessantly at war and had neither the time to work nor guarantees as to the proceeds that work would have brought him (Sismondi 1991 [1827]: 528). So, unlike the majority of the proponents of the modern theory of natural law, Sismondi did not regard peace as the human race's initial condition in society. What is more, as the overall condition of mankind was war, nor did the absence of hostility hold out a guarantee of peace.

Sismondi took a different line on the armed forces, which he depicted as a body integrated into society, the social fabric and the very concept of society. Society needed an army to keep the order established by the nation on the home front and to defend it on land and sea. So Sismondi regarded the troops as the nation's 'guardian' population: they did a job that was not material, not cumulative, but was nonetheless deserving of recompense; however, not being productive like labourers, their income had to be drawn not from the nation's capital, but from society's (see Sismondi (1991) [1827]: 121). Genovesi had taken a similar view, stating that 'this class of people may be referred to as the defenders of the state. It is clear that these people's keep is to be provided solely by the working classes, and chiefly by the producing classes' (Genovesi 1765: 122–123).

Under Smith's influence, Sismondi embarked on his discussion of the circulation of wealth among states, refuting mercantilist thinking[25] on international trade, first in his *Political Economy* (Sismondi 1825 [1830b]: 39), then in his *New Principles* (see Sismondi 1991 [1827]: 39–43), on account of the bans, reprisals, export bounties, restrictions and continual trade wars that it entailed. What he took into consideration was war's influence on the balance of trade and on government spending abroad. Its influence on the balance of trade was an extremely long-standing issue that took on a real diplomatic function in 1767 in Forbonnais' anti-physiocratic discourse, tending in the direction of legal despotism, as he linked it to the balance of powers. Starting out from the science of trade, Forbonnais had thus succeeded in outlining considerations on international relations and, more precisely, on the conditions for peace in Europe, as has been suggested by Demals and Hyard (2015).

Sismondi addressed the balance issue for the first time in his *Richesse commerciale*, which was specifically directed at France and set out to maintain Geneva's trade, which the statist constraints imposed under imperial economic policy were jeopardising. The work may indeed have been a theoretical treatise serving to describe the flows and funds whereby commercial wealth was built up, but it voiced the institutional and administrative interests of the Genevan community – oppressed as it was by the French Empire's protectionist system – that Sismondi was officially representing at the Chamber of Commerce. French economic policy decisions had not only enfeebled international trade and stepped up the demands made by the major powers' public debt, but had also abruptly altered a whole trading civilization, that multinational business network representing specific economic interests with which Sismondi had dealings as secretary of the Geneva Chamber of Commerce. He thus argued that a strong export trade in goods brought no advantage in wartime, as the profits were kept abroad to fund the armed forces or to support the allied powers (see Sismondi 1803: i, 223). This line of argument, which was not new, might have been drawn from Montesquieu, who addressed modern states' dynamics of war and conquest and their sterile victories in the *Réflexions sur la monarchie universelle en Europe* (ca. 1734):

> When a Monarch sends an Army into enemy country, he sends at the same time a part of his treasury so that the army can subsist; he enriches the country he has begun to conquer, and quite often he puts it in a position to drive him out.
>
> (Minuti 2015: 89)

War – Sismondi continued – not only did not buoy up the trade balance, but constituted a sacrifice for the country involved in it. Be that as it might, as *raison d'état* came into play, it was not the economist's place to pronounce on the utility of war, but the ruler's.

The passage from the *Richesse commerciale* that we have just considered, with its important chapter on the 'Balance des importations et exportations', moves us on to the different views on production and its outlets at the beginning of the nineteenth century. The controversy surrounding overproduction, which had its roots in Say's *Traité*, was settled between 1819 and 1827. Although this is not the place to go into Torrens' and McCulloch's positions, which are well known, taking in the line of argument advanced by the Genevan (Sismondi 1824) and Say in the *Revue Encyclopédique* (Steiner 2003), to which they both contributed regularly, it is worth pointing out that the dispute was one of the first analyses of economic crises. Sismondi's considerations (1820), which brought the concepts of production, distribution and consumption into play, thus still falling within the moral category that marked the criteria of political economy in its infancy, as is borne out by the work of Smith (1759), undoubtedly sprang from the crisis in Europe's production and financial system: due to the slump in the farming industry, the conversion of the war economy post-1815 – when the troops' return home made for an influx of manpower to be employed – and the tremendous debts the powers had run up. To put it in a nutshell, Sismondi voiced the fear that the pursuit of economic domination among the states would foster the most cut-throat brands of competition and that both the exploitation of labour and 'aggressive' (warlike) market conquest behaviour would prove decisive in achieving success.

The initial phase of depression, which followed the wars, the international strain over the continental blockade, and the Restoration, saw the rise of the static concept of capitalism that, as is well known, was to become the butt of Sismondi's economic writings from then on. His observations on the workings of the international economy (Bientinesi 2011), in the aftermath of the Napoleonic Wars, identified in Britain, the only country showing a capitalistic form of development, the results of an overproduction crisis due to the enlargement of production capacity during the war, in excess of the capacity sufficient to meet the needs of the population in peacetime (Parguez 1973; Saint Marc 1976). Examining the reasons for the growth achieved by British trade and goods manufacturing during the war, Say (1815) pieced together a detailed scenario dominated by the dealings of the European speculators, who not only bought goods in Britain, but procured the money for paying for them from the same nation, and cheaply so.

This wide range of models explaining the devastating scope and the genesis of the British post-war crisis thus includes the interpretation put forward by Sismondi in his most ambitious work of economic synthesis, his *Political Economy*. The economist identified the direct cause of the crisis in under-consumption on the part of the working class, whose purchasing power was insufficient to take up the nation's annual output.[26] However, one factor will be obvious to anyone who dwells on the pages he devoted, in 1817, to this first incisive account of the British crisis, which he attributed to the disastrous direction taken by competitive capitalism. In his desire to argue that general market saturation crises of the type he was describing were not only possible, but were also inevitable periodic phenomena bound up with the stage reached by capitalistic development, Sismondi removed them from the context of war and its consequences, both in general terms, as phenomena, and in terms of immediate current affairs.[27] Paradoxically, however, it was Ricardo, the man most faulted for setting out from abstract principles[28] when discussing economics, who gave a more incisive account of the phenomenon that same year by defining his formula regarding the link between currency and foreign trade in terms of the comparative cost principle, thus entering into irreversible collision with Sismondi:

> The commencement of war after a long peace, or of peace after a long war, generally produces considerable distress in trade. [...] It must be remembered too that the retrograde condition is always an unnatural state of society.
>
> (Ricardo 1817: 365, 367)

We have observed that Sismondi wanted to create a cause and effect link neither between economic imbalances and wars nor between the restoring of peace and countries' return to prosperity; albeit indisputable, the circumstance would, indeed, weaken his theoretical edifice blaming capitalism as such for the phenomenon of recurrent, hence systemic crises. The philosophical inspiration drawn from history on which this approach is based may help understand it.

In the explanation set out by Sismondi, the European continent's political conditions had suffered an irreparable upheaval in the sixteenth century, as a result of the wars attributable to Charles V. The hallmark of that period in history lay in the process of decline that could be glimpsed in it. He appraised the positive political and territorial situation that had preceded that historical watershed in institutional terms, citing the self-government practised by the Italian republics and the European cities that enjoyed municipal privileges.

The outstanding merit that Sismondi attributed to the 'republics' lay in their freedom, in the sense of obedience to the laws that each territorial entity had laid down for itself. This consideration is strengthened by the comparison between free governments (which increased in population, knowledge, virtue and wealth) and the hereditary ones, into which the remainder of Europe was divided. The latter, too, increased in wealth, but through conquest.

Sismondi believed that a redistribution of wealth, a task political economy was called upon to perform, was to be hoped for only where freedom reigned. So if freedom was the crucial condition for government to be fair in its work of creating the conditions for the people's prosperity, it had to be achieved at any price, even through war. Even Switzerland, his little native country, could not consider itself immune from wars until it had ensured its liberal institutions' security. Following this line of reasoning, Sismondi preferred the use of the force that sprang from a revolution to evolution when the time came to demand Italy's freedom from the oppression thrust upon it by the Restoration – after the failure of the 1831 revolts – and did not hesitate to consider it a rightful people's uprising in a nation split between patriots and absolutists (see Sismondi 1832: i, 23).[29]

As noted above, it would be a mistake to think it possible to identify Sismondi's thinking on war with one uniform 'point of view' or a 'position' adopted once and for all. The Genevan economist perceived a yawning gap between the theory advanced by legal thinking and the trading nations' actual practice, not least because his contribution on the power organization model was decisive inasmuch as it was heir to the enormous effort to bring together the whole body of previous knowledge of political law. The rent – between the international community ideals propounded by the eighteenth century philosophers and the raw reality of the mercantile conduct of war that continued to accompany the events of his day almost incessantly – produced a split in the logic of Sismondi's analysis between his economic and historical writings and those on current affairs. Hence his work's undoubted lure, and also the reader's equally undoubted difficulty in setting out on the right road, opting for a single entry point, or rather, a single work on which to lay a single interpretative foundation. There is, however, no doubt that, out of dismay at the measures ordered under the continental blockade, he began during the Empire years to modify the attitude to war set out in his first economic work coming out fully in favour of free trade. It is the most deplorable form of government (despotism) there that prevents peace, in the sense of the mutual acknowledgement of utility among peoples, from setting in by fettering the capitalists' freedom of action (1803: i, 263). An initial shift in his approach came about at the end of the Napoleonic era, when 'Europe needs peace' (Sismondi 1814a: 6). Sismondi admitted that, the greater governments' awareness of pecuniary values, the greater their attachment to their craving for power and he subordinated the importance of Europe's balance of payments to its political balance (Sismondi 1814b: 36). This meant that, if the accumulation of wealth was not a nation's chief goal, it had to be sacrificed to everything that did not ensure a nation's security and safety. After Vienna, he was to embark on a line of reasoning, in the first edition of the *Nouveaux Principes* (1819), in which he urged that a country should have an autonomous defence sector and sovereignty over food supplies.

Still hoping that the peoples of Europe would win their independence, something the constitutional moves in Spain and the Kingdom of the Two Sicilies (1820–1821) had failed to achieve, Sismondi adopted an interventionist approach. He saw the solution for Italy as lying in a strong executive power that would rearm it against Holy Alliance oppression. Might (in the form of an army for waging war abroad and a national guard for the home front) thus had to take priority over the dream of all individual rights being guaranteed, a good legal system and good municipal institutions (Sismondi 1935: 479). This approach, moreover, went hand in hand with his aspiration to come up with a solution to wars based on an appraisal both of the interests at stake among the states and of the various concurrent international laws, which he saw as the indispensable foundation for a fair verdict (Sismondi 1830a).

So what lives on in his thinking is the scepticism with which he eyed an utterly irenicist view of society and his attempt to identify restraints on wealth accumulation wars among nations. Despite its brutality, the French Revolution, he asserted, led, via the confiscation and sale of the national assets, to the formation of a new class, that of the 'smallholders', who were averse to violence (Sismondi 1991 [1827]). These smallholders, who were good citizens in peacetime, were valiant soldiers in wartime, he wrote: they did not see their homeland as an abstract idea; in the event of it being threatened from outside, they saw their own fields under threat as well. This scheme of things, in which a society made up of small owners was in itself the deterrent to war, inevitably laid him open to rebuttals and criticisms that underlined the limited, flimsy prospects its patriarchal system enjoyed, with the major farming estates carved up into smallholdings (Ressi 1820: 68–69).[30] Indeed, how could Sismondi's 'patriarchal' nation sustain a war against Europe's major seafaring and war-waging nations if it came under threat?

Notes

1 My thanks to Francesca Sofia and Maria P. Casalena for their elucidatory and valuable comments on this essay. Last, by no means least, the advisor Luca Michelini is gratefully acknowledged.
2 Some scholars have considered the European war, waged between 1792 and 1815, the 'first total war' on account of its perversity; see Blanning (1986), Bell 2007), Rapport (2013). The 'first total war' concept is explained in historical terms by the mass conscription of 1793 (*Décret de la Convention Nationale du 23 Août 1793, l'an seconde de la république Françoise une et indivisible*), which triggered the militarisation of civil society with a general mobilisation to ward off invasions on France's borders and avert a civil war within it.
3 Louvois, Louis XIV's war minister and an opponent of Colbert, wrote in his political testament: 'There is an alliance between war and trade [...]. They are two pillars that, together, hold up the edifice of the state, and one cannot fall without toppling the other' (Louvois, 1695: 414).
4 For instance, when discussing the long-drawn-out war between Turkey and Greece, Sismondi expatiates on militias, armies and likely post-war European geopolitical scenarios, but the chief nucleus of his line of argument is political and concerns nations' self-determination and right to self-government as opposed to tyranny; see Sismondi (1825), (1827a), (1827b), (1829); Sofia (2013), Barau (2015). With regard to the Algiers expedition, Sismondi asserts that the hegemonic colonising countries must in any case respect the law of the peoples they bring into subjection. The work is an appeal to the French Government to show a libertarian trait marking it out from British imperialism; see Sismondi (1830a). See Bertholet (2015) on violence in Sismondi's writings as a 'historian.'
5 'Civil wars have at least this advantage: they force leaders to try to please the people, to endeavour to earn a love that gives them strength'; Sismondi (1832, I: 34–35).
6 Although historians' attention focused traditionally on conventional warfare, waged by regular forces, Sismondi cast an attentive eye on the brutal European wars of religion and, albeit not underrating the military aspect of sectarian persecution, also took other battlefields for those 'ideological' clashes into consideration, such as those on which the church, the family and education were at work.
7 Noah's study (2001) addresses the phenomenon of war in terms of economic thought up to the present day, but completely ignores Sismondi's contribution in his treatment of it.
8 Say presents said law in Chapter 22 of the first edition of the *Traité* (1803), which is entitled 'Des debouches', and in Chapter 15, under the same heading, in subsequent editions of the work.

9 Demographic aspects are intrinsically bound up with those of war in Malthus's work (see Noah 2001: 140–141); relationships between economic progress and war emerge in Mill, while McCulloch states his views on freedom of trade and the pacific mission of political economy, whereas Ricardo focuses on the economic and financial side of international conflicts. Say, however, formulates the newest solution to the problem, drawing it from his fundamental conception of trade, the *loi des débouchés*.

10 Colbert wrote in a report to Louis XIV on 22 October 1664: 'All the occupations must be cut down to those that can be of use, as are farming, trade, and warfare on land and on sea. If Your Majesty can manage to confine the whole of his population to these four occupations, it may be said that he is the lord of the world' (Clément 1869: 3).

11 It was subsequently to fall to a member of the Coppet Group, Benjamin Constant, to hold out a systematic representation, built on a progressive philosophy of history, of the age of peace, in which the nations would acknowledge that trade brought greater advantages than war (Constant 1997 [1819]).

12 'The overall purpose of a state is obviously to acquire all the means of might available to it, meaning to strike the most precise balance between its territorial output and the extent of its rule and between its territorial output and its active population' (Forbonnais 1767: i, 56).

13 See the paper by A. Alcouffe and F. Coulomb, 'Pacifism of the French liberals in the late 19th and early 20th centuries' presented at the 18th ESHET Conference, Lausanne, 2014, in this connection.

14 Examined by several scholars, commencing with Heckscher's ground-breaking exploration (1964) [1922] and then, with differing results, by Crouzet (1987), Magnusson (1994) and, more recently, Cardoso (2013) and Stern-Wennerlind (2014).

15 Smith (1776) [1904]: Book II, chapter III, para. 4.

16 When at war, indeed, a state demanded extraordinary capital and had to be capable of procuring money with the least possible loss. It was common practice for states to build up monetary reserves, both with a view to conquests and for defence purposes; this practice of setting funds aside in peacetime had also met with the favour of Hume (*Of Public Credit*, 1752), who had stubbornly decried the rise in the public debt in wartime; see Hume (1987: 349–365).

17 Smith (1790) [1759]: Part VII, Section IV, chapter IV, para. 37.

18 Smith (1790) [1759]: Part VII, Section III, chapter II, para. 8.

19 Sismondi had discussed *L'Esprit des lois* (1748), examining the condition of the *peuples libres* in his *Etudes des sciences sociales*.

20 Letter to Bianca Milesi Mojon dated 25/10/1840 (Royal Archives, The Hague, G16-A. 443/61).

21 Letter to Bianca Milesi Mojon dated 17/10/1840 (Royal Archives, The Hague, G16-A. 443/60).

22 This was an expression recently coined by Bentham (1780), by which he meant the 'principles of legislation in matters betwixt nation and nation' (see Bentham 1823 [1789]: i, X).

23 'In war and negotiation, therefore, the laws of justice are very seldom observed. Truth and fair dealing are almost totally disregarded. Treaties are violated; and the violation, if some advantage is gained by it, sheds scarce any dishonour upon the violator. (…). In war, not only what are called the laws of nations, are frequently violated, without bringing (among his own fellow-citizens, whose judgments he only regards) any considerable dishonour upon the violator; but those laws themselves are, the greater part of them, laid down with very little regard to the plainest and most obvious rules of justice.' Smith (1790) [1759]: Part III, chapter III, para. 84.

24 Smith argued that the mother country's interference with the colonies' economy inhibited the latter's economic development, without the mother country gaining anything, except in terms of national glory. The *Wealth of Nations* closes with this very observation: 'It is surely time that Great Britain should free herself from the expense

of defending those provinces in time of war, and of supporting any part of their civil or military establishments in time of peace, and endeavour to accommodate her future views and designs to the real mediocrity of her circumstances' (Smith 1776 [1904]: Book II, chapter III, para. 92).

25 'A large sect enjoying political accreditation' (Sismondi 1803: 189–190).

26 The 'change of course' in Sismondi's economic thinking, embodied in the 'Political Economy' entry, which came out in January 1825, in Thomas Carlyle's English translation, in the *Edinburgh Encyclopædia* edited by David Brewster, who had commissioned it. The original text in French, *Économie politique*, has now been reprinted (Sismondi 2016 [1817]). The composition of the encyclopaedia entry may be dated precisely from the unpublished letter in English that David Brewster wrote (from Venlaw by Peebles) to Sismondi (in Geneva) on 14 July 1817 (Sezione di Archivio di Stato di Pescia, Fondo Sismondi 25.124). This new document completes the episode previously analysed (see Gislain 2013).

27 The fact that he does not link war to economic crises is a detail that has been noted (see Coulomb (2004: 109), and it is all the more surprising considering Sismondi's modus operandi.

28 'Political economy, in order to be really useful, must not teach […] what *necessarily has* to happen, but show how what really happens is the consequence of another real event' (Say 1819: lxv).

29 See also Casalena 2015.

30 See also Sofia 2016.

References

Ashworth, L.M. (2003) 'The Limits of Enlightenment: Inter-State Relations in Eighteenth Century Political Thought', *Studies on Voltaire and the Eighteenth Century*, 9, 110–140.

Barau, D. (2015) 'Penser dans l'actualité: Sismondi à propos de la guerre d'indépendance de la Grèce', in Descendre, R. and Fournel, J.-L. (dir.), *Langages, politique, histoire. Avec Jean-Claude Zancarini*, Lyon, Ens Éditions, available on http://books.openedition.org/enseditions/5365.

Bell, D.A. (2007) *The First Total War: Napoleon's Europe and the Birth of Warfare as We Know It*, Houghton Mifflin, Boston, MA.

Bentham, J. (1823) [1789] *An Introduction to the Principles of Morals and Legislation*. A new edition, corrected by the author, W. Pickering, London, 2 v.

Bertholet, M. (2015) 'Anarchic violence or liberal violence? The Italian Middle Ages at the turn of the Enlightenment: From Muratori and Voltaire to Sismondi', *Dix-Huitieme Siecle*, 47(1), 475–500.

Bientinesi, F. (2011) 'Notes on Sismondi and (dis)Equilibria in International Trade', *Il pensiero economico italiano*, 19(2), 93–104.

Blanning, T.C.W. (1986) *The Origins of the French Revolutionary Wars*, Longman, London.

Cardoso, J.L. (2013) 'Lifting the Continental Blockade: Britain, Portugal and Brazilian Trade in the Global Context of the Napoleonic Wars', in Coppolaro, L. and McKenzie, F. (eds.) *A Global History of Trade and Conflict since 1500*, Palgrave Macmillan, Basingstoke, 87–104.

Casalena, M.P. (2015) 'Liberté, souveraineté et décadence dans l'historiographie de Sismondi', *Annali Sismondi*, 1(1), 47–66 (available on http://annalisismondi.unibo.it/about).

Clément, P. (1869) *Lettres, instructions et mémoires de Colbert, publiés d'après les ordres de l'Empereur*, t. VI, Imprimerie Impériale, Paris.

Conder, J. (1817) 'Art. I. 1. A Solemn Review of the Custom of War', *The Eclectic Review*, 7 (January), 1–24.

Condillac, E.B. (1997) [1776] *Commerce and Government Considered in Their Mutual Relationship*, translated by S. Eltis, Edward Elgar, Cheltenham.

Constant, B. (1997) [1819] 'De la Liberté des anciens comparée à celle des modernes', in *Écrits politiques*, ed. by M. Gauchet, Gallimard, Paris, 589–619.

Coulomb, F. (2004) *Economic Theories of Peace and War*, Routledge, London; New York.

Crouzet, F. (1964) 'Wars, Blockade, and Economic Change in Europe, 1792–1815', *Journal of Economic History*, 24, 567–588.

— (1987) *L'économie britannique et le blocus continental*, 2nd ed., Economica, Paris.

Demals, T. and Hyard, A. (2015) 'Forbonnais, the Two Balances and the Economistes', *The European Journal of the History of Economic Thought*, 22(3), 445–472.

Di Reda, R. (1998) *Libertà e scienza del governo in Sismondi*, vol. II. *J.C.L. Sismondi, Essais sur les constitutions des peuples libres*, Roma, Jouvence.

Forbonnais, F. (1767) *Principes et observations œconomiques*, Marc Michel Rey, Amsterdam.

Forget, E.L. (1999) *The Social Economics of Jean-Baptiste Say: Markets and Virtue*, Routledge, New York.

Galice, G. and Miqueu, C. (2012) *Penser la République, la guerre et la paix sur les traces de Jean-Jacques Rousseau*, Slatkine, Genève.

Genovesi, A. (1765) *Delle lezioni di commercio, ossia d'economia civile*, Fratelli Simone, Napoli.

Gislain, J.J. (2013) 'La conversion de Sismondi', *Cahiers d'Économie Politique*, 64(1), 111–134.

Heckscher, E.F. (1935) *Mercantilism*, Allen and Unwin, London, 2 v.

Heckscher, E.F. (1964) [1922] *The Continental System: An Economic Interpretation*, Peter Smith, Gloucester, MA.

Hume, D. (1987) *Essays Moral, Political, and Literary*, ed. by E.F. Miller, revised edition, Liberty Classics, Indianapolis, IN.

Juglar, C. (1862) *Des crises commerciales et de leur retour périodique en France, en Angleterre et aux États-Unis,* Guillaumin et C.ie, Paris.

Louvois, F.-M. (1695) *Testament politique*, Le Politique, Cologne.

Magnusson, L. (1994) *Mercantilism: The Shaping of an Economic Language*, Routledge, London and New York.

Marchal, A. (1931) *La conception de l'économie nationale et des rapports internationaux chez les mercantilistes français*, Impr. Georges Thomas, Nancy.

Melé, D. (1999) 'Early Business Ethics in Spain: The Salamanca School, 1526–1614', *Journal of Business Ethics*, 22(3), 175–189.

Moreau, C. (1824) *State of the Trade of Great Britain with All Parts of the World … from the Year 1697 to 1822 …; État du commerce de la Grande-Bretagne avec toutes les parties du monde …*, Treuttel and Würtz, London.

Minuti, R. (2015) *Una geografia politica della diversità. Studi su Montesquieu*, Liguori Editore, Napoli.

Mitrany, D. (1933) *The Progress of International Government*, Allen & Unwin, London.

Montesquieu, C.-L. de Secondat de (1748) *De l'esprit des loix*, Barrillot et Fils, Genève.

Noah, H.-M. (2001) 'De la problématique de la guerre dans la pensée économique', *Canadian Journal of Development Studies*, 22(1), 135–164.

Parguez, A. (1973) 'Sismondi et la théorie du déséquilibre macro-économique', *Revue économique*, 24(5), 837–866.

Paulet-Grandguillot, E. (2012) 'Entre réfutation et inspiration: Sismondi lecteur de Rousseau', in *Jean-Jacques Rousseau devant Coppet*, sous la direction de F. Lotterie et G. Poisson, Slatkine, Genève, 151–202.

Pii, E. (1998) 'Montesquieu e l''esprit de commerce'', in D. Felice (ed. by), *Leggere l'Esprit des lois'. Stato, società e storia nel pensiero di Montesquieu*, Liguori, Napoli, 165–201.

Rapport, M. (2013) *The Napoleonic Wars: A Very Short Introduction*, Oxford, Oxford University Press.

Ressi, A. (1820) 'Osservazioni sull'Opera del Signor L.C.L. Simonde de Sismondi, Nuovi Principj di Economia Politica, ossia della ricchezza nei suoi rapporti con la popolazione, Parigi 1819', in Id., *Dell'economia della specie umana*, v. 4, Stamperia e Libreria di Pietro successore di Bolzani, Pavia, 47–114.

Ricardo, D. (1817) *On the Principles of Political Economy, and Taxation*, John Murray, London.

— (1997) *The Social Contract and Other Later Political Writings*, 5th ed., Gourevitch, Cambridge University Press, Cambridge.

Rousseau, J.J. (2008) [1755–1761] *Principes du droit de la guerre. Écrits sur la paix perpétuelle*, J. Vrin, Paris.

Saint Marc, M. (1976) 'Sismondi et les déséquilibres économiques', in *Histoire, socialisme et critique de l'économie politique*, Hors séries, 21, *Economies et sociétés*, 10(6), 1217–1230.

Say, J.-B. (1803) *Traité d'économie politique*, 1st ed., Déterville, Paris, 2 v.

— (1815) *De L'Angleterre et des Anglais*, Arthus Bertrand, Paris.

— (1819) *Traité d'économie politique*, 4th ed., Déterville, Paris, 2 v.

Silberner, E. (1946) *The Problem of War in Nineteenth Century Economic Thought*, Princeton, NJ, Princeton University Press.

Sismondi, J.C.L. (1803) *De la Richesse commerciale ou Principes d'économie politique appliqués à la Législation du Commerce*, J.J. Paschoud, Genève, 2 v.

— (1810) 'Du papier-monnaie et des moyens de le supprimer', *Pallas*, 2(1), 3–66.

— (1814a) *Considérations sur Genève dans ses rapports avec l'Angleterre*, John Murray, Londres.

— (1814b) *De la philosophie de l'histoire*, John Murray, Londres.

— (1815) 'De l'Angleterre et des Anglais', *Journal Général de France*, 5 May, 3–4.

— (1820) 'Examen de cette question: le pouvoir de consommer s'accroît-il dans la société avec le pouvoir de produire?', *Annales de législation et de jurisprudence*, 1, 111–144.

— (1824) 'Sur la balance des consommations avec les productions', *Revue encyclopédique*, 22, 264–298.

— (1825) 'Considérations sur la guerre actuelle des Grecs et sur ses historiens', *Revue encyclopédique*, 26, 382–398, 703–716; 27, 61–80.

— (1827a) 'De l'intervention des peuples en faveur de la Grèce', *Revue encyclopédique*, 33, 655–669.

— (1827b) 'De la Grèce au commencement de 1827', *Revue encyclopédique*, 34, 305–319.

— (1829) 'Conséquences que l'on peut désirer ou craindre pour la civilisation, de la guerre des Russes dans le Levant', *Revue encyclopédique*, 41, 5–31.

— (1830a) 'De l'expédition contre Alger', *Revue encyclopédique*, 46, 273–296.

— (1830b) 'Political Economy', *Edinburgh Encyclopædia*, conducted by D. Brewster, 3rd ed., vol. 17, W. Blackwood, Edinburgh, 37–80.

— (1832) *Histoire de la renaissance de la liberté en Italie, de ses progrès, de sa décadence et de sa chute*, Treuttel et Würtz, Paris, 2 v.

— (1933) *Epistolario*, I. *1799–1814*, ed. by C. Pellegrini, La Nuova Italia, Firenze.

— (1935) *Epistolario*, II. *1814–1823*, ed. by C. Pellegrini, La Nuova Italia, Firenze.

— (1836) *Etudes sur les sciences sociales*, t. I. *Etudes sur les constitutions des peuples libres*, Treuttel et Würtz, Paris.

— (1991) [1827] *New Principles of Political Economy of Wealth in Its Relation to Population*, transl. and annotated by R. Hyse; with a foreword by R. Heilbroner, Transaction Publishers, New Brunswick and London.

— (2016) [1817] 'Économie politique', in Bridel, P., Dal Degan, F. and Eyguesier, N. (eds.) *Œuvres économiques complètes*, IV. *Écrits d'économie politique, 1816–1842*, Economica, Paris, 35–153.

Smith, A. (1790) [1759] *The Theory of Moral Sentiments*, A. Millar, London, 2 v.

— (1904) [1776] *An Inquiry into the Nature and Causes of the Wealth of Nations*, ed. by E. Cannan, 5th edition, Methuen & Co., London, 2 v.

Sofia F. (1983) *Una biblioteca ginevrina del Settecento: i libri del giovane Sismondi*, Edizioni dell'Ateneo & Bizzarri, Roma.

— (2013) 'Addition aux œuvres de Sismondi', in Kapossy, B. and Bridel, P. (dir. by) *Républicanisme moderne et libéralisme critique. Modern Republicanism and Critical Liberalism*, Slatkine, Genève, 207–225.

— (2016) 'Ressi Adeodato', in *Dizionario Biografico degli Italiani*, Istituto dell'Enciclopedia Italiana Treccani, Roma, forthcoming.

Steiner, P. (2003) 'Say, les idéologues et le Groupe de Coppet. La société industrielle comme système politique', *Revue Française d'Histoire des Idées Politiques*, 18(2), 331–353.

Stern, P.J. and Wennerlind, C. (eds.) (2014) *Mercantilism Reimagined. Political Economy in Early Modern Britain and Its Empire*, Oxford University Press, New York.

Vattel, E. de (1995) [1758] *Le Droit des Gens, ou Principes de la loi naturelle, appliqués à la conduite et aux affaires des nations et des souverains*, with an introduction by A. de Lapradelle, W.S. Hein, Buffalo, N.Y., 3 v.

Williams, D.L. (2014) *Rousseau's* Social Contract: *An Introduction*, Cambridge University Press, Cambridge.

9 How to Pay for the War

Military Spending and War Funding in Italian Economic Thought (1890–1918)

Rosario Patalano

Introduction

This essay examines Italian Economic thought regarding military spending and war finance between the end of colonial expansion and the end of the World War I.

In the last decades of the nineteenth century, most Italian economists held anti-militarist opinions. In particular, the *Giornale degli Economisti* proposed a reorganization of the national army in the direction of reducing costs and inefficiencies, acquiring a central role for liberal and democratic political components unfavourable to rearmament and colonial expansion. The defeat at Adua (1896) marked the peak of militant anti-militarism among Italian economists. This anti-militarist front was broken only at beginning of the twentieth century, when the colonial problem came to the fore in the context of economic expansion, under Giolitti's governments. In this new political context (concluded with the Italian conquest of Libya, in 1911), military spending was utilized to support the growth of national industry, and public opinion, motivated by nationalist groups, began to show consensus on colonial expansion. Italian economists focused attention on the colonial economy and the financial means required for the war effort. The experience of the Libyan colonial war was at the basis of Federico Flora's essay on war finance, the first systematic treatise on this topic published in Italy (Flora, 1912). Flora proposed a pragmatic view of the problem of war finance, in contrast with 'Smithian dogmatism', predominant among Italian economists. The experience of World War I confirmed Flora's opinion that modern conflicts could be subsidized only with great expansion of the public debt, in the form of loan and paper-money circulation. However, most economists proposed again, during and after the war, Smithian dogmatism as the best financial policy (Einaudi, 1914; Pantaleoni, 1916).

The 1890s: militant antimilitarism and military efficiency

Italy's adhesion to the Triple Alliance was prompted by the need to seek defence against the anti-Italian hostility of the French Third Republic, and indeed by a historical left hankering after the role of a great power and colonial expansion. As a result, the Italian government was driven to rearm and to build up the country's armed forces (see Figure 9.1) (Rochat and Massobrio 1978: 86–96).

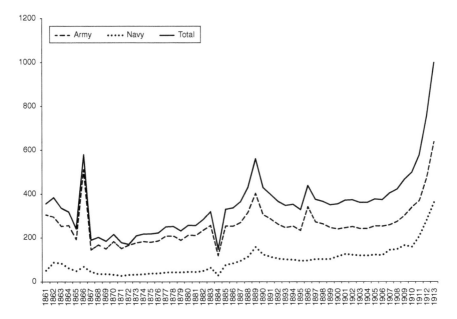

Figure 9.1 Military spending in Italy (1861–1913).

Source: Our elaboration on data from Ragioneria Generale dello Stato and Rochat-Massobrio (1978): 67–68

The ideas of the generation of economists who had been directly involved in the vicissitudes of the Risorgimento and had had first-hand experience of the fight for national unity were enshrined in Gerolamo Boccardo's *Dizionario della Economia Politica e del Commercio* (Boccardo, 1857), containing a number of entries dedicated to the *Political economy of war*, with 'general economic considerations on this great social issue' (Boccardo 1857 vol. II: 417).

Boccardo himself addressed the particular topic of military expenditure in the entry *Eserciti Stanziali* (Standing Armies) (Boccardo 1857 vol. II: 137–147), clearly showing the influence of Gustave de Molinari and the French liberal school (Michel Chevalier and Frédéric Bastiat) (Silberner 1957: 94).

While not taking a distinctly antimilitarist stance, Boccardo argued in favour of an army reduced to the bare essentials (Boccardo 1857 vol. II: 139) and based on an efficient core around which to aggregate territorial militias, following the example of countries like Switzerland, Sweden and, above all, Prussia with its *Landwher* (Boccardo 1857 vol. II: 145–146). It was a preference that reflected the waning warlike spirit amongst the populations, seen as an inevitable effect of technological development (Boccardo 1857 vol. II: 140).

Boccardo's proposal for reform, favouring the idea of the armed nation, was in essence taken up again in the 1890s, when Italian economic culture showed a decidedly antimilitarist orientation, deploring the increase in military expenditure and the waste it involved. In particular, the *Giornale degli Economisti* became a reference point for the liberal and democratic components who were opposed to the policy of rearmament and colonial expansion represented at the highest level by Francesco Crispi.

Support for this position lay in the state of economic crisis, which led to the unsustainability of military expenditure financed with the public debt and increasingly heavy taxation, weighing mostly on the poorer classes. In this state of affairs the antimilitarist positions found wide consensus in public opinion, no longer enchanted by Risorgimento rhetoric.

Maffeo Pantaleoni, Vilfredo Pareto and Antonio De Viti De Marco were in the front line in this battle against military expenditure, calling for a reduction in the interest of containing public spending, which in turn was seen as a first step towards tackling the economic depression (Cardini 1981: 103–104). However, the journal did not limit itself to criticism but went on to advance proposals, in particular with a view to reorganising the army.

The basic points of the proposal for reform advanced by the *Giornale degli Economisti* were presented by Captain Tito Molinari (under the pseudonym of Tiberio Squilletta) between September and October 1892.

The idea of the *armed nation* was identified with the plan for reorganisation of the army which could satisfy the needs of national defence at the minimum cost (Squilletta 1892a: 187).

The choice was presented as inevitable given the financial burden of maintaining the permanent Armed Forces. According to the data provided by the author himself, in the decade 1880–1890 the great powers as a whole channelled about a third of their revenues (28%) into military expenditure (see Figure 9.2). This burden proved all the heavier on taking into account the interest on the public debt, resulting from the resort to loans necessitated by the wars previously waged (Squilletta 1892a: 196).

To avoid such financial burdens, the need was to reduce standing armies drastically, favouring recruitment on a regional basis with a view to defence,

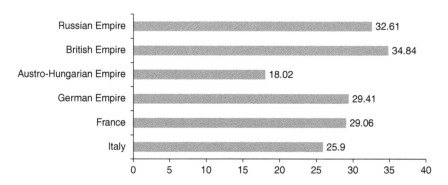

Figure 9.2 Percentage of national revenue employed in military spending (1880–1890).
Source: Our elaboration on data from Squilletta (1892a): 190.

and not aggression (Squilletta 1892a: 195; Squilletta 1892b: 352–375; Squilletta 1892c: 430–473; Molinari 1894).

This line of reform was widely endorsed by the productive middle classes in the last decade of the nineteenth century. And much the same line was taken by the industrialist Giuseppe Colombo, a member of Parliament and Minister of Finance in the Di Rudinì government, in contrast with the Minister of War, Luigi Perroux, who proposed only a slight containment of expenditure, confirming the organisation of the army emerging from the Ricotti reform[1] (Cardini 1981: 106–108).

Generalised resort to small professional armies (superseding the model of the armed nation still to some extent adopted by Prussia–Germany) corresponded to the idea of modern war as conflict limited in space and time, conducted with efficient use of resources and settled with the decisive battle. This idea of short, limited war harked back to a very great extent to the experience of the last few European conflicts (from the Crimean War to the Franco-Prussian War) and the campaigns for colonial conquest, ignoring the example of the American Civil War, which represented the first case of total and long-lasting war with an enormous cost in terms of men and means (Preston and Wise, 1970). Experience of the three major conflicts in the 20 years prior to the Great War (the Spanish-American War, the Russian-Japanese war and the Boer War) would bear out the idea of the short war conducted with efficient use of men and means. At the same time, there began to emerge the central role of naval power, which was increasingly bearing the brunt for wars waged on fronts distant from the national borders. Again, this 'maritime' aspect of modern warfare reinforced the idea that hegemony was to be achieved primarily at the level of technological efficiency.

In these same years military thinking was still profoundly influenced by the great lessons drawn from experience of the Napoleonic wars by Karl von Clausewitz and Antoine-Henri Jomini[2] at the beginning of the century. It is hardly surprising that the plans drawn up by the general staff in the following decade aimed at swift encirclement (German *Schlieffen Plan*) and counteroffensive (French *Plan XVII*), which should bring a rapid end to the conflict.

If this was how the general staffs saw it, the antimilitarist front based its aversion to war on the optimistic idea that given the close and intricate network of economic relations between industrialised societies, the idea of embarking on a plan for military hegemony proved totally irrational (and indeed the identification of militarism with protectionism derived from this assumption, Giretti 1900: 568). An overview of these ideas was presented by the Polish economist Jan Bloch in his weighty work in six volumes, *Budushchaya Voina* (*The War of the Future in its Technical, Economic and Political Relations*).[3] Here he set out to demonstrate that the enormous destructive power attained by modern armies had now made the geographical delimitation of conflict impossible, and thus any recourse to armed conflict between the European powers was no longer economically viable, for it would prove immensely destructive and the victor would go unrewarded. Given this state of affairs, only small-scale wars were possible. At the beginning of the twentieth century these ideas were given new circulation by the British journalist Norman Angell in *The Great Illusion* (1910), a pamphlet that was to become a sort of *manifesto* of the world pacifist movement in the period of the *Belle Époque*. Both authors had succeeded in coming up with a realistic response, of an economistic nature, to the problem of war, superseding the traditional ethical view of the issue (Weinroth 1974; Biocca 1980).

Smithian dogmatism and pragmatism on the eve of the Great War

The Italo-Turkish conflict from September 1911 to October 1912 faced Italy for the first time with the problem of financing a modern war. In the debate that developed during the war, Luigi Einaudi, writing in the journal of which he was also editor *La riforma sociale*, reiterated the traditional anti-militarist and anti-colonialist position of the Italian 'liberist' economists (Einaudi 1911).

As Einaudi pointed out, if the advantage of territorial conquests was by no means guaranteed, what was absolutely certain was the economic sacrifice that the Libyan venture cost Italy. Following the example of Adam Smith (1776),[4] Einaudi deemed taxation the principal means to pay for the war given the scant or indeed lacking budget surplus to fall back on:

> Taxation educates, debt corrupts. Taxation forces the citizens to face up to realities, to show strong will, and all the stronger, indeed, the readier they are to pay to obtain the object of their desires; debt leaves the doubt that the will is weak, or that it only exists if there is little or nothing to pay
>
> (Einaudi 1911: 638)

Moreover, taxation can prove equitable, weighing directly on the middle classes, the petty bourgeoisie and the traditionally nationalistic sectors of urban artisanship responsive to the appeal of military expeditions (Einaudi 1911: 638). At the same time, taxation should not affect the lowest incomes or the commercial and industrial classes. A residual share of the financing, Einaudi deemed, was to be derived from loans, finding the necessary capital at home and abroad (Einaudi 1911: 639).

This position was largely shared by the liberal economists, who would never break their ties with *Smithian dogmatism*, reasserting the principle that the expenses of war should mainly be based on taxation.[5] On the other hand, despite the positions taken by Antonio De Viti De Marco little attention was paid to the principle of Ricardian equivalence (De Viti De Marco 1893).

However, the war for the conquest of Libya saw the antimilitarist front of the Italian economists giving way, and the problem of financing the war was addressed in more general, pragmatic terms in a study by Federico Flora (1912), defined as 'one of the best Italian monographs on war finance' (Griziotti 1918b; 272), and which clearly anticipated the serious problems that were soon to arise in financing the Great War with notable lucidity.

Flora's study sought to determine not only which resources were best suited to meet the expenses of war, but also the 'timing and degree of their use according as to whether the need was to launch, maintain or terminate a campaign, aiming at deriving a system of eliminating all uncertainty in the choice of the most expedient measures for States at war' (Flora 1912: 646).

Flora also set out to demonstrate that long-lasting conflict was sustainable without necessarily resorting to inflation. Only States unprepared for war – Flora observed – were obliged to resort to the most immediate and harmful source through the issuance of currency, but combining strategic-military planning with the planning of financial means, the minimum sacrifice of lives would be insured by the minimum waste of assets (Flora 1912: 647).

Table 9.1 shows the characteristics and most appropriate uses of the various sources of financing for war according to Flora.

When Treasury resources are available conflict can be entered upon in more advantageous conditions than those of the other belligerents, and without having to wait for loans or revenue from taxes. For this reason, 'one of the responsibilities of financial policy is not to exhaust Treasury resources in peacetime, with the possibility to draw upon them on the outbreak of hostilities' (Flora 1912: 647–648).

However, given the growing economic role of the State and the development of welfare legislation, the possibility of ample budget surpluses of social legislation

Table 9.1 War finance instruments according to Flora (1912)

Source	Instruments	Burden	Purpose
Treasury	Cash in Hand deriving from budget surplus and war chest	Light	Effective in the brief period. A rapid instrument for great sums because generally exempt from preliminary legislative approval
	Obligatory and optional loans by agents appointed for collection, public and private credit institutes	Heavy in unfavourable market conditions or high public debt	
	Issue of Treasury Bonds Short-term bonds		
Public borrowing	Creation of inconvertible paper money	Heavy, due to inflationary pressure	For immediate, urgent needs
	Short-maturity bonds (Extraordinary Treasury Bonds)	High interest rate	For immediate, urgent needs
	Long-term redeemable debt	High interest rate	To finance long-lasting conflicts
Taxes	Increase in rates of ordinary direct and indirect taxes	Inequitable distribution of burden	Increase in public revenues in the least possible time
	Introduction of extraordinary taxes	Possible distortive effects	

seems increasingly remote. Similarly, resort to war bonds is in general unusual in modern States, which use whatever state reserves of precious metals there may be to support the currency, to the advantage of the community as a whole. A more immediate solution is to source obligatory and optional loans from public (as the *Cassa depositi e prestiti*) and private credit institutes. If the resources available on the public credit institutes appear limited, falling back on bank loans may prove burdensome if political and market conditions are unfavourable, or if the public debt is very high. To be avoided, according to Flora, are long-term loans, which indissolubly tie the banks to the Treasury, while preference should go to the very short-term loans, equivalent to commercial loans, in the form of advances with low interest, the opening of current accounts guaranteed by public property or assets, or Treasury bond or debt certificate discounts (Flora 1912: 651).

Issue of *Treasury Bonds* is of use in meeting the first needs of war. This, according to Flora, is a great resource given the extraordinary availability favoured by financial cosmopolitanism (Flora 1912: 652). However, in this case, too, the amount and conditions of borrowing are strictly related to the financial solidity represented by the level of the country's public debt. With regard to public borrowing, Flora distinguishes between inconvertible paper money and long-term and short-term loans. Supply of inconvertible paper money is the most immediate way to access resources, but also, as mentioned above, the most dangerous in view of the inflationary pressure it generates. Nevertheless, Flora is pragmatic in distinguishing certain cases in which forced circulation can be resorted to without compromising the stability of prices.

Inconvertible paper money can, for the immediate needs of war, serve to utilise the metal reserves available at the issuing banks, 'the modern State's sole war chest', and not only to increase the existing money circulation (Flora 1912: 655). However, the paper money should never exceed the total of metal reserves available (in general, at the beginning of the last century the bank laws stated that the metallic reserve should cover from a third to a half of the convertible paper money) and any additional issue should be suspended as soon as the premium on the national exchange began to increase. The fiat currency should then be abolished at the end of the war, using the revenue from extraordinary war taxes.

Obviously, the metallic reserve will not suffice to cover the total cost of the war, and resort to borrowing becomes inevitable. An immediate source lies in short-term loans (Extraordinary Treasury Bonds), which represent 'scientifically, the form best suited to the day-to-day needs of the war and the interests of the contracting parties' (Flora 1912: 655). Use of this instrument, with short-term maturity, is dictated by the rising trend in the interest rate typical of times of war. The bonds representing the loan must be placed with national or foreign bank consortiums for immediate payment of the sum. However, resort to this type of loan becomes increasingly burdensome in proportion with the duration of the conflict, the amount of the current public debt and the increase in the rate of interest (Flora 1912: 657–658). Repayment of these loans must be made as soon as the war is over with the issue of a covered consolidated loan, in the meantime covering interest service with extraordinary taxes.

The longer the war lasts, the more pressing the need will be to resort to long-term borrowing, with destruction of capital constantly raising the interest rate, making short-term borrowing no more than a temporary expedient (Flora 1912: 659). With regard to the use of this instrument, Flora takes an anti-Smithian position:

> The writers of the past rejected the principle, arguing that taxes can suffice for the needs of war, saving the States the cost of loan management and service. The historical facts prove just the contrary. There have been wars financed solely with loans, but there are no records of wars fuelled with taxes alone. Even the countries that depended most on taxes failed to cover more than a *third* of their overall war expenditure. And doctrine made the reasons for this clear. Not only are loans less harmful to the national economy than heavy taxation, but they represent the only possible expedient to collect the billions needed for war. The slow, limited revenue from such new taxes as the citizens can still reasonably bear will not suffice. What is needed is a good part of the available wealth created on an increasingly large scale, at home and abroad, by savings, restriction in the scope for use, and the growing inequality in the distribution of assets occurring in the most developed countries.
>
> (Flora 1912: 659)

Resort to this 'colossal' source of financing enables even the weakest States to engage in war, long and costly as it may be, absorbing the available capital without interfering with the performance of productive activities.

For the advantages of long-term borrowing to materialise fully, Flora observes, it is necessary to introduce certain management principles which States generally fail to observe:

a   The best solution for the purposes of war is to forego perpetual debt in favour of redeemable loans with long maturity, convertible and repayable with a periodic draw by lot (Flora, 1912: 661–662).

b   There should be no issues below the par that oblige the State to repay sums far higher than those received (Flora, 1912: 660). In general belligerent States mistakenly issue below the par to reduce the interest burden to the minimum rates.

c   A part of the bonds, small as it might be, should always be placed abroad to enhance their negotiability. This applies above all to the poorest countries which, by placing bonds abroad, avoid the immediate removal from the economy of the circulating capital necessary to fuel the domestic productive process and to import the goods and resources needed for the war effort (Flora 1912: 663).

d   It is advantageous to issue sizeable bonds even when war is coming to an end, because the conditions benefit both the winners, due to the rise in the rate on bonds that follows peace, and the vanquished, due to the increase in national revenues that occurs at the end of the war (Flora 1912: 664).

The limit to resort to borrowing is obviously set by the level of the interest rate, which, Flora observes, does not depend on military successes but on the progressive exhaustion of the country's productive capacities (Flora 1912: 663). If the sums necessary for interest service rise so high as to absorb 40% of the ordinary revenue, it will be difficult avoid bankruptcy (Flora 1912: 665).

It is therefore necessary gradually to substitute taxation for borrowing: 'the resources that at the outbreak of hostilities are drawn from borrowing must ultimately be obtained from taxation [...]. And the greater the sum of bonds issued, the faster this must be done' (Flora 1912: 665).

Resort to taxation to bear the cost of war is inevitable, Flora argues. On the outbreak of war application of taxes cannot immediately yield truly appreciable revenues: a sudden increase in taxes from 20% to 50% would obviously bring about an economic crisis proving more disastrous than the war itself, and no country could bear it (Flora 1912: 666). Taxation, therefore, has a complementary role, serving to avoid excessive increase in the public debt, provide the Treasury with resources to pay for the debt service, boost the country's credit, distribute the costs of war over all the social classes, and limit consumption for the purpose of boosting productive activity and encouraging saving (Flora 1912: 666).

Ordinary taxes or cuts in expenditure (which can only be marginal) cannot suffice for the needs of war, but specific war taxes have to be brought in from the very outbreak of hostilities, and their application prolonged after the end of hostilities to yield an appreciable revenue rapidly without aggravating the economic conditions of the country. Light, temporary taxation is of no use in bearing the costs of war (Flora 1912: 667). To facilitate implementation of the new taxes in wartime as well as increase in the ordinary taxes, the peacetime taxation system must be conceived from the outset in elastic terms in order to yield the necessary additional revenue without severe shock or delay (Flora 1912: 668). The first tax to be raised must be the income tax, which, being universal, equitable and productive constitutes the basic tax for war finance. The cost of war must then weigh upon the indirect taxes, in particular on consumption and business transactions, to be applied universally with no exceptions, so as to avoid distortive effects (Flora 1912: 670).

Ultimately, taxes can be raised without distortive or inequitable effects only if the national system of taxation is ordinarily immune from the outset. If the ordinary peacetime system is inequitable care must be taken to prevent the cost of war from aggravating the distortive effects, raising only the less onerous taxes more readily tolerated by the national economy (Flora 1912: 678).

The conclusions of Flora's study, based 'on careful observation of the facts' (Flora 1912: 678), lead to a precise formula for war finance policy: 'the Treasury begins the war, borrowing supports it, taxation brings it to its end' (Flora 1912: 678).

> The Treasury, with the State coffers, the statutory advances of the banks, the ordinary banks, allows for rapid mobilisation and instant opening of hostilities; the metallic reserve of the issuing banks, through the circulation of fiat paper money already in place, extraordinary Treasury bonds and borrowing

with long maturity yield the huge sums necessary for the campaign in the shortest possible time; finally, a combination of income tax and indirect taxes on consumption spreads the costs of the war amongst a variable number of businesses without upsetting the balance of the budget, harming the productive forces faced with responsibility for reconstruction of the property destroyed, or altering the natural distribution of wealth. With simultaneous resort to the three sources – mainly the Treasury in the initial period, borrowing during the war, and taxation at the end – the costs of war can be covered at a minimum cost for the community as a whole and most advantageously for the States at war.

(Flora 1912: 678)

Over and above the findings he arrives at, which are much like those advanced by Henry C. Adams a few years before (Adams 1887: 134–142),[6] in his study Flora leaves behind the antimilitarism of the Italian economists, legitimising war, now seen as a sustainable eventuality even for the poorest belligerents thanks to the financial wealth accumulated as a result of general economic progress. In this respect we see the economist beginning to take on a neutral role as technical organiser of the war effort, upon which he is not expected to give any value judgement.

Financing total war: the realities and the theoretical debate

At the outbreak of the First World War, nobody in Italy – neither the military nor the politicians, nor indeed the economists – was prepared for the idea of a long war of attrition with consequent enormous expense of resources and men.[7] As early as the autumn of 1914 it was already becoming clear that the war would be one of attrition, calling for huge material resources. Already severely proven by the recent colonial war for Libya, the country appeared far from ready to bear the financial and material weight of total war.

This was one of the main arguments in favour of neutrality, widely shared by the political class still engaged with the government of Giovanni Giolitti. But Italy's entry into war was the result of the political choice practically forced on Parliament by public opinion, represented in this case by a – politically speaking – highly active minority.

Bracing itself for the war effort, Italy had in the first place to mobilise the necessary human resources and supply them with efficient armament in a very short time. To this end, the entire productive system had to be rapidly converted and subordinated to the needs of the war. It was then necessary to formulate a supply policy geared to boosting production and transferring the material to the front. Poor in raw materials as it was, Italy had no choice but to establish a sufficiently centralised control of foreign trade. Obviously, the vast deployment of troops and material could not function without preparing for adequate financial resources. For the most satisfactory results, the need was to plan and centralise choices in production and consumption, both military and civil, as much as possible in order to avoid both collapse on the front and popular uprisings at home.

Italy had no real experience of planning production, although the subject had been raised in lucid analytic terms by Enrico Barone as early as 1908 (Barone 1908), receiving scant attention. Moreover, in Italy the leading liberal tradition had always been extremely diffident about any attempt to substitute state intervention for the invisible hand of the market (Einaudi 1915; 1920; 1933), although the subject was not entirely neglected in the Italian literature. We might take, for example, certain positions adopted by Francesco Saverio Nitti regarding the need to define an *Organisierter Kapitalismus,* above all for the supply of energy sources and raw materials (subsequently central to his activity as Minister during the closing stages of the war).

However, the pressing needs of the war called for mechanisms for centralisation and direct state intervention, setting up public bodies for the supply of raw materials, a state monopoly on currency exchange, regulation of foreign trade, while bringing in obligatory consortiums between producers and bank cartels.

The expenditure of wealth entailed by the war was largely implemented through public spending, as was the case with the other states at war. The exceptional costs (see Table 9.2) which the Italian state had to bear could be covered by raising either taxes or the public debt, while the reduction of day-to-day costs not directly involved in the war effort proved decidedly marginal and ephemeral.[8] The governments that led the country during the war made use largely of public borrowing financed in various ways (see Table 9.4), while limiting resort to taxation (see Table 9.3), both for technical reasons, the Italian fiscal system being antiquated and inefficient, and as a matter of political expediency since placing

Table 9.2 War costs 1914–1918 in US dollars, at pre-war rates of exchange

August 1914–June 1915	607.840.000
July 1915–June 1916	1.670.300.000
July 1916–June 1917	2.826.440.000
July 1917–June 1918	3.946.920.000
July 1918–October 1918	1.345.000.000
Unpaid liabilities	20.000.000.000
Interest on war debt to Oct. 31, 1918	724.000.000
Total	13.120.500.000

Source: Bogart (1920): 159.

Table 9.3 Increases in taxation alone during the war period

	Amount	*Increase*
1914–1915	265.000.000	
1915–1916	339.800.000	74.800
1916–1917	481.600.000	142.600.000
1917–1918	601.820.000	120.220.000

Source: Bogart (1920): 158.

the burden of the war directly on taxation would prove extremely unpopular (see Figure 9.3).

Experience of the First World War as total war must have brought the realities of financing a long and wasting war to the centre of the attention of the Italian economists.[9]

The financing of the Great War confirmed the conclusions of Flora's study, according to which the major burden of the war would be borne by the public debt in the various forms of borrowing and fiat currency.

The choice to place the burden of the war basically on borrowing was already clear at the outbreak of the war, observing the experience of Germany and Great Britain. It was Luigi Einaudi who focused in particular on the mechanism controlling the allocation of debts, seeking to define the limits. 'There do not exist – remarked Einaudi – nor can exist in any country readily available monetary

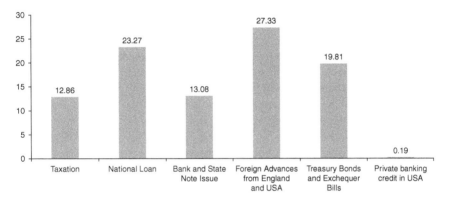

Figure 9.3 Sources of paying for the war in percentage (1915–1918).

Source: *Our elaboration on data from Bogart* (1920).

Table 9.4 Number of fiscal sources in US dollars, at pre-war rates of exchange (1914–1918)

Mobilisation loan	200.000.000
1st war loan	229.200.000
2nd war loan	602.800.000
3rd war loan	797.100.000
4th war loan	1.224.600.000
State note issue	339.740.000
Bank note advances	1.376.500.000
Advances from England to April 1919	2.065.000.000
Advances from United States to April 1919	1.521.500.000
3 and 5 years Treasury Bonds	650.000.000
3 and 12 months Exchequer Bills	1.950.000.000
Private banking credit in U.S.	25.000.000
Total	10.981.440.000

Source: Bogart (1920): 160.

resources sufficient to cover even remotely the huge war debts of the present day' (Einaudi 1914: 886). War loans can be taken on either by issuing fiat paper currency or through the banking system.

Inconvertible paper money is inevitable in such urgent conditions, but extremely dangerous, creating *ex novo* paper money that makes it possible to collect the future debt. Issue of paper money serves in the first place to pay the State's suppliers and creditors, and eventually becomes almost entirely absorbed by the bank system insofar as it is surplus liquidity which can find no useful outlet given the doldrums in investment opportunities caused by the war (Einaudi 1914: 886–888). Thanks to the surplus liquidity the State is able to issue bonds and obtain resources to pay for the goods and services needed to wage war. In this way, the forced, non-interest-bearing loan represented by nonconvertible paper money is replaced with voluntary, interest-bearing loan (Einaudi 1914: 888). This mechanism, implemented mainly in Germany, can be applied repeatedly to finance the needs of a prolonged war. A similar method consists in issuing paper money on the strength of the guarantees given on public debt instruments or bonds in private hands. The liquidity thus introduced into the economic circuit is then reabsorbed by the government bonds, etc. This mechanism 'at first sight might seem a joke, for the State, needing to borrow 1 billion, prints the banknotes and lends them to the capitalists, who return them to the State, receiving an exchange 1 billion in bonds. Thus the State eventually finds itself with a debt of 1 billion at 5%, and 1 billion in the banknotes it has created' (Einaudi 1914: 890).

Actually – Einaudi pointed out – the operation proves rather more virtuous than simple issue of fiat paper money, insofar as:

a   to the new bond corresponds a debt for the bonds given in pawn. To rid himself of the burden of interest to be paid, the capitalist will have to save and gradually pay off his debt; in this way, the liquidity created to issue the bond will be destroyed with further liquidity, which will return to the State;

b   the State acquires control over future savings, and not only current savings (Einaudi 1914: 891).

Another method for issuing securities, applied mainly in Great Britain, consists in a series of entries in the account books of the banks and clearinghouses. In this case it is the banks that in part use the available deposited savings while in part creating fiduciary means of payment, opening credit lines to their customers (Einaudi 1914: 893). The banks underwrite the loan and then issue it to their clients; the underwriting is carried out opening a credit line to the State, or in other words entitling the State to draw cheques on the banks and hand them on to their suppliers and creditors, who, in turn, have them credited to their accounts in the same banks (Einaudi 1914: 896). The new savings that progressively become available will flow into the banks thanks to the high interest rates. The operation that began with opening of credit by the banks to the State will be concluded when the clients, having accumulated sufficient savings, buy the bonds representing the loan from the banks, thereby contributing to pay off the State's debt to the same banks (Einaudi, 1914: 896).

The mechanism delineated by Einaudi seems to anticipate the 'monetary or capital circuit' policy, proposed by the Minister of Finance Thaon de Revel, which served as a basis to finance the war economy between the invasion of Ethiopia (1935) and the Armistice (1943) (Gattei and Dondi, 1990; Gattei 2008). The aim of the circuit policy, much like that proposed by Einaudi, was to absorb surplus liquidity both directly, through taxation and public loans, and indirectly, through the intermediation of the bank system.

Einaudi returned to the subject of war finance in 1915, when it had become clear that Italy found itself in a war that would prove long and costly. The experience of the other countries at war constituted for Einaudi further confirmation to reiterate the *Smithian dogma*. War brings about the destruction of enormous masses of capital and available savings, which have to be disinvested and transformed into money to meet the needs of war (Einaudi 1915: 466). These losses of national wealth are aggravated by the economic turbulence resulting from the issue of fiat banknotes as the principal means to finance the war. This, Einaudi pointed out, was an expedient Italy had already tried out, albeit on a relatively small scale, during the war in Libya, and it now appeared necessary to support the new, more challenging war effort that had begun in May 1915.

Although resort to the 'scourge' of fiat currency was by then inevitable, Einaudi favoured keeping it within clearly set limits: (1) first of all, issue of paper money should always be limited to public ends relating to war finance, and not to satisfy particular interests; (2) this in turn should be coordinated with the issue of domestic war bonds, 'in such a way that the former be preparatory for the latter', thereby avoiding inflationary pressures (Einaudi 1915: 471); (3) increase, and above all, sharp fluctuations of the premium should be controlled through resort to foreign loans (Einaudi 1915: 472).

A long and costly war will also entail equally hard sacrifices to repair the damage once peace has been restored. According to Einaudi, the taxes would have to be raised by many hundreds of millions a year, with the burden falling mainly on the middle and upper classes, while no economic reward was to be expected from the annexation of reclaimed territories (Einaudi 1915: 476).

When the war had come to an end, Einaudi drew up his ideal scheme for war finance management (Einaudi 1933). The resources for the war are to be drawn from the annual flow of national income, and the major economic problem lies in modifying the relation between public goods and private goods in the distribution of the national income flow (Einaudi 1933: 30). It is then necessary to adjust the structure of consumption, transferring wealth to the State to be used for the purposes of war. This goal can only be achieved with adequate resort to taxation (Einaudi 1933: 30), effectively controlling inflationary trends and excess profit resulting from the war (Einaudi 1933: 31, 35–36).[10]

A comprehensive analysis of war finance was offered by Maffeo Pantaleoni in a substantial contribution published in the *Giornale degli Economisti* in 1916 (Pantaleoni 1916).[11]

War, Pantaleoni pointed out, can never be perfectly planned in economic terms since it always comes as a shock to an industrial society that is not organised militarily and shows particularly marked division of labour (Pantaleoni 1916: 165). War breaks into the routine of economic life bringing with it a bundle of new needs (war needs), giving rise to a utility and cost ladder, and introducing a specific demand curve in addition to the other existing goods (Pantaleoni 1916: 169, 171).

Thus war eats into the flow, distribution and volume of income, and so bears a real cost, consuming useful goods, whether already available or to be provided by the productive system, while also consuming useful services, diverting them from their ordinary use. Moreover, the consumption is of present, and not future, goods and services. Even if a country acquires these goods on debt, pledging its present goods against future goods, another country has necessarily had to acquire the goods for which it feels the need. (Pantaleoni 1916: 171). Here, obviously, reference to the needs of the war applies only to such goods as are directly or indirectly related to the war effort.

Ultimately, war changes the economic equilibrium, leading to alteration in all the terms of trade. In fact, there is a rise in the prices of the direct and capital goods serving for the needs of war. Demand for present goods of much the same kind is faced with a supply of heterogeneous – not only present, but also future – goods (Pantaleoni 1916: 178). The goods that do not serve the needs of war fall in price, above all if it is necessary to sell them to acquire war material, while the prices of material serving directly or indirectly for the needs of war will rise.

The cost of war is given by the 'utility of the material to be made available' to sustain the war effort, or in other words the opportunity cost, calculated as if 'each of the things made available had served the purpose it served in peacetime, or the productive forces – the capital goods – that produced them had remained in use for the production of those utilities whose production had been determined by the peacetime price system' (Pantaleoni 1916: 173).

The cost is to be measured as a current of water is measured, in terms of flow of both human and material resources. If the war is limited, it may be said to have available the stock of existing goods and the flow of those added during the war (apart from the human resources). If the war proves particularly costly it eats into the stock, and if it is prolonged then the existing stock is progressively exhausted (Pantaleoni 1916: 179).

Thus the maximum limit to the sustainability of the war is represented by the reserves of national capital immediately transformable into material serving for the war. Only circulating capital has the property of being immediately transformable into war material. Essentially, war entails a rapid destruction of capital securities, resulting in a rise in the interest rate due to the increase in their marginal utility (Pantaleoni 1916: 181). Greater quantities of capital to draw upon can be made available through resort to the international market or exploitation of occupied and colonial territories.

The government pays the costs of war with resources taken from the citizens by means of both taxation and the proceeds on bonds, for it can pay nothing directly, not being a 'manager of the citizens' wealth' (Pantaleoni 1916: 195).

Since war is a transfer of resources the costs must always be paid with metallic currency. Hence the exceptional need for precious metals that arises, the destruction of paper and credit surrogates, the general slowing down of the velocity of circulation of money, the onset of widespread hoarding and, finally, speculative premium on the existing monetary stocks (Pantaleoni 1916: 197).

The dire need for money entailed by a long conflict for which the governments – including the Italian government – were not prepared gave rise to a severe problem of financing that had to be solved very rapidly, for the needs of war did not arise gradually but came in one great wave.

The first source of financing was to be taxation, but the costs of war cannot be distributed leaving the fiscal systems intact or bringing in light taxes that would not generate sufficient revenue (Pantaleoni 1916: 449).

The need is to create a 'partly new finance', in the first place imposing radical economies on the public administration and implementing overall reform of the fiscal system, introducing a new personal property tax and new fiscal monopolies (Pantaleoni 1916: 467–470). The reforms are to be implemented dismantling the system of bureaucratic constraints on economic activity, guaranteeing freedom for labour, contracts and trade, and eliminating all forms of customs protectionism (Pantaleoni 1916: 451). *Laissez-faire* reforms – according to Pantaleoni – would favour post-war recovery.

Financing by means of taxation was the classical Smithian issue that Pantaleoni returned to in dogmatic terms. Dogmatic, too, were the *laissez-faire* reforms held necessary, and the rejection of state intervention (Pantaleoni 1916: 383). This was an unrealistic position, in contrast with the trend towards state intervention (again defined generically as socialism) and planning, which was the main upshot in all the countries at war, including Italy.

Nevertheless, Pantaleoni took cognizance of the general resort to borrowing as the principal means to finance the war effort. Even here, however, he took a dogmatic approach. He distinguished between domestic and foreign debts, and debts 'disguised' in the form of issue of fiat paper money (Pantaleoni 1916: 199).

The creation of domestic debt does not affect the wealth of a country insofar as it amounts to transference of assets from private parties to the State in exchange for state credit. Payment of interest and paying off the debt are merely distributive matters. 'A domestic debt – Pantaleoni remarked – never weighs on the future generations, for it is already paid by the present generation. The domestic debt from this point of view is the same thing as a tax, which is not paid by future generations' (Pantaleoni 1916: 201).

The debt underwritten by foreign citizens in practice nationalises the foreign capital, leaving the national capital intact. Payment of the loan increases the circulation of fiat currency in the recipient country, raising the level of prices and reducing exports. By contrast, currency circulation and prices fall in the country the capital comes from, where the exports increase. 'The Americans have lent to the Europeans the money with which the Europeans have paid them, which is tantamount to having lent them goods' (Pantaleoni 1916: 204).

The most dangerous debt lies in fiat currency, for with it – Pantaleoni observed – the government deprives the citizens of goods and gives them banknotes which endow them with analogous power over other citizens. But this is, of course, an illusory power, for the banknotes will be exchanged not for goods, but for other pieces of paper (Pantaleoni 1916: 208).

Pantaleoni once again evokes the traditional diffidence towards the public debt, which appears to amount to no more than an asymmetric relationship between citizens and State in which the debtor 'can disappear' or perpetually renew the debt without ever honouring it, resorting, like the German government, to issue of paper currency and facilitating speculation (Pantaleoni 1916: 463–466). Equally firm was Pantaleoni's opposition to every form of property tax or tax on the excess profits of war (Pantaleoni 1917: 228, 230).

In the following years, as the war effort progressed, Pantaleoni qualified many of the dogmatic positions he had taken on the use of foreign loans, the role of political prices and state intervention (Ruini 1940: 30–32).[12]

Among the Italian economists, the dogmatic approach began to give way to a more pragmatic viewpoint. On the very eve of Italy's entry into war, an article by Gustavo Del Vecchio in 1915 anticipated some of the problems of financing that would become central to debate in the 1930s. For Italy the major obstacle in the way of entry into war, according to Del Vecchio, was not financing the war, which could be achieved with bonds and paper currency, but the constraint of keeping the balance of payments on an even keel. How was Italy to find resources to pay for the grain, coal, raw materials and industrial products it could not go without, while its main sources of revenue – silk, emigration, foreign industrial activities – will bring in far more limited assets than before, 'and it will be difficult, if not impossible, to resort to deferment of payments in forms of international credit to any appreciable degree' (Del Vecchio 1915: 3–4). Without preliminary accumulation of strategic goods and raw materials in our warehouses, entry into war becomes an unrealistic eventuality.

With regard to financing, Del Vecchio held that the war was to be financed with a mixture of instruments, in part with extraordinary taxation, in part with bonds and in part with paper currency (Del Vecchio 1915: 8–9).

Del Vecchio returned to the issue of the sustainability of the war, in contrast with the pessimistic previsions of Norman Angell, in a contribution in 1916 (Del Vecchio, 1916). His aim was to identify the sources of war finance able to ensure the longest possible resistance and economic independence (Del Vecchio 1916: 2–3). The war effort, he held, could be financed with various sources: boosting labour productivity, reducing per capita consumption, use for the purposes of war and destruction of the savings which would be transformed into new capital in peacetime, exhaustion of circulating capital, destruction of capital stock and inflow of capital from abroad (Del Vecchio 1916: 13). Contrary to the expectations of a large part of the economists, the modern countries possess these sources to a considerable degree and are able to stand up to the pressure entailed with the war effort for a long period of time (Del Vecchio 1916: 13). This unexpected resistance, according to Del Vecchio, resulted from the increase 'in productive energies before the war, imperfectly evaluated by the economic statistics' (Del Vecchio, 1916: 13). Ultimately, 'the increase in economic strength is even greater than the increase in the needs entailed by the war effort' (Del Vecchio 1916: 13). Experience had shown that 'the economic system has shown returns and performance beyond all expectations, and has brought about general and particular trends in production and consumption to the extent of exceeding even the most favourable expectations. The cost of the war has in general been borne with less strain than had been foreseen even by the most optimistic' (Del Vecchio 1916: 16).

The sustainability of the war was also enhanced by the resources obtainable through international trade, not only with the neutral countries, but even with the belligerent States themselves thanks to contraband (Del Vecchio 1916: 14).

Monetary policy, too, according to Del Vecchio, contributed to enhancing the sustainability of the war effort. The huge issue of paper currency and substantial opening of credit lines mitigates the negative effects of the war on money circulation. If, in fact, the outbreak of war brings about a general fall in the rate of securities in the belligerent countries, the need for moratoriums, the closing of the stock exchanges, resort to import of gold and an expansive monetary policy produce 'contrary phenomena' (Del Vecchio 1916: 19), insofar as the massive issues and opening of new credit lines, and indeed the issue of national debt bonds, constitute 'a sort of quasi currency thanks to the great facility in obtaining advances on it' (Del Vecchio 1916: 21).[13]

The pragmatic approach to war finance was again taken up by Benvenuto Griziotti[14] in the final months of the war, in a series of articles for *Riforma Sociale* and the *Giornale degli Economisti* (Griziotti 1917; 1918a, 1918b, 1918c). What was being contested was the idea advanced by Flora that the war effort could only rest on taxation to a minimal extent. Historical experience of war – Griziotti pointed out – shows that resort to taxation has been made widely, becoming the primary financing instrument in Great Britain (Griziotti 1918b: 271). There is no general rule, therefore, but the financial conduct of war behaviour is to be determined on the basis of the economic conditions of each country, distinguishing between the fiscal, economic and political effects of each instrument employed (Griziotti 1918b: 274).

To finance the Italian war, Griziotti proposed that alongside bonds and extraordinary tax should be levied on property in excess of 10,000 lire, serving also to census the taxable capital and prepare the ground for future 'more drastic resort to taxable sources' (Griziotti, 1918b: 282). Essentially, Griziotti was following in the direction indicated by Einaudi, who looked to the social classes that would benefit from it most directly for resources to finance the war (Griziotti 1918a: 307).[15]

Conclusions

Pacifism and Smithian dogmatism were the main features that characterised the thinking of the Italian economists about war finance up until the Libyan colonial war. The needs arising from the realities of the war led to a change in direction, towards a more pragmatic viewpoint which was summed up in the fundamental contribution by Federico Flora, legitimising resort to alternative instruments to finance the public debt in various forms of borrowing and fiat currency.

The financing of the Great War bore out the conclusions of Flora's study, to the effect that the major burden of the war would be sustained with borrowing. However, this opinion was still contested by the liberal and freed-trade economists, and in particular by Pantaleoni and Einaudi, who reaffirmed during the hostilities their critical position on resort to borrowing and paper currency inflation.

The tax/debt alternative was, however, eventually superseded by new contributions (emblematic here was the position taken by Del Vecchio) pointing out, precisely on the evidence of the First World War, that the main obstacle facing Italy was not the problem of defining the appropriate instruments to finance the war – which could be settled with bonds and fiat paper currency – but the constraint constituted by the poverty in raw materials fundamental for the conduct of war and, indeed, to ensure geopolitical autonomy.

Thus debate on war finance was framed within a new economic perspective in which programming the exploitation of strategic resources was considered a preliminary condition to sustain the war effort. The problem would become central in the 1930s, when the foreign policy of the fascist regime started to bare its teeth, culminating with the Italo-Ethiopian colonial war. The issue of resources was then to be incorporated in the propaganda for autarky following upon the Abyssinian War.

Notes

1 Cesare F. Ricotti Magnani, minister of War of the Kingdom of Italy (1870–1876; 1884–1887; 1896), implemented an important military reform (called *Ordinamento Ricotti*), reorganizing the *Italian army* on the Prussian model (short period of military service, extension of conscription to all able-bodied men, creation of permanent army, divided in mobile militia and reserve).

2 On the differences between the two authors, cf. Preston and Wise (1970): chapter XV.

3 Originally published in Russian, and then translated and summarised in English under various titles, cf. Bloch (1899a), (1899b). Apparently, the work left a profound impression on Czar Nicolas II. Bloch also participated in the First Hague Conference (1899) on the laws of warfare, but without any success at the political level.

4 In Chapter 3 of Book V of his *Wealth of Nations*, Adam Smith, argued that financing with taxes was preferable to resorting to public: «Were the expense of war to be defrayed always by a revenue raised within the year, the taxes from which that extraordinary revenue was drawn would last no longer than the war. The ability of private people to accumulate, though less during the war, would have been greater during the peace, than under the system of funding. War would not necessarily have occasioned the destruction of any old capitals, and peace would have occasioned the accumulation of many more new. Wars would, in general, be more speedily concluded, and less wantonly undertaken. The people feeling, during continuance of war, the complete burden of it, would soon grow weary of it; and government, in order to humour them, would not be under the necessity of carrying it on longer than it was necessary to do so. The foresight of the heavy and unavoidable burdens of war would hinder the people from wantonly calling for it when there was no real or solid interest to fight for' (Smith 1776, vol. II: 560–561).

5 Exemplary, in this respect, is the observation by Giulio Alessio: «Taxation is the only rational way to deal with the expenses of war' (Flora 1912: 665).

6 According to Adams, the ratio between borrowing and extraordinary taxes should vary from year to year as the war proceeds, in such a way that borrowing predominates over taxes at the beginning of the war, and taxes yield most of the war revenue at the end. Borrowing can more urgently respond to the need for means that could hardly be covered with taxes in the first year of war, given the political and economic expediencies. As the war continues it becomes ever more politically acceptable to bring the weight of the war to bear on taxes, the operation also being facilitated by the rise in incomes resulting from war expenditure. Positions very close to those of Flora were shown during the war by Edwin R. A. Seligman and Robert M. Haig (Seligman, Haig 1917: 9–10).

7 In the summer of 1915, as reported by *The Economist* (June 26 1915), in Italy the conviction was still widespread in public opinion that the war should not last more than four months, with the cost calculated not to exceed four million lire.

8 «The government endeavoured to introduce economy by a decree of November 18, 1915, by which it suspended all new appointments of public servants, ordained that the number of commissioned public officials be reduced by one-fifth, reduced office expenditures from 10 to 20 per cent, and took other measures looking to the same end' (Bogart, 1920: 145).

9 For a general reconstruction of the financing of the Great War, see Alberti (1915), Virgili (1916), Falco (1983), Gabriele (2008).

10 On Einaudi and the problem of war, see Faucci (2016).

11 Cf. on the contribution by Pantaleoni, Ruini (1940: 28–32). According to Ruini: «Pantaleoni is the economist who has advanced further than any other in contextualising the economic problems of war within the general framework of theory' Ruini (1940: 28). See also Ruini (1941) and Barucci (2016).

12 A similar position to Pantaleoni's was taken by Luigi Amoroso (Amoroso 1916: 498–499). Dogmatic Smithian positions were also taken by Augusto Graziani (Graziani 1916b, 1917b, 1917, 1917b, 1918) with regard to financing war with taxation. Francesco Saverio Nitti also proposed the classical model of financing war expenditure, based on the reduction of domestic consumption (Nitti 1916: 56).

13 On the issue of state intervention, too, Del Vecchio adopted a pragmatic position: «State intervention is simply a form through which what would also be done without it can be achieved with greater speed and facility. One of the most widespread errors among economists is to consider the operation of the State as essentially alien to the economy, while it often comes about as a spontaneous and inevitable economic reaction' (Del Vecchio 1916: 25).

14 Also essentially pragmatic in approach is the contribution by Camillo Supino, who held the conduct of war to be strictly related to economic power (Supino 1916: 226).

15 Similar ideas on 'income conscription' emerged in debate in the Anglo-Saxon countries (Sprague 1917). Opposition to property taxes and excess war profits was raised by Maffeo Pantaleoni and Attilio Cabiati (Pantaleoni 1917; Cabiati 1915a, 1915b).

References

Adams, H.C. (1887) *Public Debt*, Appleton, New York.

Alberti, M. (1915) 'Gli insegnamenti economici del conflitto europeo: La guerra ed il regime doganale', *Giornale degli Economisti e Rivista di Statistica*, Serie terza, Vol. 50 (Anno 26), No. 1, January 1915, 16–43.

Amoroso, L. (1916) 'Il costo della guerra', *Giornale degli Economisti e Rivista di Statistica,* Serie terza, vol. 53, Anno 27, No. 6, December 1916, 489–512.

Angell, N. (1910) *The Great Illusion. A Study of the Relation of Military Power in Nations to Their Economic and Social Advantage,* G.P. Putnam's & Sons, New York.

Barone, E. (1908) 'Il Ministro della Produzione nello Stato Collettivista', *Giornale degli Economisti*, September/October, 2, 267–293, 392–414, 1908. English Translation

'The Ministry of Production in the Collectivist State' in von Hayek, F. (ed.) (1935), *Collectivist Economic Planning*, 245–90, reprinted in Marchionatti, R., ed. (2004), *Early Mathematical Economics, 1871–1915: The Establishment of the Mathematical Method in Economics*, v. IV, Taylor & Francis, 227–63.

Barucci, P. (2016) 'Pigou, Pantaleoni e la teoria economica della guerra', *Il pensiero economico italiano*, Anno XXIV/2016, No. 1, 19–30.

Biocca, D. (1980) 'Il pacifismo e "La Grande Illusione" di Norman Angell', *Studi Storici*, 21, No. 3 (July–September, 1980), 595–607

Bloch, I.S. (1899a) *Is War Now Impossible? Being an Abridgment of 'The War of the Future'*. Richard Grahant, London.

— (1899b) *The Future of War: In its Technical, Economic, and Political Relations*, English translation by R. C. Long. Ginn, Harvard.

Boccardo, G. (1857) *Dizionario della Economia Politica e del Commercio*, vol. II, Bocca, Turin.

Bogart, E.L. (1920) *Direct and Indirect Costs of the Great World War*, Second (Revised) Edition, Oxford University Press New York.

Cabiati, A. (1915a) 'Problemi finanziari della guerra: L'imposta speciale sui sovra-profitti', *Giornale degli Economisti e Rivista di Statistica*, s. III, Vol. 51, Anno 26, No. 6, December 1915, 409–442.

— (1915b) *Problemi finanziari della guerra*, Athenaum, Rome.

Cardini, A. (1981) *Stato liberale e protezionismo in Italia*, Il Mulino, Bologna.

De Viti de Marco, A. (1893) *'La pressione tributaria dell'imposta e del prestito'*, *Giornale degli economisti*, VIII [1893], 38–67; then in *Contributo alla teoria del prestito pubblico*, in *Saggi di economia e finanza*, Edizioni Giornale degli Economisti, Rome, 61–123.

Del Vecchio, G. (1915) 'Economia e finanza di guerra' *Giornale degli Economisti e Rivista di Statistica*, s. III, Vol. 50, Anno 26, No. 1, January 1915: 1–15.

— (1916) 'Questioni di economia teorica relative alla guerra', *Giornale degli Economisti e Rivista di Statistica*, s. III, Vol. 53, Anno 27, No. 2, August 1916, 1–40.

Einaudi, L. (1911) 'A proposito della Tripolitania. Considerazioni economiche e finanziarie', *La Riforma Sociale*, XVIII, vol. XXII, 597–649.

— (1914a) *Le finanze della guerra e delle opere pubbliche*. Bona, Turin.

— (1914b) 'Di alcuni aspetti economici della guerra europea', *La Riforma Sociale*, XXI, vol. XXV, 865–899.

— (1915) 'Guerra ed economia', *La Riforma Sociale*, XXII, XXVI, 6–7, June–July 1915, 454–482, then in *Prediche*, Laterza, Bari, 1920, 1–42.

— (1920) *Prediche*, Laterza, Bari.

— (1933) *La condotta economica e gli effetti sociali della guerra italiana*, Laterza, Bari.

Falco, G. (1983) *L'Italia e la politica finanziaria degli alleati, 1914–1920*, ETS, Pisa.

Faucci, R. (2016). 'Croce ed Einaudi sulla Grande Guerra', *Il pensiero economico italiano*, XXIV/2016, No. 1, 31–40.

Flora, F. (1912) *Finanze della guerra*, Luigi Beltrami, Bologna: published in *La Riforma Sociale*, anno XIX, vol. XXIII, s. III, 641–681.

— (1917) *Manuale della Scienza delle Finanze*. Giusti, Livorno.

Gabriele, M. (2008) 'Il finanziamento della Grande Guerra' in Gentilucci C.E. (ed.), *Storia economica della guerra*, Atti del Convegno Varallo, 21–22 September 2007, Società Italiana di Storia Militare. Quaderno 2007–2008, 103–118.

Gattei, G., and Dondi, A. (1990) 'La teoria della "economia di guerra" in Italia (1939–1945)', *Quaderni di storia dell'economia politica*, 1990, nn. 2–3, 359–376.

Giretti, E. (1900) 'I popoli e la lotta contro il militarismo', *Giornale degli Economisti*, s. II, Vol. 20, Anno 11, 550–569.

Graziani, A. (1916a) *La guerra e le leggi economiche. Memoria letta alla R. Accademia di scienze morali e politiche della Società Reale di Napoli*, Federico Sangiovanni & Figlio, Napoli.

— (1916b) *Finanze di guerra e riforma tributaria. Per un sistema d'imposte per contingente*, Società tipografico editrice nazionale.

— (1917a) 'Di alcuni sofismi sulle spese di guerra', *La Riforma Sociale*, 245–250.

— (1917b) 'La diversa pressione tributaria del prestito e dell'imposta', *Giornale degli Economisti e Rivista di Statistica*, s. III, Vol. 54, Anno 28, No. 3 (March 1917), 129–164.

— (1918) 'Gli insegnamenti di Ricardo e la guerra presente', *La Riforma Sociale*, 352–359.

Griziotti, (1917) 'La diversa pressione tributaria del prestito e dell' imposta', *Giornale degli Economisti e Rivista di Statistica*, Serie terza, Vol. 54, Anno 28, No. 3 (Marzo 1917): 129–164.

— (1918a) 'Come ripartire il carico delle spese della guerra', *Giornale degli Economisti e Rivista di Statistica*, Serie terza, Vol. 56, Anno 29, No. 6, June 1918, 297–329.

— (1918b) 'Prestiti e imposte nelle finanze di guerra', *La Riforma Sociale*, Fasc. VII–VIII, July–August 1918, 270–290.

— (1918c) 'La politica dei prestiti di guerra', *Giornale degli Economisti e Rivista di Statistica*, s. III, Vol. 57, Anno 29, No. 2, August 1918, 37–66.

Molinari, T. (pseudonimo T.M.) (1894) 'Economie militari', *Giornale degli Economisti*, s. II, Vol. 8 (5) (May 1894), 490–503.

Nitti, F.S. (1916) *La guerra e la pace*, Laterza, Bari.

Pantaleoni, M. (1916) 'Fenomeni economici della guerra'. *Giornale degli Economisti e Rivista di Statistica,* March 1916, 157–211; May 1916, 381–400; June 1916, 449–470: pubblicato anche come *Estratto dal Giornale degli economisti e Rivista di statistica*, Athenaeum, Rome, 1917.

— (1917) 'Le tre internazionali', in *Tra le incognite*, Bari: Laterza.

Preston, R.A. and Wise, S.F. (1970) *Men in Arms: A History of Warfare and its Interrelationships With Western Society*. Praeger Publishers, New York.

Rochat, G., and Massobrio, G. (1978) *Breve storia dell'esercito italiano dal 1861 al 1943*. Einaudi, Turin.

Ruini, C. (1940) *L'economia di guerra*. Laterza, Bari.

— (1941) 'Rassegna di studi sulla politica economica e finanziaria di guerra', *Studi economici, finanziari e corporativi,* Anno I (s. I), n. 1, April 1941, 113–154.

Seligman, E.R.A. and Haig, R.M. (1917) *How to Finance the War*, Division of intelligence and publicity of Columbia University.

Silberner, E. (1957) *La guerre et la paix dans l'histoire des doctrines économiques*, Sirey, Paris.

Smith, A. (1776) *An Inquiry into the Nature and Causes of the Wealth of Nations,* Strahan, London.

Sprague, O.M.W. (1917) 'The Conscription of Income', *The Economic Journal*, Vol. 27, No. 105 (March 1917), 1–15.

Squilletta T. (pseudonym of di Tito Molinari) (1892a) 'La nazione armata: studio di un nuovo ordinamento dell' esercito', *Giornale degli Economisti*, s. II, Vol. 5(3) (September 1892), 183–221.

— (1892b) 'La nazione armata: studio di un nuovo ordinamento dell' esercito', *Giornale degli Economisti*, s. II, Vol. 5(3) (October 1892), 344–375.

— (1892c) 'La nazione armata: studio di un nuovo ordinamento dell' esercito', *Giornale degli Economisti*, Serie Seconda, Vol. 5(3) (November 1892), 428–478.

Supino, C. (1916) *Le fonti economiche della guerra*, Zanichelli, Bologna (already published in *Scientia*, Vol. 19, (1916), n. 42–43, 212–229).

Virgili, F. (1916) *Il costo della Guerra europea. Spese e perdite. Mezzi per fronteggiarle.* Treves, Milano.

Weinroth, H. (1974) 'Norman Angell and the Great Illusion: An Episode in Pre-1914 Pacifism', *The Historical Journal,* Vol. 17, No. 3 (September 1974), 551–574.

10 Productive Powers and War in Friedrich List's Theory of Economic Development

Stefano Spalletti

> War is nothing but a duel between nations, and restrictions of free trade are nothing but a war between the powers of industry of different nations.
>
> (List [1827] 1909: 154)

Friedrich List is an important figure in economic thought and policy.[1] Because of the deep political dimensions of his thought, he is the most widely read German economist after Marx, even though he may be included in the older and less studied group of the 'romantic' exponents of German economic culture. Nevertheless, according to the literature, he also belongs to the circle of 'liberal' economists who are fascinated with modern industry. Regarding war and conflicts, the first categorisation explains clearly List's focus on the concept of the productive powers of a nation because these forces owe much to the versions of German romantic strength and organicism (Bronk 2009: 329). In this particular tradition, the productive forces serve the spiritual and intellectual capital of the nation and contribute to its material growth. Spiritual and intellectual capital evolves slowly and needs nurturing, protection and security. Because even the brief destruction of labour's productive power could affect the nation's economy in the long term, it must be avoided (Daastøl 2015: 14).

Several concepts and some principles – but not a method – of war economics can be applied to List's thought. His ideas about conflict, security, nationalism and imperialism can be analysed as outcomes of particular choices related to the economic development of a nation. While traditional economic models assume that economic behaviour is peaceful, List treats both production and exchange as means of acquiring the wealth of a nation. He clearly conceives the study of conflicts in terms of what might be called a macro approach to the economics of war (Anderton and Carter 2009: 2), including interstate conflicts but not intrastate conflicts. While Szporluk (1985: 125) expressed doubt about List's declarations of support for the ideal of universal harmony and peace, Earle (2010: 246) specified that the primary concern of List's political and economic issues is power even though he links it with welfare. Coulomb (2004: 25) definitively stated that List's theory extends beyond power to the development and organization of a national economy and its security.

This essay explores several ways in which List combines conflict and economics by referring to some often-coherent pieces of thought about modifications in trade, production and development. All these items are subject to the influence of conflict. List's conception of the productive powers of a nation remains a central argument for the potential long-term development and of a nation's security. In this perspective, List's cultural framework belongs to German organicism, in which economic factors are interdependent of social and institutional ones and where economic agents and the national economy are seen as a mutually constitutive whole (Greenfield 2001: 204). List's concept of war focuses on ideological motivations and stresses the contingent elements of emergency. Specifically, on one hand, List's reference to the economics of war translates the traditional mercantilist self-centredness into a modern version of the relationship between the objectives of national security and those of economic development. This is discussed in section 2, which explains that the old opposition between liberalism and mercantilism remains relevant (Dunne and Coulomb 2008: 14; Fontanel and Chatterji 2008: 2) but without a particular ideological aspect, and is closest to the practice of economic policy. On the other hand, common arguments about nationalism and imperialism align with List's vision of war and conflicts, as described in section 3. Here, the historical analysis offers an ideological base to contrast classical political economy. The attacks on Adam Smith concern protective measures and the encouragement of nation building. In this perspective, List's position remains influential despite the world's domination by the free market economy (Stander 2014: 86).

A short (but necessary) summary of List's macroeconomic thought

The economic stages of the nation

The end of the European Wars in 1815 opened a new age in international trade and commercial competition between Europe and America. With Alexander Hamilton, List's experience in the USA and the related debate on protectionism and industrialization, led to the conception that economic development stemmed from economic forces divided into heterogeneous national entities. In this framework, the cosmopolitical economy is no longer the main logical background used to explain and accomplish national development. While the cultural traditions of German organicism and public institutions attempted to substitute the traditional (English) theory of the factors of production by the theory of the powers of production, an historical model addressed the sequence of the plausible, gradual growth of a nation. List unlocks the German tradition by explaining the economic growth of a nation through the Renaissance theory of economic stages, which divides human history into qualitatively different stages. Within this framework, the stage theory underlines different aspects of economic growth: List focuses on the type of production, Karl Bücher on the geographical dimension, Karl Marx on social conflict, Bruno Hildebrand on the system of payments, whereas contemporary authors focus on the technological aspects of economic growth (Reinert 2000: 195; 197).

List's theory comprises a savage stage, a pastoral stage, an agricultural stage, an agricultural and manufacturing stage and, finally, an agricultural, manufacturing and commercial stage. Only in the last stage may the entire human race attain prosperity. In the progression toward a cosmopolitical economic world, a fundamental passage is from the agricultural stage to the agricultural and manufacturing stage of a single nation, specifically when the productive powers are able to facilitate the main objective of the development of a nation: industry. In contrast, a simple agrarian society remains populated by 'primitive peasants [...] without culture, knowledge or any competitive spirit', without 'mental powers [...] adequately used or properly developed' (List [1837] 1983: 53).

The productive powers of the nation

The powers of production are instruments used to increase the potential wealth because 'the prosperity of a nation is not [...] greater in the proportion in which it has amassed more wealth (i.e. values of exchange), but in the proportion in which it has more developed its powers of production' (List [1841] 1904: 117). List's analysis connects the power of production with economic nationalism. In this relationship, the national system of political economy brings to the forefront the central process of the stages of evolution. Chapters 9 to 12 in List's *Natural System* (1837) explains the progression from an ignorant agricultural society to an educated and industrial nation. In the first fully agricultural stage of economic development, the physical and mental power of human beings is not sufficiently mature. In the industrial stage, economic maturity promotes the growth of material and intellectual factors of production, and 'those engaged in industry become more familiar with the advances made in scientific knowledge the more quickly – and the more successfully – will new discoveries and inventions be applied to industry in a practical way' (List [1837] 1983: 67). In the language of modern economics, List emphasizes the importance of human capital (Spalletti forthcoming 2016; Kiker 1968) and criticizes the idea of saving, which is promoted by the classical school:

> [Smith] does not consider that this theory of savings, which in the merchant's office is quite correct, if followed by a whole nation must lead to poverty, barbarism, powerlessness, and decay of national progress. Where everyone saves and economises as much as he possibly can, no motive can exist for production. Where everyone merely takes thought for the accumulation of values of exchange, the mental power required for production vanishes [...] The building up of the material national capital takes place in quite another manner than by mere saving as in the case of the rentier, namely, in the same manner as the building up of the productive powers, chiefly by means of the reciprocal action between the mental and material national capital.
>
> (List [1841] 1904: 184)

A nation with economic agents that point solely at the classical definition of real and monetary saving, and not at productive powers, 'would give up the defence of the nation from fear of the expenses of war, and would only learn the truth after all its property had been sacrificed to foreign extortion, that the wealth of nations is to be attained in a manner different to that of the private rentier'(Ibid.).

As the importance of the productive powers expands, the role of the nation-state in nurturing and defending the national wealth must increase; the definition of the nation-state as the protector and nurturer of the national productive powers is always valid (Levi-Faur 1997a: 172). When the productive powers appear to be close to the aims of the nation-state, the boundaries of the political economy become a decisive topic in the social and political sciences. In a neo-mercantilist key, Earle (2010) gave a general lecture on the relationship between the power of capital (traditional and human) and economic development, which combined the military vision of Smith, Alexander Hamilton and List. Earle underlined the organicist origin of List's reasoning, which describes a nation of separate individuals with common government laws, rights, institutions, history, glory, security and so forth. The nation must defend its material and mental capital, even in founding colonies and begetting new nations. Hence, List's ideas draw on the 'basic concepts of Pan-Germanism and National Socialism, such as *Lebensraum*, the *Drang nach Osten*, naval and colonial expansion, the impermanency of frontiers, the permanent allegiance of the *Auslanddeutsche* to the fatherland, and the desirability of a Continental bloc against Anglo American power' (Earle 2010: 260). Like Hamilton, List is a primary figure both in the revival of mercantilism in the modern world of the nineteenth century and in the inevitability of war in the capitalistic system. While Smith accepts only limited military intervention,[2] List emphasises that economic power is an instrument of national unification, acknowledging that 'the individuals may be very wealthy; but if the nation possesses no power to protect them, they may lose in one day the wealth they gathered during ages, and their rights, freedom, and independence too' (List [1827] 1909: 160).

The neo-mercantilist wars at the light of the of the economic stages and productive powers

Another decisive neo-mercantilist concept is the assertion that 'power secures wealth and wealth increases power, so power and wealth, in equal parts, are benefited by a harmonious state of agriculture, commerce and manufactures within the limits of the country' (List [1827] 1909: 163). In this perspective, the theory of stages, complete with productive forces, is particularly explanatory. The passage from one economic stage to another takes place by modifying several economic factors (e.g., population growth, capital accumulation, technical exchanges etc.) and considering several non-economic variables, such as wars and their consequences, which make the provision of a manufacturing power necessary. In particular, when war has broken out, it works as a prohibitive system. List takes into account the several interests and attitudes of socio-economic groups, such as agricultural, industrial and commercial producers. The relationships are well designed in a historical and economic prospective; moreover, they are sufficiently compact, and they provide interesting points of view.

The passage from a fully agricultural stage to a stage in which some external manufactured goods are exchanged with internal agricultural products is a key. This is true both in the development of productive powers and in analysing the nature of war. During war, 'the agriculturist living in one country is by it forcibly separated from the manufacturer living in another country' (List [1841] 1904: 147). On one hand, the main consequence is to reduce the farmer's labour, thus depriving 'the tiller of the soil of the means wherewithal to purchase manufactured goods, and to produce raw material and food for the manufacturer' (List [1841] 1904: 43). On the other hand, war destroys the manufacturers because

> hostilities interfere with the importation of raw material and with the exportation of goods, and because it becomes a difficult matter to procure capital and labour just at the very time when the masters have to bear extraordinary imposts and heavy taxation; and lastly, the injurious effects continue to operate even after the cessation of the war, because both capital and individual effort are ever attracted towards agricultural work and diverted from manufactures, precisely in that proportion in which the war may have injured the farmers and their crops, and thereby opened up a more directly profitable field for the employment of capital and of labour than the manufacturing industries would then afford.
>
> (Ibid.)

Furthermore, war interrupts the proximity between agriculture and manufacturers, because the economic

> prosperity of the corn-cultivating interest requires that the corn millers should live in its vicinity, so also does the prosperity of the farmer especially require that the manufacturer should live close to him, so also does the prosperity of a flat and open country require that a prosperous and industrial town should exist in its centre, and so does the prosperity of the whole agriculture of a country require that its own manufacturing power should be developed in the highest possible degree.
>
> (List [1841] 1904: 128)

In the case of war, the primary sector of the economy falls into ruin because while the manufacturer, 'especially if he belongs to a nation powerful at sea, and carrying on extensive commerce' can find support from the agriculture of other accessible countries, 'the inhabitant of the purely agricultural country suffers doubly through this interruption of intercourse' (List [1841] 1904: 147).

The destiny of agriculture is very important in the progression of the stages and in the development of productive powers. However, the fortune of a purely agricultural country is influenced by the economic policy for the manufacturers and industries. Because it is highly influential,

> the nation should not be dependent on the chances and changes of war in respect of its machinery, this particular branch of manufacture has very special claims for the direct support of the state in case it should not be able under moderate import duties to meet competition. The state should at least encourage and directly support its home manufactories of machinery, so far as their maintenance and development may be necessary to provide at the commencement of a time of war the most necessary requirements, and under a longer interruption by war to serve as patterns for the erection of new machine factories.[3]

> (List [1841] 1904: 251–252)

Without a machinery-oriented manufacturing, the condition of dependence is greater in nations that, in times of war, are not able to sell 'their agricultural products and thereby the means of purchasing the manufacturing products of the foreigner' (List [1841] 1904: 241). In this case, the end of war becomes strategic. In fact, in peacetime, 'the exertions and the sacrifices may have been by which the agricultural nation during the time of war has called into existence manufactures and works, the competition of the manufacturing supremacy [...] will again destroy all these creations of the times of necessity' (Ibid.).

In Chapter 24 of the *National System* (1841), List attempts to show the historical process of prosperity and calamity that occurs in nations until they reach a mature division of labour and a complete confederation of their powers of production. In Chapter 15, List also demonstrates the relationship between war and productive powers. According to him, the event of war is comparable to an exogenous decision to face an external prohibitive tariff system in international trade. The classical school 'does not perceive that war effects a compulsory prohibitive system, and that the prohibitive system of the custom-house is but a necessary continuation of that prohibitive system which war has brought about' (List [1841] 1904: 253). It could be argued that List is wrong because the classical economists consider issues of national security in their observations. In the stage theory, List inserts war as a possible issue, but also Adam Smith's approach to offensive warfare is indirectly related to levels of national growth. According to Goodwin's description of the chapter 'Of the Expenses of the Sovereign or Commonwealth' in book 5 of *The Wealth of the Nation*, Smith's opportunity-costs of war increase with the advent of manufacturing.[4] Therefore, in the manufacturing stage, the advantages that a nation may obtain in defeating a neighbouring area decline, whereas the opportunity costs of the hostilities increase. Considering a manufactural or industrial stage of development, even if a nation wins a war militarily, it can lose economically. In this stage, it is not rational to expect further welfare-maximization for the nation (Goodwin 1991: 24–25).

Nevertheless, there is another strong reasoning behind List's attention to international political economy. In the *Natural System*, he explains clearly that

> in time of war, every country is forced to establish factories to make goods that were formerly imported from abroad in exchange for products made at home. The result is the same as that achieved by a prohibitive fiscal policy in peacetime. The nation is forced to demand great sacrifices from consumers in order to create new industries. Moreover, this happens just when the means available for the establishment of manufactures have been reduced to a minimum.
>
> (List [1837] 1983: 32)

The main positive consequence of this is that when a purely agricultural nation is no longer able to sell its goods abroad:

> It thereby becomes acquainted with the great advantages of a manufacturing power of its own, it becomes convinced by practical experience that it has gained more than it has lost by the commercial interruptions which war has occasioned. The conviction gains ground in it, that it is called to pass from the condition of a mere agricultural state to the condition of an agricultural-manufacturing state, and in consequence of this transition, to attain to the highest degree of prosperity, civilisation and power.
>
> (List [1841] 1904: 147–148)

In short, when war 'leads to the change of the purely agricultural State into an agricultural-manufacturing state is therefore a blessing to a nation'(Ibid.). This happens because war recalls into existence the systems of protection. List's point of view supports the interests of a manufacturing nation – especially of the second and third rank – to retain a protective policy. War is responsible for the system of protection:

> On the one hand, in the less advanced manufacturing nations commercial industry, on the other hand, in the most advanced manufacturing nation agricultural production, becomes stimulated in an extraordinary manner, indeed to such a degree that it appears advisable to the less advanced manufacturing nation (especially if war has continued for several years) to allow the exclusion which war has occasioned of those manufactured articles in which it cannot yet freely compete with the most advanced manufacturing nation, to continue for some time during peace.
>
> (List [1841] 1904: 248)

Therefore, protective tariffs are indispensable both during and after the war. Only the industries that manufacture luxury goods require less public attention and deserve to be less protected because they demand technical sophistication, they do not reach the overall mass of production, and their disruption in the event of war does not affect the vital interests of the nation (List [1841] 1904: 251).

There is another point of interest in List's view on the economics of the war. In contrast to Smith, List considers the war an event capable of creating productive consumption. With regard to direct military expenditures, he does not

> believe that the dominant schools are in the right when they contend that all consumption which is not directly reproductive – for instance, that of war – is absolutely injurious without qualification […] Strictly speaking, material wealth may have been consumed unproductively, but this consumption may, nevertheless, stimulate manufacturers to extraordinary exertions, and lead to new discoveries and improvements, especially to an increase of productive powers.
>
> (List [1841] 1904: 43)

Productive power remains a permanent economic requirement to achieve an augmented dimension of the internal demand for military goods. This is a further reason for criticism of the English political economy that reverts to a certain exclusion of politics from economic science with the consequence of an unjustifiable carelessness in the tract of nationality. In his political system, List pays particular attention to the wars between nations. In England's case, where 'perpetual internal peace has stimulated industrial progress at home, while England's naval supremacy has prevented any decline in trade abroad' (List [1837] 1983: 46), the productive powers of the nation have been developed in spite of the civil war. Therefore, every 'normal' war between nations produces expansion in foreign trade. Furthermore, 'the history of the last century also teaches us that every war which the powers of the Continent have waged against one another has had for its invariable result to increase the industry, the wealth, the navigation, the colonial possessions, and the power of the insular supremacy' (List [1841] 1904: 338).

If war has the power to enliven manufacturing, peace can destroy it. In order to avoid this regression in the evolution of stages, 'judicious laws, forbearance for securing productive powers [are needed] against foreign aggressions, foreign events, foreign laws and regulations, foreign capital, industry, and policy' (List [1827], 1909: 240). The bi-directional interpretation of history distinguishes List's model from the similar and well-known model of Walt Rostow, which logically identifies all societies according to their economic dimension (e.g., traditional society, preconditions for take-off, take-off, drive to maturity and age of high mass-consumption). The idea of the progress of nations is in line with List's theory of stages, but there are also many differences. For our interests, while in List's analysis, the possibility and desirability of war are fully provided for, in Rostow's investigation, war can be only partially connected to the stages of growth. Rostow points out that in colonial conflicts, the element of power is remote and derivative because the proximate goal is trade. Regarding wars of regional aggression, Rostow's references are territories close to the new nation's own borders (i.e., Bismarck's military operations against Denmark, Austria and France from 1894) (Rostow 1991: 113). When this attitude toward 'reactive nationalism' (Rostow's term) recalls the unifying element, it becomes an historical determinant in passing traditional society, and it is closest to List's economic development in stages. Rostow also focuses on the British parameter, historically arguing the various economic consequences of war and relativizing Great Britain's path to wealth. List made a similar statement in his theory of economic development by stages. The results are similar because 'war emerges [...] as a national economic enterprise, a form of communal capital investment'.[5] Precisely, in the course of British history, the great shifts in social and political power are the consequences of war. War is not responsible for these shifts, but it influences their timing and their rate (Rostow 1953: 165). The logical stages in Rostow's theory are unbiased compared with the stage theories of the German Historical School, which oppose the English classical economists and their acceptance of an economics devoid of interstate conflicts. These latter theories are also against free trade although they partially emulate the British hegemony as in List's case. Because the developmental experiences of each country are always historical in their circumstances, their interventionist policies differ accordingly.

From the standpoint of political relations, List's model deals with an international order that depends upon the hegemony of the British in the world of political economy. List's approach readily accepts a fully functioning theory of hegemonic stability, that is, an order created by a single or a few dominant superpowers (Germany potentially included). As J. Shield Nicholson (List [1841] 1904) notes in his introduction to the English translation of the *National System*, the target of German expansion is heavily influenced by the gain of powers of production and by the defence of industrial independence in the case of war. Hence, List's theory of trade enacts a specific historical phase that is translatable into military strength and is responsible for a new starting point in a substantial assessment in international political economy. Several authors correctly state that the roots of economic nationalism are in the mercantilist writers of the seventeenth century. Hamilton and List modernised the eighteenth-century mercantilist thesis by identifying national power through the development of manufacturing (Gilpin, 1987: 180). However, it is possible to view this approach as a neo-mercantilist proposition in the modern economic capacity to reach military strength (Kennedy 1987: xvi) and the ability to mobilize the underlying economic and industrial capacity of a nation to produce power during war. Without exception, the relation between war and mercantilism always leads to endless commercial wars, as Heckscher (1955: 25) and Silberner (1939: 117–118) noted, while the epistemological construction of List's nationalism promotes a mercantilism of both practice and analysis (Brubaker 1996: 15).

Under the conditions of classical free trade, the result would be 'a universal subjection of the less advanced nations to the supremacy of the predominant manufacturing, commercial, and naval power' (List [1841] 1904: 103; Andreatta 2001: 33). Therefore, for List, as for the mercantilists of the seventeenth and eighteenth centuries, power is a necessary condition for wealth because of the trade-off between the interests of the power (of production) and wealth of the state in the long-term. There is a long-term harmonic relationship between these two ends (Keohane 1984: 23), and war is inherent in the mercantilist system because economic life is mobilized for political purposes. The mercantilist framework postulates a continuous search for national economic growth. Thus, in contrast to Coulomb (2004: 28), for List there is no confusion between economic and military matters or between defence and economic security matters. List seems aware of the Keohane trade-off, and the only unwelcome effect of his theory is the consequence of the revival of mercantilism in the unstable Europe in the economic nationalism after 1870, that is, totalitarian economics, totalitarian states and finally totalitarian war. List's greatest mistake is his (non-explicit) viewpoint on the future minor recourse to the conflicts in the perspective of cosmopolitical economy. However, a gradual path toward a cosmopolitical world and peace is utopic because of the changing nature of war.

Conflict and the economic doctrines of nationalism and imperialism

It is not a mere question of appeal. List's image as a German nationalist is not because of his visionary nature, his ability as a journalist or his extraordinary activism (Henderson in List [1837] 1983: 13), or his character as an agitator (Tribe 1995: 36). The main reason for his success is the power of an evocative message directed at a precise subject: the German bourgeoisie is the best example of a people that love industry, order, thrift, moderation, perseverance, endurance in research and in business, honesty after improvement, measure of morality, prudence and circumspection (List [1841] 1904: 66). As an economic subject, this class is capable of projecting its own image of its economic and social character into an organic and national body. Moreover, the roots of this evolution, once again, are in the concept of productive powers and in their defence. List's nationalism stems from both national identity and nationalist sentiment. It reveals an epistemological stance in which the economic actors have different characteristics despite the 'homo oeconomicus'. In much of List's work, nationalism is at the root of his belief in protectionism for infant industries. However, it is useful to remember this ontology with regard to nationalism (Helleiner 2003: 25, 31).

How does war affect the theoretical causation of List's protectionism? Although the relationship between war and protectionism is well known and is not an original concept, war assumes a particular role in the making of productive powers. In the origin of the criticism against Smith's political economy, List discovers the hypothesis of a 'stable' lack of wars. In fact, 'The theory of Adam Smith and of his disciple Dr Cooper' provides 'neither for peace nor for war, neither for particular countries nor for particular people' (List [1827] 1909: 160). Therefore, 'although here and there he [Smith] speaks of wars, this only occurs incidentally. The idea of a perpetual state of peace forms the foundation of all his arguments' (List [1841] 1904: 98). In consequence, the classical school of economics 'does not take into account the influence of war on the necessity for a protective system' (List [1841] 1904: 253).

If – as discussed above – the spirit of war is intended to protect the nation, List rapidly goes beyond the idea of war as a dialectic means of religious or temporal supremacy, which existed in Europe until the late Medieval Age. He considers the modern remuneration of the work as the foundation for increasing labour productivity and wealth, while the end of the religious wars leads to the statement of an intellectually and mobile society to substitute the stratified societies of the *Ancien Régime* (Senghass 1991: 455–456). However, in the national and military aspects of the free and industrious Italian Renaissance city-states, List sees weaknesses in the modern forms of political and economic organization. All city-states were vulnerable as

> German cities, founded by an absence of security in the open country, grew powerful and wealthy by the contest against the robbers of the age by which they were forced to unite their individual strength. Philip's hangmen created the union of the Netherlands, and the wars of the new republic against Spain elevated her to a degree of wealth and power that was never thought of before. So events which seemed at first destructive to individuals, and had, indeed, destructive effects for the present generation, became a cause of happiness for posterity. Therefore, that which had seemed to weaken the human race served to elevate its powers. Look at the histories of England and France, and every page will confirm this truth.
>
> (List [1827] 1909: 219–220)

This weakness inhibits development and leads to the arrest of the bourgeoisie's self-awareness as the driver of economic process. In this interpretation of the historical process of the European expansion, List states that only homogenous communities with large-scale territories may prosper. City-states are too small to survive the principles of liberalism without market and military power, as the dominance of Great Britain demonstrates. The correct scale is provided only by the spread of nation-states and, in the case of Germany, by its future unification. From 1866, with the formation of a conservative-liberal Prussian-dominated German state, List's national project became a concrete application combined with Bismarck's foreign policy and wars (Patomäki 2008: 78–80).

According to the nationalistic approach, the idea of a 'normal nation' may be found initially in the spirit of Zollverein and its boundaries. In List's opinion, Zollverein is in fact a measure that

> cannot be considered complete so long as it does not extend over the whole coast, from the mouth of the Rhine to the frontier of Poland, including Holland and Denmark. A natural consequence of this union must be the admission of both these countries into the German Bund, and consequently into the German nationality, whereby the latter will at once obtain what it is now in need of, namely, fisheries and naval power, maritime commerce and

colonies. Besides, both these nations belong, as respects their descent and whole character, to the German nationality. The burden of debt with which they are oppressed is merely a consequence of their unnatural endeavours to maintain themselves as independent nationalities, and it is in the nature of things that this evil should rise to a point when it will become intolerable to those two nations themselves, and when incorporation with a larger nationality must seem desirable and necessary to them.[6]

(List [1841] 1904: 143; Earle 2010: 249–250)

List's view of war highlights at least three items in Lebensraum's argument. First, as Tribe (1995: 63) pointed out, he uses military metaphors to illustrate the function of the railway network, which connects the idea of space with the transport structure of economic utility. By the creation of a customs union, war, defence and security determine the theoretical consequences of the economic and geographical boundaries established by railways.[7] Second, Britain has already become a super-nation also through military choices. Moreover, the USA has developed a strong economic force capable of competing with Britain and with Russia, even if they are still expanding their frontiers and searching for a definitive national identity to promote their industries (Stander 2014: 86). When List became a citizen of the USA, he was well aware of this ambitious goal, combined with the specific protection of the manufacturers. From this moment forward, the influence of Hamilton's *Report on Manufactures* (1791) and Daniel Raymond's *The Elements of Political Economy* (1823) became crucial (Tribe 1995: 34–35).

The third item brings to the fore the political and economic question of the imperial nature of development. In colonialism, the impulse to acquire a sufficient or even a large territorial scale concerns equilibrium. Colonialism represents an entry that is necessary to avoid the excessive advantages in favour of one or another nation in political and military solutions. According to Ince (2013: 14), in the division and balance of agriculture, manufacturing and commerce, that is the stage theory of development represented by British economic history, not a national but an imperial structure matures. The reason for this view is List's articulated theory of economic development, which remains within the historical horizon of first the British and second the American economic experience, both of which are imperial in nature.[8] To be precise, Ince considers List's national economy as both an anti-imperial and an imperial concept. On the one hand, it moves from a criticism of free trade to British imperialism. On the other hand, List's nation-state attempts to reproduce international relations at a global level through the concept of the members of an expanded circle of state-powers (Ince 2013: 3).

Conclusions

List's theory emphasises the organized power of a dominant capital group that is capable of creating an economic order in society (Bichler and Nitzan 2009: 29). In List's case, this group is the bourgeoisie, who is employed in manufacturing and industry, thus expressing the power of the entire nation. Power recalls force, military design and war. Several ideas are related to these items in List's work. Nevertheless, the results that can be gained by the application of any military theory are poor, especially with the reference to the 'decision making' theoretical core of neoclassical economics (e.g., Brauer and van Tuyll 2008: 6). Only the criticism of the classical political economy, which is mediated by the arguments of the German Romantic movement and the (successive) Historical School, link List's contribution to war to the analysis of economic development. Similar to other German military authors, List does not agree with an articulated system of military theory but instead focuses his analyses on the historical evolution of the concrete and moral forces (Gat 1992: 100). Views of historical economic evolution cannot consist of a simply mercantilist representation of international relations as a zero-sum game, especially because of the conflicts that take place between states to obtain wealth. Instead, List should be read as a modern author compared to the writers in the bullionist age of the seventeenth century. According to Levi-Faur's (1997b: 366) definition, List is a neo-mercantilist: if the productive powers are also material power and human power (human capital), the rationality of an international conflict can change logically. Bullion is a concrete form and source of wealth, while human capital is a productive factor that can be augmented almost indefinitely. Therefore, productive powers must be defended on the territorial scale, and they should be protected as necessary components of manufactural and industrial development.

List's assertions about the neo-mercantilist nature of war do not correspond to the quest for hegemony by engaging in continuous conflict. List and the Historical School explain economics in terms of political rivalry, which may lead to nationalism or even imperialism. However, his outcomes are not those of an economist who permanently thinks according to a Clausewitzian mode. He remains the romantic dreamer of a political hegemony in which war is linked to history mainly for the defence of the development of a national economy. He always attempts to take into account strategies that are adequate for facing reality. For List, reality is not the peaceful Smithian society of free trade.

Notes

1   This essay is the result of the discussions in two different papers on Friedrich List. The first, about productive powers and education, was presented at the conference 'To Freedom via Prosperity', which was dedicated to the 225th Anniversary of Friedrich List's birth, October 8–10, 2014, at the University of Reutlingen. The second, which is about productive powers and war, was presented at the conference 'Economist and the war', which was organized by the Italian Association for the History of Economic Thought, December 11–13, 2014, at the University of Pisa.
2   According to List, Smith did not ignore the fact that the world was divided into many nations, each of which pursued its own economic and political interests. Smith made clear that the first duty of a sovereign was to protect the country from invasion by another state, and this duty could be performed only by maintaining a military force. He also declared that the art of war was the noblest of the arts. He approved of bounties on the export of sailcloth and gunpowder to encourage the production of commodities that would be of vital importance to a country in times of war. Finally, he declared that since

defence 'is of much more importance than opulence, the act of navigation is, perhaps, the wisest of all the commercial regulations of England' (Adam Smith, *An Inquiry into the Nature and Causes of the Wealth of Nations*, vol. 1, p. 408, Everyman edition, quoted in List [1837] 1983: 11). This remark indicates the need to engage circumspectly with List as a historian of economic ideas, particularly when he comments on several of Smith's conclusions. According to Watson, this is an interesting and urgent point to clarify. The framework of comparison between Smith and List, in fact, 'tends to be repeated, pretty much verbatim, by so many who have written about the National System for an IPE audience. In this way, though, they import its historiographical weaknesses into their own work' (Watson 2012: 4).

3   A major instrument of national security was 'the influence of railways upon the shifting balance of military power [...] List saw sooner than anyone else that the railway would make the geographical situation of Germany a source of great strength, instead of one of the primary causes of her military weakness' (Earle 2010: 255). Railways are both commercial and military issues. As military issues, they are instruments of geo-economic security.

4   'both because of the complexity of weapons and because as few as one one-hundredth of the manufacturing population could be spared without loss of production' (Goodwin 1991:24).

5   In his analysis, war has five sources: 'increases in home production; increased borrowing or gifts from abroad; decreases in home consumption; decreases in forms of investment other than war; and by the depletion, in one form or another, of the accumulated national capital' (Rostow 1953:161).

6   Moreover, the building of a larger nationality requires that population, mental and material means of a state, in the case of underutilization, do not take the way of the emigration (the case of German citizens immigrating to the United States).

7   The reference is to the article *Deutschlands Eisenbahnsystem in militärischen Beziehung*, published by List in the *Eisenbahn-Journal* in 1836: 'The needs of industry and communication will compel the railway systems of the larger Continental nations to assume the form of a network, concentrating on the interior principal points and radiating from the centre to the frontiers' (quoted in Tribe, 1995: 63). Wendler (2015: 173) mentions List's view on the new means of transport and on their capability to render the wars more expansive and devastating.

8   Ince (2013: 4) explains that the imperial List's horizon, instead of a gesture toward economic decolonization and independence, culminates in an early vision of the Global North as the exclusive locus of techno-industrial civilization.

References

Anderton, C.H. and Carter, J.R. (2009) *Principles of Conflict Economics. A Primer for Social Scientists*, Cambridge University Press, Cambridge.

Andreatta, F. (2001) *Mercanti e guerrieri: interdipendenza economica e politica internazionale*, Il Mulino, Bologna.

Bichler, S. and Nitzan, J. (2009) *Capital as Power. A Study of Order and 'Creorder'*, Routledge, London.

Brauer, J. and van Tuyll, H. (2008) *Castles, battles, and bombs: how economics explains military history*, University of Chicago Press, Chicago, IL.

Bronk, R. (2009) *The Romantic Economist. Imagination in Economics*, Cambridge University Press, Cambridge.

Brubaker, R. (1996) *Nationalism Reframed: Nationhood and the National Question in the New Europe*, Cambridge University Press, Cambridge.

Coulomb, F. (2004) *Economic Theories of Peace and War*, Routledge, London and New York.

Daastøl, A.M. (2015) 'Austerity Versus Productive Investment: Two Traditions in Capital Formation and Growth', in Backhaus, J. (ed.) *Great Nations at Peril*, Springer, Berlin, 77–118.

Dunne, P. and Coulomb, F. (2008) 'Peace, War and International Security: Economic Theories', in Fontanel, J. and Chatterji, M. (eds.) *War, Peace, and Security*, 6, *Contributions to Conflict Management, Peace Economics and Development*, Emerald Group Publishing, Bingley, 13–36.

Earle, M.E. (2010) 'Adam Smith, Alexander Hamilton, Friedrich List: The Economic Foundations of Military Power in Makers of Modern Strategy', in Paret, P., Craig, G.A. and Gilbert, F. (eds.) *Makers of Modern Strategy from Machiavelli to the Nuclear Age*, Princeton University Press, Princeton, NJ, 217–261.

Fontanel, J. and Chatterji, M. (2008) 'Introduction: The Controversial Economic Question of Peace and War', in Fontanel, J. and Chatterji, M. (eds.) *War, Peace, and Security*, 6, *Contributions to Conflict Management, Peace Economics and Development*, Emerald Group Publishing, Bingley, 1–12.

Gat, A. (1992) *The Development of Military Thought: The Nineteenth Century*, Clarendon Press, Oxford.

Gilpin, R. (1987) *The Political Economy of International Relations*, Princeton University Press, Princeton, IL.

Goodwin, C.D. (1991) 'National Security in Classical Political Economy', in Goodwin, C.D. (ed.) *Economics and National Security. A History of Their Interaction*, Annual Supplement, 23, *History of Political Economy*, Duke University Press, Durham and London, 23–35.

Greenfeld, L. (2001) *The Spirit of Capitalism: Nationalism and Economic Growth*, Harvard University Press, Cambridge, MA.

Heckscher, E.F. (1955) *Mercantilism*, 2 vols., Allen and Unwin, London.

Helleiner, E. (2002) 'Economic Nationalism as a Challenge to Economic Liberalism? Lessons from the 19th Century', *International Studies Quarterly*, 46(3), 307–329; also in TIPEC working paper, 02/3.

Ince, O.U. (2013) *Imperial Origins of the 'National Economy*, paper presented at the Annual Convention of the American Political Science Association, September, Chicago, IL.

Kennedy, P. (1987) *The Rise and Fall of the Great Powers*, Random House, New York.

Keohane, R.O. (1984) *After Hegemony: Cooperation and Discord in the World Political Economy*, Princeton University Press, Princeton, NJ.

Kiker, B.F. (1968) *Human Capital in Retrospect*, University of South Carolina, Columbia, NY.

Levi-Faur, D. (1997a) 'Friedrich List and the Political Economy of the Nation-State', *Review of International Political Economy*, 4(1), 154–178.

— (1997b), 'Economic Nationalism: From Friedrich List to Robert Reich', *Review of International Studies*, 23, 359–370.

List, F. [1827] (1909), 'Outlines of American Political Economy', in Hirst, M. (ed.) *Life of Friedrich List and Selections from his Writings*, Smith, Elder & Co., London, 147–286.

— [1837] (1983) *The Natural System of Political Economy*, Henderson W.O. (ed.), Franks Cass, London.

— [1841] (1904) *The National System of Political Economy by Friedrich List*, Nicholson, J.S. (ed.), Longmans Green and Co., New York and Bombay.

Patomäki, H. (2008) *The Political Economy of Global Security: War, Future Crises and Changes in Global Governance*, Routledge, London.

Reinert, E.S. (2000) 'Bücher and the Geographical Dimensions of Techno-Economic Change. Production-Based Economic Theory and the Stages of Economic Development', in Backhaus, J. (ed.) *Karl Bücher Theory – History – Anthropology – Non Market Economies*, Metropolis-Verlag, Marburg, 177–222.

Rostow, W.W. (1953) *The Process of the Economic Growth*, Clarendon Press, Oxford.

— (1991) *The Stages of Economic Growth: A Non-Communist Manifesto*, Cambridge University Press, Cambridge.

Senghass, D. (1991) Friedrich List and the Basic Problems of Modern Development, *Review*, 14(3), 451–467.

Silberner, E. (1939) *La guerre dans la pensée économique du XVIe au XVIII siècle*, Recueil Sirey, Paris.

Spalletti, S. (forthcoming 2017) 'Friedrich List's Economics of Education' in Hagemann, H., Seiter, S. and Wendler, E. (eds.) *Through Wealth to Freedom*, Routledge, London and New York.

Stander, S. (2014) *Why War. Capitalism and the Nation-State*, Bloomsbury, New York, London, New Delhi, Sydney.

Szporluk, R. (1985) *Communism and Nationalism. Karl Marx Versus Friedrich List*, Oxford University Press, Oxford and New York.

Tribe, K. (1995) *Strategies of Economic Order: German Economic Discourse, 1750–1950*, Cambridge University Press, Cambridge.

Watson, M. (2012) Friedrich List's Adam Smith Historiography and the Contested Origins of Development Theory, *Third World Quarterly*, 33, 459–474.

Wendler, E. (2015) *Friedrich List (1789–1846). A Visionary Economist with Social Responsibility*, Springer, Berlin.

11 Keynes on the Role of the 'Insane and Irrational Springs of Wickedness' in War

Ted Winslow

Keynes arranged in his will to have two, and two only, of his unpublished writings published after his death. These appeared in 1949 as *Two Memoirs* (X: 385–451).[1] Interpretive writing on Keynes has focused mainly on the second, 'My Early Beliefs'. What has been primarily of interest is the first part concerned with the relation of the early beliefs of Keynes and the other members of Bloomsbury to G.E. Moore's *Principia Ethica*. Keynes there identifies a critical appropriation of the latter with his own mature 'religion' defined as 'one's attitude towards oneself and the ultimate (X: 436)'. He elaborates this as the ontological idea of an objective and knowable 'good' combined with the anthropological idea of human being as the being able to know this 'good' and actualize it in a truly good life. In *The Economic Consequences of the Peace*, he identifies this anthropological idea with 'the universal element in the soul of man (II 189)'.

The second part of the memoir has, however, largely been ignored. In it is found the main point made in both memoirs. Keynes claims that he and the other members of early Bloomsbury adopted a view of human nature that was, in one key respect, 'disastrously mistaken (X: 447)'. This belief was that 'human nature is reasonable', that:

> the human race already consists of reliable, rational, decent people, influenced by truth and objective standards, who can be safely released from the outward restraints of convention and traditional standards and inflexible rules of conduct, and left, from now onwards, to their own sensible devices, pure motives and reliable intuitions of the good.
>
> (X: 447)

This ignored, he now claims, the fact of 'there being insane and irrational springs of wickedness in most men' so that 'civilisation was a thin and precarious crust erected by the personality and the will of a very few, and only maintained by rules and conventions skilfully put across and guilefully preserved (X: 447)'.[2]

The first memoir, 'Dr Melchior: A Defeated Enemy', illustrates these points by representing Melchior as someone who understood both the fact and its implications. It does this by means of an account of their joint participation in the negotiations ending in the Treaty of Versailles. As Keynes had made clear in *The Economic Consequences*, both the war and the negotiations that ended it had revealed the important role played by the 'insane and irrational springs' in 'practical affairs' and, hence, the necessity to take account of such springs in rational discussion of such affairs (X: 449).

For Keynes then, these springs were the source of the 'deeper and blinder passions' (X: 449) having their most destructive expression in war. The paper aims to elaborate this interpretive thesis and support it with textual evidence. It begins with an examination of Keynes's understanding of irrationality, particularly in the form he makes 'the essential characteristic of capitalism'. It then examines the role he assigns to it in his account of 'economic' and 'spiritual' possibilities for our grandchildren. Finally, with this as background, it focuses on the relation Keynes claims exists between the 'insane and irrational springs of wickedness' and war.

The 'springs' as instincts

It can be reasonably inferred from Keynes's other discussions of irrationality that he conceived these 'springs' as 'instincts' concerned with sex and death. This conception is implicit, for example, in his discussions of the motives whose dominance he makes 'the essential characteristic of capitalism'. In 'The End of Laissez-Faire' he claims this characteristic is 'the dependence upon an intense appeal to the money-making and money-loving instincts of individuals as the main motive force of the economic machine' (X: 293)

In 'Economic Possibilities for Our Grandchildren' he describes 'the love of money as a possession' as a somewhat disgusting morbidity, one of those semi-criminal, semi-pathological propensities which one hands over with a shudder to the specialists in mental disease' (X: 329). In his 1927 review of H.G. Wells's *The World of William Clissold*, he implicitly invokes a Freudian explanation of business motives to explain why business men cannot be recruited to what Wells had called 'the open conspiracy'.

In *Clissold*, Wells had addressed the questions:

> why should not we begin to reap spiritual fruits from our material conquests? If so, whence is to come the motive power of desirable change? ... From whence are we to draw the forces which are 'to change the laws, customs, rules, and institutions of the world'? 'From what classes and types are the revolutionaries to be drawn? How are they to be brought into co-operation? What are to be their methods?
>
> (X: 318)

He had pointed to business men as potential recruits for this project:

> We must persuade the type of man whom it now amuses to create a great business, that there lie waiting for him yet bigger things which will amuse him more. This is Clissold's 'open conspiracy'. Clissold's direction is to the Left—far, far to the Left; but he seeks to summon from the Right the creative force and the constructive will which is to carry him there.
>
> (X: 319)

According to Keynes, however, the nature of their motivation makes businessmen immune to such an appeal. They lack the capacity for the sublimation of '*libido*' into a rational 'creed', a 'true religion', such a 'spiritual' project requires:

> Why do practical men find it more amusing to make money than to join the open conspiracy? I suggest that it is much the same reason as that which makes them find it more amusing to play bridge on Sundays than to go to church. They lack altogether the kind of motive, the possession of which, if they had it, could be expressed by saying that they had a creed. They have no creed, these potential open conspirators, no creed whatever. That is why, unless they have the luck to be scientists or artists, they fall back on the grand substitute motive, the perfect *ersatz*, the anodyne for those who, in fact, want nothing at all—money. Clissold charges the enthusiasts of labour that they have 'feelings in the place of ideas'. But he does not deny that they have feelings. Has not, perhaps, poor Mr Cook something which Clissold lacks? Clissold and his brother Dickon, the advertising expert, flutter about the world seeking for something to which they can attach their abundant *libido*. But they have not found it. They would so like to be apostles, but they cannot. They remain business men.
>
> (X: 319–320)

Consistent with this, in *A Treatise on Money*'s discussion of '*auri sacra fames*', he explicitly invokes 'the Freudian theory the love of money, and of gold in particular', as insightfully connecting this 'love' with *Eros*, the sex instinct (VI: 258–259 note 1).[3]

Freud's final theory of the instincts added to this a death instinct. Interpreted in Freudian terms, this appears in Keynes's economics in derivative forms whose purpose, as with derivatives of the sex instinct, is to allay the anxiety that the functioning of the instinct in its original form provokes. One such derivative is explicit or implicit denial of mortality. Implicit denial is found in the second irrational motivation Keynes identifies with the money motives in 'Economic Possibilities for Our Grandchildren' – 'purposiveness' (IX: 329–330). This is an irrational interest in saving and accumulating by means of which the 'purposive' individual is 'trying to secure a spurious and delusive immortality for his acts by pushing his interest in them forward into time', i.e. by implicitly denying the *certain* fact that '*in the long run* we are all dead' (IV: 65). This connection is also pointed to in *The General Theory*'s account of the role of 'animal spirits' in capitalist 'enterprise':

> It is safe to say the enterprise which depends on hopes stretching into the future benefits the community as a whole. But individual initiative will only be adequate when reasonable calculation is supplemented and supported by animal spirits, so that the thought of ultimate loss which often overtakes pioneers, as experience undoubtedly tells us and them, is put aside as a healthy man puts aside the expectation of death.
>
> (VII: 162)

The 'Freudian theory of the love of money, and of gold in particular', identifies this 'love' with a particular stage of childhood development in which the sexual and death instincts are fused together in a 'canalised' form of sadistic aggression. In the concluding chapter of *The General Theory*, Keynes explicitly represents 'opportunities for money-making and private wealth' as able to act as further 'canalized' expressions of such 'dangerous human proclivities':

> dangerous human proclivities can be canalised into comparatively harmless channels by the existence of opportunities for money-making and private wealth, which, if they cannot be satisfied in this way, may find their outlet in cruelty, the reckless pursuit of personal power and authority, and other forms of self-aggrandisement. It is better that a man should tyrannise over his bank balance than over his fellow-citizens; and whilst the former is sometimes denounced as being but a means to the latter, sometimes at least it is an alternative.[4]
>
> (VII: 374)

For this reason,

> The task of transmuting human nature must not be confused with the task of managing it. Though in the ideal commonwealth men may have been taught or inspired or bred to take no interest in the stakes, it may still be wise and prudent statesmanship to allow the [capitalist] game to be played, subject to rules and limitations, so long as the average man, or even a significant section of the community, is in fact strongly addicted to the money-making passion.
>
> (VII: 374)

Keynes on 'the ideal social republic of the future'

'My Early Beliefs' adopts the idea of 'religion' understood as 'one's attitude towards oneself and the ultimate' (X: 436) as a potentially rational subject of study, a study through which it is possible to reach 'objective standards' and 'reliable intuitions of the good' (X: 447). It is the 'branch of religion' Keynes elsewhere identifies with 'practical idealists', and elaborates as one of 'two distinct sublimations of materialistic egotism', the one 'in which the ego [...] is merged in the pursuit of an ideal life for the whole community of men' (IX: 254). As his identification of capitalism with irrational 'money motives' indicates, his 'imagined ideal social republic of the future' (XXI: 241) would not be capitalist. The key ontological and anthropological ideas constituting this imagined ideal were those pointed to above, the ontological idea of 'being' as including an objective and knowable 'good' and the anthropological idea of 'human being' as the being potentially able to know this 'good' and actualize it in a 'good life' in an 'ideal commonwealth'.

What Keynes means by the 'good' is spelled out explicitly in the first part of 'My Early Beliefs'. He there associates his own view primarily with the view found in G.E. Moore's *Principia Ethica*.[5] For Moore, 'good' is a characteristic of states of mind, of 'timeless, passionate states of contemplation and communion, largely unattached to 'before' and 'after'' (X: 436). Such states are 'organic unities' in the sense that the goodness of any part depends upon its relations to the whole. Thus the goodness of the 'state of mind of being in love' depends 'not merely on the nature of one's own emotions, but also on the worth of their object and on the reciprocity and nature of the object's emotions' (X: 436). 'A beloved person, beauty and truth' constitute the subjects of these good states of mind:

> The appropriate subjects of passionate contemplation and communion were a beloved person, beauty and truth, and one's prime objects in life were love, the creation and enjoyment of aesthetic experience and the pursuit of know-ledge. Of these love came a long way first.
>
> (X: 436–437)

An 'ideal life for the whole community of men' was a life in which these non-economic 'goods' were actualized. Imagined in this way, it was 'on the extreme left of celestial space' (IX: 309). Such a community would be the full develop-ment and actualization of self-conscious 'reason' – 'the universal element in the soul of man'.

For it to become practicable, reason had to be substituted for 'blind instinct'. Both in their individual and collective lives, individuals had 'to substitute moral and rational motive as their spring of action in place of blind instinct' (XVII: 453). Human development understood from this perspective was 'the endeavour by civilised man to assume conscious control in his own hands away from the blind instinct of mere predominant survival' (XVII: 446).

Keynes viewed this development as a two-stage process. It was first necessary to solve what he called 'the economic problem'. This required the developments in science and technology, along with the accumulation at compound interest of productive facilities embodying these, that would produce the solution – 'material abundance'. He claimed capitalism, i.e. the domination of economic motivation by the money-making and money-loving instincts, was the most efficient way of doing this. It was for this reason that:

> For at least another hundred years we must pretend to ourselves and to everyone that fair is foul and foul is fair; for foul is useful and fair is not. Avarice and usury and precaution must be our gods for a little longer still. For only they can lead us out of the tunnel of economic necessity into daylight.
>
> (IX: 331)

Given, however, that 'opportunities for money-making and private wealth' formed only a 'weak and precarious crust', the more 'vulgar passions' boiling underneath remained serious obstacles in the way of solving even this problem. Throughout his writing Keynes points to what amount to more direct expressions

of the sex and death instincts, overpopulation and war, as the main obstacles in the
way of developing the requisite 'material abundance':

> The principles of pacifism and population are absolutely necessary pre-
> requisites of any good life at all being possible for the mass of men.
>
> (XVII: 450)[6]

Keynes remained relatively optimistic, however, that the 'economic problem'
would ultimately be solved

> assuming no important wars and no important increase in population, the *eco-*
> *nomic problem* may be solved, or be at least within sight of solution, within a
> hundred years. This means that the economic problem is not—if we look into
> the future—*the permanent problem of the human race.*
>
> (IX: 326)

In a draft for his 1943 maiden House of Lords speech on the Beveridge Report,
he writes:

> Moreover, to make a bogey of the economic problem is, in my judgment, griev-
> ously to misunderstand the nature of the tasks ahead of us. [...] It is not any fear
> of a failure of physical productivity to provide an adequate material standard of
> life that fills me with foreboding. The real problems of the future are first the
> maintenance of peace, of international co-operation and amity, and beyond that
> the profound moral and social problems of how to organise material abundance
> to yield up the fruits of a good life. These are the heroic tasks of the future.
>
> (XXVII: 260–261)

When, however, the economic was given its proper instrumental role, the understanding and management of this role in the body politic would be 'like dentistry', i.e.
instrumental to non-economic 'matters of greater and more permanent significance':

> But, chiefly, do not let us overestimate the importance of the economic prob-
> lem, or sacrifice to its supposed necessities other matters of greater and more
> permanent significance. It should be a matter for specialists – like dentistry.
> If economists could manage to get themselves thought of as a humble, com-
> petent people, on a level with dentists, that would be splendid!
>
> (IX: 332)[7]

Much more serious was the obstacle the 'insane and irrational springs' put in
the way of the 'spiritual' prerequisite of an ideal social republic – the full development and actualization of 'the universal element in the soul of man':

> There is no reason, therefore, why the inhabitants of Europe, if they have
> wisdom, need fear their material surroundings. They can still see a Golden

Age in front of them and travel towards it. If Europe is to suffer a decline, it will be due, not to material, but to spiritual causes.

(XVII: 445)

Ultimately, the money-motives were incompatible with the ideal:

> To me it seems clearer every day that the moral problem of our age is con-
> cerned with the love of money, with the habitual appeal to the money motive
> in nine-tenths of the activities of life, with the universal striving after indi-
> vidual economic security as the prime object of endeavour, with the social
> approbation of money as the measure of constructive success, and with the
> social appeal to the hoarding instinct as the foundation of the necessary pro-
> vision for the family and for the future [...] A revolution in our ways of
> thinking and feeling about money may become the growing purpose of con-
> temporary embodiments of the ideal.
>
> (IX: 269)

When, however, both the 'material' and the 'spiritual' obstacles to the actualization of the ideal had been eliminated, we would be free

> to return to some of the most sure and certain principles of religion and tradi-
> tional virtue – that avarice is a vice, that the exaction of usury is a misdemean-
> our, and the love of money is detestable, that those walk most truly in the paths
> of virtue and sane wisdom who take least thought for the morrow. We shall
> once more value ends above means and prefer the good to the useful. We shall
> honour those who can teach us how to pluck the hour and day virtuously and
> well, the delightful people who are capable to taking direct enjoyment in things,
> the lilies of the field who toil not, neither do they spin.
>
> (IX: 330–331)

The 'insane and irrational springs of wickedness' and war

According to Keynes, war results from and exacerbates the weakness of the 'rules
and conventions' maintaining the 'thin and precarious crust' of 'civilisation'. It
is the re-emergence of the 'dangerous human proclivities' in a relatively uncana-
lised form. At the beginning of *The Economic Consequences*, he points to these
proclivities as the cause of the First World War, a war that had, he claimed, 'overturned the foundations on which we all lived and built':

> Moved by insane delusion and reckless self-regard, the German people over-
> turned the foundations on which we all lived and built.
>
> (II: 2)

Keynes claimed the conduct of the war had expressed an even more extreme
form of the irrationality at issue, a form characteristic of the 'militarist mind'.

In 'Melchior', Admiral Browning, a 'stupid and callous militarist' (X: 395), and Marshall Foch, with a mind that was 'in the strict sense, militarist', a 'narrow intellect' from which 'nine-tenths of the affairs of mankind are blotted out' (X: 391), are pointed to as exemplifying the 'militarist' type. In *Essays in Biography*, he makes use of Churchill's *The World Crisis, 1916–18*, to paint a more detailed picture of the type (X 46–57). He calls Churchill's book

> in its final impression on the reader, a tractate against war – more effective than the work of a pacifist could be, a demonstration from one who loves the game, not only of the imbecility of its aims and of its methods, but, more than this, that the imbecility is not an accidental quality of the particular players, but is inherent in its spirit and its rules.
>
> (X: 52)[8]

Unfortunately, public policy was not immune to influence by the same 'insane and irrational springs' so that it often contributed to the breakdown of the 'outward restraints of convention and traditional standards and inflexible rules of conduct' keeping them at bay. 'Melchior' illustrates this (and thus illustrates the general point about human irrationality made in the second memoir) by means of an analysis of that part of the Treaty negotiations in which Keynes and Melchior had played key roles.

Keynes claimed the irrationality involved in the causes and conduct of the war was also at work in the Treaty negotiations. In *The Economic Consequences* (II: 2–4), he claimed that the Peace ran the risk of 'completing the ruin, which Germany began' of 'the delicate, complicated organization' holding the more dangerous expressions of 'the insane and irrational springs of wickedness' at bay. He quotes a passage from Thomas Hardy's *The Dynasts* to characterize the irrationality at play:

Spirit of the Years

> Observe that all wide sight and self-command
> Deserts these throngs now driven to demonry
> By the Immanent Unrecking. Nought remains
> But vindictiveness here amid the strong,
> And there amid the weak an impotent rage.

Spirit of the Pities

> Why prompts the Will so senseless-shaped a doing?

Spirit of the Years

> I have told thee that It works unwittingly,
> As one possessed not judging.
>
> (II: 4)[9]

'Melchior' is focused on the negotiations, in the first months of 1919, to re-supply Germany with food. Keynes's account of them utilizes the ideas about human irrationality and its implications for the development and maintenance of civilisation elaborated in 'My Early Beliefs'.

The war, he claims, had seriously weakened the capacity of the 'outward restraints of convention and traditional standards and inflexible rules of conduct' to hold at bay the 'dangerous human proclivities'. In particular, in Russia these passions had broken through in the form of the revolution. In Germany, the effects of the war and of German defeat, particularly the effect of the state of semi-starvation brought about by the Allied blockade, had seriously weakened the barriers to a similar eruption there, an eruption Keynes suggests could take the form of either 'Bolshevism' or 'reaction' (X: 397; II: 83–185). The re-supply of Germany with food was an essential first step in protecting Germany and the rest of Europe from such an eruption, *i.e.* in protecting civilisation from the 'the insane and irrational springs of wickedness'.

The problem was that the irrationality characteristic of the peace negotiations in general also characterized the negotiations for re-supply. The main expression of this was French refusal to allow Germany to use its remaining gold and other liquid assets to buy food. On the other hand, Germany, in a state of nervous collapse brought on by defeat, was proving unable to defend its interests in the matter, interests that, given the threat posed by the vulgar passions, were also Europe's.

In the preface to the French edition of *The Economic Consequences*, Keynes had claimed of the French role in the peace negotiations as a whole that the 'fundamental interests of France were all betrayed by those with whom M. Clemenceau had surrounded himself'. Moreover, the evidence that had accumulated since the signing of the Treaty that it 'is not being executed and cannot be executed' was not changing their minds:

> The plainer it becomes that the treaty is not being executed and cannot be executed, the more apparently, do French statesmen blind their eyes and muffle their ears and seek to alter facts by denying them. I appeal, therefore, beyond her politicians to the *intelligence* of France, to that element in the French mind which delights to see things as they are and to draw the consequences; and also to that idealism which is the child of humanity and good sense.
>
> (II: xix–xxii)

A major feature of French irrationality concerned gold – the *auri sacra fames*, an aspect of what, in the memoir, Keynes calls 'the grasping sterility of France, which in spite of what Clive [Bell] and Roger [Fry] may say, *is* France' (X: 403). The French insisted the Germans not be allowed to use their remaining gold to buy food. It was to be reserved for the payment of reparations. Keynes treats French attitudes to Germany's gold as 'money-motives' understood in the above way, i.e. as an irrational expression of instincts. These attitudes were personified in the negotiations by the French Finance Minister, Louis-Lucien Klotz, whom Keynes held 'chiefly responsible' for delaying re-supply:

> If any individual is to be picked out as chiefly responsible for prolonging the dreadful privations of Central Europe, it must certainly be the celebrated Monsieur Klotz.
>
> (X: 56)

Irrationality about gold constitutes one of the main expressions of 'the money-making and money-loving instincts'. As pointed out above, the one instance where Keynes explicitly mentions 'the Freudian theory of the love of money, and of gold in particular', is in his discussion of the relation of the gold standard to *auri sacra fames* in *A Treatise on Money* (VI: 258–261):

> Dr Freud relates that there are peculiar reasons deep in our subconscious why gold in particular should satisfy strong instincts and serve as a symbol.
>
> (VI: 258)

In the bibliographic footnote providing references for the particular Freudian theory involved, he says of a prophecy made by Ernest Jones in one of the articles listed there:

> The following prophecy, written by Dr Jones in 1917, may be reckoned, per-haps, a success for the psycho-analytic method: 'The ideas of possession and wealth, therefore, obstinately adhere to the idea of 'money' and gold for defi-nite psychological reasons. This superstitious attitude will cost England in particular many sacrifices after the war, when efforts will probably be made at all costs to reintroduce a gold currency' (*op. cit.* p. 172 [see Jones 1961, p. 129]).
>
> (VI: 258–259 note 1)

Keynes frequently points to India as an example of the impediment the irra-tional 'love of the precious metals' puts in the way of economic development. He does this as early as *Indian Currency and Finance* (I: 69–71; 116–117). He also does it in *The General Theory*:

> The history of India at all times has provided an example of a country impov-erished by a preference for liquidity amounting to so strong a passion that even an enormous and chronic influx of the precious metals has been insuf-ficient to bring down the rate of interest to a level which was compatible with the growth of real wealth.
>
> (VII: 337)

Keynes also frequently singled out France as a place where the gold fetish was particularly strong. In a February 1933 *Daily Mail* article, he makes explicit use of

Freudian language in describing France as 'the last home of the bullionist complex and of ultra-conservatism in all matters concerning cash' (XXI: 231).

In 1932 he connected this complex with a change in Indian attitudes to which he had looked forward in *Indian Currency and Finance* (I: 69–71). In that year Indian hoards were beginning to be disgorged, and this, combined with the increased productivity of African mines, was flooding the world with gold, much of which was ending up in the Bank of France. Keynes gleefully envisaged the following outcome for 'our modern Midases':

> The Indian farmer and the African miner need only a little time to achieve the inevitable conclusion. The day must come, and not too far off, when our modern Midases will be filled to the teeth and choking. And that, perhaps, will be the moment which the irony of heaven will choose for granting to our chemists the final solution of the problem of manufacturing gold, and of reducing its value to that of a base metal.
> Witness the famous tale that Ovid told.
> Midas the king, as in his book appears,
> By Phoebus was endowed with asses' ears.
>
> (XXI: 71–72)[10]

In the case of the negotiations to re-supply Germany with food, the Americans and British were able, in no small part because of the combined efforts of Keynes and Melchior, to prevail over French irrationality. Lloyd George, about whose psychology and general role in the negotiations Keynes was highly disparaging (X: 20–26), managed, in this instance, to be highly effective. After the negotiations had dragged on for some months without success because of French intransigence, he managed, at an 8th March 1919 meeting of the Supreme War Council, to remove the obstacle constituted by French *auri sacra fames* by means of a rhetorical 'onslaught' on Klotz's gold fetishism and obliviousness to German starvation and the threat of Bolshevism (X: 422–423).

Through another private meeting, Keynes enabled Melchior to make sure that Germany, in the final round of the negotiations, would make the concession (the unconditional surrender of its ships) necessary to free her gold for re-supply. To the great disappointment of the French, Melchior was able to get the Germans to do what was necessary. This brought the matter to a successful conclusion:

> There were many technical details to settle and we sat in conference with Melchior and the food experts for a long day. But all was settled now and the food trains started for Germany.
>
> (X: 426)

Throughout this account, Melchior is represented by Keynes as understanding both that there were 'insane and irrational springs of wickedness in most men' and that, in consequence, 'civilisation was a thin and precarious crust erected by the personality and the will of a very few, and only maintained by rules and conventions skilfully put across and guilefully preserved'. He was aware of the irrationality at work in the negotiations, including the irrationality at work on the German side, aware of what Keynes, in a letter to Vanessa Bell, described as 'the amazing complications of psychology and personality and intrigue which make such magnificent sport of the impending catastrophe of Europe (Keynes, as quoted in Skidelsky 1983, p. 363)'. Melchior skilfully negotiated in the light of this awareness (X: 403). He was also aware of the danger the 'deeper and blinder passions' posed to civilisation. He was therefore able to foresee the further danger posed, both to Germany, where the civilised 'crust' had already been severely weakened by the war and defeat, and to Europe as a whole, by the effect on these passions of the mass starvation that would follow a failure to re-supply Germany with food, a danger evident in the Russian revolution that was already threatening to spread west.

Keynes reports the following encounter between himself, Melchior and 'three young Germans' at the start of their first private meeting:

> I waited for some minutes on the landing and then saw Melchior approaching. 'May I speak to you privately?' I asked him. He led me along the passage and entered one of the rooms. At the farther end of it were three young Germans; one was strumming loudly on a piano, one a fat ungainly creature in his shirt-sleeves bellowed a raucous tenor, the third sprawled on a table. 'Excuse me', said Melchior, 'but I'd be much obliged if for a few minutes I could have this room for a private conference'. They roared at him vulgarly. Did he not know that this was the hour of the day when music was permitted in that place? And had he forgotten—pointing to his cigarette—that smoking was prohibited there before five o'clock? We went farther down the passage. With a shrug of his shoulders, 'Here', he said, 'you have a picture of Germany in revolution. These are my clerks'.
>
> (X: 414)

Aware of the dark forces in human nature, Melchior also understood the necessity this created for strict and precise adherence to the 'Tablets of the Law', for 'the outward restraints of established conventions, standards and rules of conduct'. Recounting what Melchior had told him, in their final meeting in Amsterdam after both had resigned, of the last days at Weimar preceding German signature of the Treaty, Keynes writes:

> I also understood most clearly, then for the first time, how dwellers in Eastern Germany look to the East and not Westwards. The war for him had been a war against Russia; and it was the thought of the dark forces which might now issue from the Eastwards, which most obsessed him. I also understood better than before, what a precisian he was, a strict and upright moralist, a worshipper of the Tablets of the Law, a Rabbi. The breach of promise, the breach of discipline, the decay of honourable behaviour, the betrayal of undertakings by the one party and the insincere acceptance by the other of impossible

conditions which it was not intended to carry out, Germany almost as guilty to accept what she could not fulfil as the Allies to impose what they were not entitled to exact – it was these offences against The Word which so much wounded him.

(X: 428)

In the final paragraph of the essay, Keynes contrasts the delight and laughter provoked in the American Paul Warburg with the more appropriate and insightful sense of tragedy and sadness provoked in Melchior by Keynes's reading to them the chapter on President Wilson from *The Economic Consequences*, a chapter detailing the contribution made by the flaws in Wilson's character to the tragedy of the Treaty:[11]

My book was not then out, and I had with me the manuscript of my chapter on the President. After lunch I read it to them [Melchior and Warburg] [...] I noted its effect on the two Jews. Warburg, for personal reasons, hated the President and felt a chuckling delight at his discomfiture; he laughed and giggled and thought it an awfully good hit. But Melchior, as I read, grew ever more solemn, until at the end he appeared almost in tears. This, then, was the other side of the curtain; neither profound causes, nor inevitable fate, nor magnificent wickedness. The Tablets of the Law, it was Melchior's thought at that moment, had perished meanly.

(X: 429)[12]

Subsequent events could perhaps be reckoned, as Keynes had said of Ernest Jones's 1917 prophecy, 'a success for the psycho-analytic method' as employed in this instance by Keynes himself.

Keynes used these same ideas in treating another instance of what he claimed was irrational public policy, namely 'austerity' as the appropriate policy response to economic recession and depression. In *The Economic Consequences*, he had made the following claims about the dominance of a preference for saving and accumulating in nineteenth century European economic motivation:

The nineteenth century was able to forget the fertility of the species in a contemplation of the dizzy virtues of compound interest (II: 13).[13] The duty of 'saving' became nine-tenths of virtue and the growth of the cake the object of true religion. There grew round thee non-consumption of the cake all those instincts of Puritanism which in other ages has withdrawn itself from the world and has neglected the arts of production as well as those of enjoyment.

(II: 12)[14]

In *A Treatise on Money* (V: 246) he describes those (he has Hayek particularly in mind) who believe that real wealth accumulates faster during a depression than during a boom as 'puritans of finance – sometimes extreme individualists'. He claims this irrational belief hides the real reason behind the 'gloomy satisfaction' such people get from 'the speculative and business losses, the low prices, and the high real wages, accompanied, however, by unemployment, which characterize the typical depression'. The real reason is satisfaction of an unconscious wish for punishment arising from the unconscious guilt ('suppressed reactions against the distastefulness of capitalism') accompanying the unrestricted pursuit of the vulgar hidden passions which fuels the boom.

In the original galleys of a reply to Dennis Robertson's *Economic Journal* review of the *Treatise*, Keynes explicitly connected this argument to psycho-analysis. In the last paragraph of his review (Robertson 1931: 410–411), Robertson had expressed some sympathy with the puritans of finance and suggested their policy of restraint was not 'a relic of sadistic barbarism'. In his reply, Keynes claimed the policy was indeed an expression of sadism, though of sadistic puritanism rather than barbarism, and that its explanation was to be found in psycho-analysis rather than economic analysis.

> Mr Robertson's last paragraph of all – yes! a mere relic of Sadistic – well, not so much barbarism as puritanism. But at this point psycho-analysis must take charge and economic analysis withdraw discreetly.
>
> (XIII: 238)

As in the 1930s, the economic consequences of the modern version of the policy are fuelling the eruption of 'dangerous human proclivities', proclivities of which the policy itself is, according to Keynes, an expression.

Conclusion

As treated by Keynes, war is an extreme expression of the 'insane and irrational springs of wickedness'. These are instincts concerned with sex and death, the source of the 'deeper and blinder passions'. Social forms that, in any ultimate sense, would be viewed as incompatible with 'reason' can, in the light of this fact of human nature, be judged necessary to the canalisation of such instincts into less dangerous though still imperfect forms. The strength of the instincts is such, however, that these can only be a 'thin and precarious crust' overtop the 'lava' boiling underneath. Keynes interpreted both the First World War and the negotiations that ended it in terms of these ideas. He represented the origin and conduct of the war as an eruption of the lava, an eruption arising from the weakness of the crust and weakening it still further. Moreover, the deeper and blinder passions expressed by the war also dominated the negotiations that produced the peace. The result was to weaken still further the civilized crust and so prepare the ground for the subsequent eruption of fascism and Nazism, an eruption climaxing in a further war that included genocidal industrial murder. In analysing war in this way, Keynes tied it to economic analysis.

Capitalist motives, he claimed, were canalised less dangerous forms of the instincts expressed more directly in war. In particular, 'the essential characteristic of capitalism', 'the dependence upon an intense appeal to the money-making and money-loving instincts of individuals as the main motive force of the economic machine', was a canalised expression of the sex and death instincts.[15]

Keynes also attributed a positive role to capitalist psychopathology. It was, he claimed, the most efficient way of bringing about the development of science and technology that, in combination with the accumulation at compound interest of productive facilities embodying it, would solve 'the economic problem', i.e. produce the 'material abundance' required for actualization of the 'ideal common-wealth'. The instincts were, however, ultimately the source of the more difficult 'spiritual' obstacle in the way of this actualization. This required the substitution of 'moral and rational motive' for 'blind instinct'. This, he claimed, would prove extremely difficult, particularly given that the innate strength of the instinctual element in the majority of the present population made this substitution impos-sible in their case. To the end of his life, he claimed the only way this aspect of the obstacle could be overcome was through a eugenics policy.[16] In the long run, however, 'capitalism', defined as the dominance of the money-motive, was to be transcended. Keynes's imagined 'ideal social republic of the future' was, as he himself claimed, 'on the extreme left of celestial space'.

Throughout his life Keynes expressed optimism about the power of reason to ultimately determine human belief and action.[17] By the time of the writing of 'My Early Beliefs', however, he had come to see this optimism as to a significant degree itself irrational. He says there of various instances of his appeal to reason:

> I still suffer incurably from attributing an unreal rationality to other people's feelings and behaviour (and doubtless to my own, too). There is one small but extraordinarily silly manifestation of this absurd idea of what is 'normal', namely the impulse to *protest* – to write a letter to *The Times*, call a meeting in the Guildhall, subscribe to some fund when my presuppositions as to what is 'normal' are not fulfilled. I behave as if there really existed some authority or standard to which I can successfully appeal if I shout loud enough – per-haps it is some hereditary vestige of a belief in the efficacy of prayer.
>
> (X: 448)

Notes

1   References to Keynes's *Collected Writings* take the form of the volume number followed by the page numbers.

2   In Keynes's own case there is more continuity between his early and his mature beliefs than 'My Early Beliefs' suggests. In his 1904 essay on Burke, he accepts Burke's defence of 'customary morals, conventions and conventional wisdom', a defence based on the ground that 'the part that reason plays in motive is slight'. He stresses Burke's 'disbelief in men's acting rightly, except on the rarest occasions because they have judged that it is right so to act'. It is 'just prejudices' rather than reason that must be the guide of life. Moreover, given the role such prejudices play in defending civilisa-tion from barbarism, they have to be defended from critical attack (i.e. in 1904 he sets out 'a *dictum* in which' according to 'My Early Beliefs', 'we should have been unable to discover any point or significance whatever (X: 448)'. Keynes attributes to Burke the view that, since reason plays such a small role in motivation, 'those who would

govern men must consequently, rely upon other aids; they must foster and preserve just prejudices; they must discountenance the exposure even of those prejudices which are based upon misapprehension but are beneficial in their immediate results' (Keynes 1904: 82).

3 For detailed examinations of the consistency of Keynes's treatment of psychology in his economics with psycho-analysis, see Winslow 1986, 1990, 1992 and 1995.

4 This paraphrases Freud's account, in *Civilization and Its Discontents* (Freud 1930: 112–113), of capitalist motives as a fusion of the sexual and death instincts 'canalised' by the ego's defences against anxiety.

5 'My Early Beliefs' also records Keynes's dissent from important aspects of Moore's account of the 'good', (Winslow 2010: 4–5). For a more general treatment of the development of Keynes's philosophical ideas through time, see Winslow 2003.

6 See also (II: 13) and (XVII: 454).

7 Harrod quotes Keynes as describing economists in a 1945 speech as 'he trustees, not of civilisation, but of the possibility of civilisation (Harrod 1951: 194)'.

8 Here and elsewhere, Keynes explains the 'imbecility' as due in part to 'the comparative exemption from criticism which the military hierarchy affords to the high command': 'The explanation of the incompetence with which wars are always conducted on both sides may be found in the comparative exemption from criticism which the military hierarchy affords to the high command. I have no excessive admiration for politicians, but, brought up as they are in the very breath of criticism, how much superior they are to the soldiers!' (XXI: 246).

9 On the last page of the book (II: 189), Keynes quotes an analogous insightful poetic lament from Shelley's *Prometheus Unbound*.

10 The lines of poetry are from John Dryden's *The Wife of Bath, her Tale*, a rendering of the original tale by Geoffrey Chaucer.

11 In that chapter Keynes explicitly associates these flaws and the mistakes to which they led with a 'Freudian complex': 'The reply of Brockdorff-Rantzau inevitably took the line that Germany had laid down her arms on the basis of certain assurances, and that the treaty in many particulars was not consistent with these assurances. But this was exactly what the President could not admit; in the sweat of solitary contemplation and with prayers to God he had done nothing that was not just and right; for the President to admit that the German reply had force in it was to destroy his self-respect and to disrupt the inner equipoise of his soul; and every instinct of his stubborn nature rose in self-protection. In the language of medical psychology, to suggest to the President that the treaty was an abandonment of his professions was to touch on the raw a Freudian complex. It was a subject intolerable to discuss, and every subconscious instinct plotted to defeat its further exploration' (II: 34).

12 This sense of Melchior as personifying 'the universal element in the soul of man' is also conveyed in a 1932 lecture Keynes gave in Hamburg, 'The Economic Prospects 1932' (XXI: 47–48).

13 Another implicitly Freudian identification of 'the love of money' with 'sexual love' occurs in 'The End of Laissez-Faire': 'Just as Darwin invoked sexual love, acting through sexual selection, as an adjutant to natural selection by competition, so the individualist invokes the love of money, acting through the pursuit of profit, to bring about the production on the greatest possible scale of what is most strongly measured by exchange value' (X: 284).

14 As indicated above, as irrational 'purposiveness' saving and accumulating are a means for securing 'a delusive and spurious immortality', an irrationality deriving, according to Freudian theory, from the anxiety provoked by the death instinct. Also as indicated above, they express the 'instincts of Puritanism' as a further canalisation of the sex and death instincts previously transformed and fused together as sadistic aggression. This understanding of them is consistent with Keynes characterization of 'austerity' as an expression of 'Sadistic [...] puritanism'.

15 Moreover, canalisation in these forms was only possible for a minority. The instincts of the majority required more direct less sublimated repression. Keynes claimed that, in the latter case, the war had broken down the forms that had worked pre-war so that these now needed to be replaced by new ones if the innate 'destructiveness' of the majority was to be held at bay (for a discussion of Keynes's idea of the reforms required, see Winslow 1990).

16 See Keynes 1946, Fishburn 1983 and Toye 2000.

17 For instance, at the end of *The Economic Consequences* he writes: 'The events of the coming year will not be shaped by the deliberate acts of statesmen, but by the hidden currents, flowing continually beneath the surface of political history, of which no one can predict the outcome. In one way only can we influence these hidden currents, – by setting in motion those forces of instruction and imagination which change *opinion*. The assertion of truth, the unveiling of illusion, the dissipation of hate, the enlargement and instruction of men's hearts and minds, must be the means' (II: 189).

References

Fishburn, G. (1983) 'Keynes and the Age of Eugenics', *The Age Monthly Review*, 3(2), Melbourne.

Freud, S. (1930) *Civilization and its Discontents*, in Freud, Sigmund, James Strachey, and Anna Freud. *The Standard Edition of the Complete Psychological Works of Sigmund Freud*, vol. XXI, Hogarth Press, London, 1953.

Harrod, R. (1951) *The Life of J. M. Keynes*, Macmillan Press, London.

Jones, E. (1961) 'The Theory of Symbolism', in *Papers on Psycho-analysis*, 5th rev. ed., Boston, MA, Beacon Press.

Keynes, J.M. (1904) 'Essay on Edmund Burke', on deposit in *The Papers of John Maynard Keynes*: JMK/UA/20, The Archive Centre, King's College, Cambridge.

— (1946) 'Opening remarks: The Galton Lecture, 1946', *The Eugenics Review*, 38(1), 39–40.

— (1971–89) *The Collected Writings of John Maynard Keynes*, edited by E. Johnson and D.E. Moggridge, Macmillan Press, London.

Robertson, D. (1931) 'Mr. Keynes's Theory of Money', *Economic Journal*, 41(163), 395–411.

Skidelsky, R. (1983) *John Maynard Keynes: Hopes Betrayed 1883–1920*, Macmillan Press, London.

Toye, J.F.J. (2000) *Keynes on Population*, Oxford University Press, New York.

Winslow, E. G. (Ted). (1986) 'Keynes and Freud: Psychoanalysis and Keynes's Account of the 'Animal Spirits' of Capitalism', *Social Research*, 53(4), 549–578.

— (1990) 'Bloomsbury, Freud, and the Vulgar Passions', *Social Research*, 57(4), 785–819.

— (1992) 'Psychoanalysis and Keynes's Account of the Psychology of the Trade Cycle', in Gerrard, W.J. and Hillard, J.V. (eds.) *The Philosophy and Economics of J.M. Keynes*, Edward Elgar, Cheltenham.

— (1995) 'Uncertainty and Liquidity-Preference', in Dow, Sheila and Hillard, J.V. (eds.) *Keynes, Knowledge and Uncertainty*, Edward Elgar, Cheltenham.

— (2003) 'Foundations of Keynes's Economics', in Runde, Jochen and Sohei, Mizuhara (eds.) *Perspectives on the Philosophy of Keynes's Economics: Probability, Uncertainty and Convention*, Routledge, London.

— (2010) 'Keynes on the Relation of the Capitalist "Vulgar Passions" to Financial Crises', *Studi e Note di Economia*, 2010 Fascicolo 3, 369–388.

Index

For Product Safety Concerns and Information please contact our EU
representative GPSR@taylorandfrancis.com
Taylor & Francis Verlag GmbH, Kaufingerstraße 24, 80331 München, Germany

www.ingramcontent.com/pod-product-compliance
Ingram Content Group UK Ltd.
Pitfield, Milton Keynes, MK11 3LW, UK
UKHW020956180425
457613UK00019B/706